GEORGE WASHINGTON AND THE CREATION OF THE AMERICAN REPUBLIC

ALSO BY WILLIAM M. FOWLER JR.

*American Crisis: George Washington and the Dangerous
Two Years after Yorktown, 1781–1783*

The American Revolution: Changing Perspectives
(edited with Wallace Coyle)

The Baron of Beacon Hill: A Biography of John Hancock

Commanding Old Ironsides: The Life of Captain Silas Talbot

*Empires at War: The French and Indian War and the
Struggle for North America, 1754–1763*

Jack Tars and Commodores: The American Navy, 1783–1815

Rebels under Sail: The American Navy during the Revolution

*Steam Titans: Cunard, Collins, and the Epic Battle
for Commerce on the North Atlantic*

Under Two Flags: The American Navy in the Civil War

William Ellery: A Rhode Island Politico and Lord of Admiralty

GEORGE WASHINGTON AND THE CREATION OF THE AMERICAN REPUBLIC

William M. Fowler Jr.

LYONS
PRESS

Essex, Connecticut

LYONS PRESS

An imprint of The Globe Pequot Publishing Group, Inc.
64 South Main St.
Essex, CT 06426
www.GlobePequot.com

British Library Cataloguing in Publication Information Available

Library of Congress Cataloging-in-Publication Data

Names: Fowler, William M., Jr., 1944– author
Title: George Washington and the creation of the American republic /
   William M. Fowler Jr.
Description: Essex, Connecticut : Lyons Press, 2025. | Includes
   bibliographical references and index. | Summary: "This book debunks the
   standard portrayal of George Washington in what is described by
   historians as the 'Critical Years' (1781–1789), a time when he was
   deeply involved in land speculation, western expansion, scientific
   farming, canal building, political affairs, and family
   matters—directing the nation toward a strong central government"—
   Provided by publisher.
Identifiers: LCCN 2024060511 (print) | LCCN 2024060512 (ebook) | ISBN
   9781493091669 cloth | ISBN 9781493091676 epub
Subjects: LCSH: Washington, George, 1732–1799 | United
   States—History—Confederation, 1783–1789 | United States—Territorial
   expansion | Federal government—United States—History—18th century |
   Constitutional history—United States | Presidents—United
   States—Biography | BISAC: HISTORY / United States / Revolutionary
   Period (1775–1800) | HISTORY / United States / General | LCGFT:
   Biographies
Classification: LCC E312.29 .F68 2025 (print) | LCC E312.29 (ebook) | NLM
   HIS036030 | DDC 973.4/1092 $a B—dc23/eng/20250415
LC record available at https://lccn.loc.gov/2024060511
LC ebook record available at https://lccn.loc.gov/2024060512

For my grandchildren

Olivia
Gray
AJ
Winter

CONTENTS

ACKNOWLEDGMENTS

Writing acknowledgments is a pleasant and important task. It usually arrives near the end of a long process—years, perhaps—of researching and writing. More important, however, it is a time of reflection, providing the author a moment to remember the people and institutions central to his/her project.

Among all of America's historic figures, no one stands more prominently than George Washington. During his lifetime, to the present day, books, articles, and movies continue to appear without end. Aside from his importance to American history, this phenomenon is due to the scores of archivists and curators who have cared meticulously for his papers. To these people, and their institutions, I owe a debt of thanks.

In this list, Mount Vernon stands high. It would be impossible to write about Washington without visiting his plantation on the Potomac. Walking the grounds, visiting the mansion, and talking with the interpreters gives a sense of the man that even his papers cannot convey. Nearby, just across the street, is the George Washington Presidential Library. It is the epicenter for Washington scholarship. But, of course, documents are mute, and it is only through the incredible work of the staff, preserving and curating the collections, that Washington's story can be told. Other institutions and staff were equally helpful. These include the Massachusetts Historical Society, the American Philosophical Society, the Historical Society of Pennsylvania, the United States National Archives, the Library of Congress, the Boston Athenaeum, the American Antiquarian Society, and the National Park

Service at Philadelphia and Boston. At every one of these stops I was greeted warmly and given the material I sought (even when I did not know quite what I was looking for). I offer a deep thanks to all.

In addition to housing physical archives, in a world of modern technology, these institutions provide online access—a tremendous benefit!

To the staff at Globe Pequot, special thanks go to Patricia Stevenson and Nancy Syrett, compassionate and skillful editors. Remaining errors are my responsibility entirely. Thanks also to the staff at the Snell Library at Northeastern University. For more than forty years it was my pleasure to be a member of the history department at this university. My colleagues offered help and encouragement (and occasionally criticism). I am grateful to them. My main job has always been teaching. It is what I like best. When students learn that I am "writing," they want to know more. Sharing my work with them (successes and failures) serves as an example—teaching and scholarship intertwined.

Finally, of course, I must turn to my family. As always, they have been my mainstay. They allowed me to retreat to my office. They were always interested in what I was doing, and they were particularly impressed when I presented them with the finished volume.

William M. Fowler Jr.
Reading, Massachusetts

INTRODUCTION

Fond of the theater, George Washington appreciated the power of performance. He was center stage at noon on 23 December 1783, when, "according to order," the Confederation Congress admitted the "Commander in Chief to a public audience." The Revolution was over, independence won. Washington had come to return his commission. He took a chair. The secretary ordered, "Silence." The president of the Congress, Thomas Mifflin, turned to Washington: "Sir, the United States in Congress assembled are prepared to receive your communications."

In a "solemn and affecting moment," as "the spectators all wept," Washington "rose and bowed" to the members. Holding the address in shaking hands, he addressed them, "happy in the confirmation of our Independence and Sovereignty" and "sanguine" that the new nation would become "respectable." After asking that they not forget their obligations to the army and the officers who had served them, "having finished the work assigned," he bid them "an affectionate farewell." Then, in a final, well-calculated moment, "he drew out from his bosom his commission and delivered it up to the president of Congress." He was taking "leave of all the employments of public life." The president responded, assuring Washington that as he retired "from the great theatre of action," he did so "with the blessings of your fellow citizens." Washington left the chamber. The entire ceremony took less than ten minutes.[1]

In this remarkable moment, General George Washington, the American Cincinnatus, put aside his sword to take up the plow. He was, once again, citizen and farmer. When a curious King George III asked his American-born portrait painter, Benjamin West, what Washington would do after the war, West responded, "They say he will return to his farm." To that the king replied, "If he does that, he will be the greatest man in the world."[2]

Whatever his intentions, Washington's departure from "public life" was brief. He was a national icon to whom a fragile republic, more likely to fail than succeed, looked for leadership. Just as his strength had held the army together in war, so now the emerging nation looked to him to bind them together in peace. His Cincinnatus-like response—putting aside the sword, declining honors, wishing to live with his family as a farmer—placed him squarely in the eighteenth-century pantheon of heroes who offered themselves in defense of their nation.

Though he was a public figure, family stood firmly in Washington's life. His aging mother required care. His brothers and their children were in constant need. His stepgrandchildren, who "made him laugh most heartily," were a light in his life.[3] Yet the world was unrelenting in its attention. In his six years of "retirement," hundreds of visitors arrived, many staying in his "well resorted tavern." For Martha, the strain of looking after the constant stream of visitors, caring for her children and grandchildren, and managing an expansive household sapped her strength.

As he minded the affairs of an extended family, Washington was also a farmer. When home, he rode nearly every day visiting his farms. He corresponded with noted agriculturists in England to learn new techniques. He likely knew more about modern methods for cultivating land and breeding livestock than any other American. He dismissed old and wasteful methods of cultivation and built an impressive greenhouse in which he gathered plants from around the world to test their adaptability to the American environment.

A master at deflection, to those who pressed him to return to public life, he responded (nearly fifty times) that he wished only to sit under his "vine and fig tree" as he immersed himself in farming, family, and private pursuits, avoiding politics. Competing with the forces that kept him close to home, however, was the centrifugal pull of national issues that drew him away from Mount Vernon: settlement of western lands, improving roads and rivers, domestic unrest, a troubled economy, and foreign threats. From personal experience, dinner table chatter, letters, and newspapers, Washington was acutely aware of the nation's peril. Nonetheless, service in the Virginia legislature coupled with nine years in the field enduring defeats and celebrating victories, all the while coping with political machinations in Congress, had taught him the risks of boldness and the wisdom of patience. Washington never disengaged from the nation he had helped found. He simply waited.

In March 1785, Washington returned to the national stage. At his invitation, delegates from Maryland and Virginia met at Mount Vernon to settle disputes over navigation on Chesapeake Bay. The success of that gathering sparked hope for a national meeting. Washington took great interest in the subsequent meeting at Annapolis and its report calling for a general convention. Although he continued to harbor doubts, a failed convention would be catastrophic. Under pressure from James Madison, John Jay, Henry Knox, and many others, he consented to go to Philadelphia.

Remaining apart from the noise of debate, Washington, with the same dignity and steady perseverance he had exhibited during the Revolution, presided over the convention. He said little, and made virtually no contributions to the final text, but his solemn presence was the force that fixed the delegates to their duty. Since he would not leave until the task was completed, they would not leave. His work in Philadelphia completed, Washington returned to Mount Vernon to await the verdict of the states.

Washington watched as debates in the state conventions proceeded. Careful to spend his ammunition wisely, in public he was cautious, but in private he did all he could to prod acceptance. As the tide of ratification swept ahead, there was little doubt about who should lead the new nation. Enjoying the support of the new nation, he prepared to take his place, once again, in the "publick theatre."

1

HOME

I am a private citizen on the banks of the Potomac and
under the shadow of my own fig tree. (GW to ML, 1
February 1784, in *GWP, Conf. Series*, 1:87)

John Trumbull, "painter of the American Revolution," was an artist from the Romantic period who, in his drive to capture historic
moments, often favored drama over reality. So it is with one of his four
paintings, displayed in the rotunda of the National Capital, depicting
scenes associated with the American Revolution. In it, he portrayed
Washington, on 23 December 1783, resigning his commission before
Congress. Trumbull presents Washington appearing before the Confederation Congress, convened in the Senate Chamber of the Maryland
State House at Annapolis. In the center of the painting, as an ethereal
light shines down from above, Washington, erect as usual, stands next
to a chair draped in a red crimson cloak symbolizing the absence of a
king. In the upper right, Trumbull, who was apt to put people into historic scenes even when they were not actually present, placed a glowing
Martha Washington, grandchildren by her side, looking down from the
balcony at the event below. Unfortunately, at that moment, she and the
children were at Mount Vernon.[1]

What Trumbull could not depict was the tension in the room.
Congress was in dire straits. In June 1783, fearing that their safety was
at risk from angry mobs, the members had made a hasty departure
from Philadelphia, spending the fall in Princeton and then settling at

Annapolis in late November. The body's peripatetic habits, an empty treasury, and a collapsing reputation discouraged attendance. Despite its momentous importance, for this event they lacked a quorum (nine states required, seven present), but, by parliamentary legerdemain, they managed to convene the meeting.

Washington, uncharacteristically emotional, grasped the precarious situation. Adding to his uneasiness was the fact that the president of the Congress, Thomas Mifflin, the person to whom he was about to hand his commission, was one of the conspirators who, according to Washington, "bore a part" in the Conway Cabal whose members five years earlier had plotted to remove him as commander in chief. Neither man trusted the other.[2]

As Washington entered, the members, offering little deference, remained seated. The secretary of the Congress, Charles Thomson, called for silence. In a hushed room, Mifflin turned to Washington, "Congress, sir, are prepared to receive your communications."[3] Succinct in his remarks, Washington, the consummate actor, concluded his speech with a dramatic flourish. James McHenry described the moment: As Washington thrust his hand into his tunic, he drew "out from his bosom his commission and delivered it up to the president of Congress."[4] Mifflin, callous to the moment, read a stiff reply "without any shew of feeling but with much dignity."[5] The ceremony finished, Washington "bid every member farewell." Anxious to return home, accompanied by Billy Lee (the enslaved African who had been by his side the entire war), and joined by his two military aides, Benjamin Walker and David Humphreys, Washington left Annapolis. By evening the party had made Georgetown, where they waited until morning to cross the Potomac. The next day, making their way through Alexandria, they reached Mount Vernon. It was Christmas Eve. Washington had come home to his beloved Mount Vernon.

This was Washington's first Christmas at home in eight years. Described by one visitor "as one of the most regular men in the world," on Christmas morning, the general rose early, beginning his "diurnal course with the sun."[6] Martha, too, was an early riser. She dressed while the general made his way down a narrow set of stairs to his study, where he washed, shaved, and, for the first time since the Revolution began, put on civilian clothes rather than the crisp blue and buff uniform of commander in chief.

In his study, preparing for the day, Washington could detect the aroma of hoecakes warming on a griddle in the nearby kitchen. Of Native American origin, and known as "Fair Virginia's pride," these simple cornmeal mush flat cakes, accompanied by hot tea, were Washington's favorite breakfast.

Unlike other parts of the mansion where "perpetual elegant hospitality exercised," Washington's study was a private place intended as refuge from the hubbub that characterized the rest of his home.[7] The walls were plain white plaster, not painted in the sumptuous Prussian blues and verdigris green that graced other parts of the mansion. The floor was constructed of plain wooden planks, but, to give it a more fashionable appearance, the pine woodwork was "grained." On the east wall was a large floor-to-ceiling bookcase, fronted by glass doors, behind which shelves groaned under the weight of more than eight hundred books and pamphlets. "Conscious of a defective education," Washington had a love of books, conceiving that "a knowledge of books is the basis upon which other knowledge is to be built."[8] Unlike John Adams and Thomas Jefferson, both of whom possessed larger and more diverse libraries, Washington's collection focused on useful knowledge. Always a farmer, he was eager to have the most recent volumes and periodicals on agriculture. Fascinated with the "new husbandry," he subscribed to the writings of English agriculturist Arthur Young. In the waning days of the war, expecting some leisure in retirement, he bought books on geography and travel, including *The Duke of Hamilton's Travels through France* (1783) and *Youngs Tour through Ireland* (1780). In May 1783, he instructed William Smith, one of the American commissioners negotiating the British withdrawal from New York City, to scour the city's bookshops and send him biographies of "Charles the 12th of Sweden, Louis XV of France, and A History of the reign of Czar Peter, the Great." Furthermore, he added, "If there is a good Booksellers Shop in the City, I would thank you for sending me a catalog."[9]

To guide him as Mount Vernon's principal architect, Washington sought titles on architecture and carpentry. With the eye of a practiced surveyor, he was equally attentive to tomes that could direct him in reshaping and improving the land surrounding the mansion. In 1759, barely a month after Martha arrived at Mount Vernon, he had bought Batty Langley's *New Principles of Gardening; or, The Laying Out and Planting Parterres, Groves, Wildernesses, Labyrinths, Avenues, Parks, etc.* (1728).[10] Politics and history ranked high. Thomas Paine's *Common Sense* (1776), a gift from the author, held a special place. Washington was also an avid reader of newspapers, often sent to him gratis. Poetry, novels, and belles-lettres were given a low priority, representing less than 10 percent of his collection.[11]

While her husband prepared for the day, Martha began her domestic routine moving through the mansion, checking on every detail. She finished her inspection in the kitchen where the enslaved staff had risen earlier to prepare the holiday menu.

Compared to later extravagant Victorian celebrations, laden with carol singing, ornate decorations, and grandiose exchanges of gifts, Christmas at Mount Vernon was simple. Holiday observances continued through 6 January.[12] In 1784, that day was an occasion of personal celebration. It was the Washingtons' twenty-fifth wedding anniversary.[13]

Before the war, following breakfast, the family usually attended Christmas services at nearby Pohick church, an Anglican congregation at which Washington served as a vestryman. This year, however, the unusual cold and snow made travel difficult. The Washingtons remained at home.[14] Joining them were two of Martha's grandchildren, four-year-old Eleanor Parke Custis and her two-year-old brother George Washington Parke Custis. With her late husband, Daniel Custis, Martha Dandridge Custis (Washington) had four children. A son, Daniel Parke Custis II, and daughter, Frances Parke Custis, died young—Daniel at age three and Frances only four. Following their father's death (1757) and Martha's marriage to George Washington (1759), the surviving children—John Parke Custis ("Jacky") and Martha Parke Custis ("Patsy")—came to live at Mount Vernon. Patsy, chronically ill, suffered from seizures. In the summer of 1773, while Mount Vernon was bustling with the usual bevy of guests, she experienced a severe attack. Carried to bed, she died, according to Washington, within a few minutes "without uttering a word, a groan or scarce a sigh." Having lost three of her four children, Patsy's death, according to her husband, "almost reduced my poor wife to the lowest ebb of misery."[15] Jacky remained at Mount Vernon, where his indolent habits worried Washington, who lamented that the young man's interests lay more in "dogs, horses and guns" than in books and business.[16]

In 1774, Jacky, age nineteen, married sixteen-year-old Eleanor Calvert, daughter of a distinguished Maryland family. Over the next six years, they had had seven children (one set of twins), with only four surviving beyond infancy: three daughters—Elizabeth Parke ("Eliza"), Martha Parke ("Patsy"), and Eleanor Parke ("Nelly")—and a son, George Washington Parke ("Wash"). In 1781, while serving as a civilian aide to Washington, Jacky contracted "camp fever" and died. Left a widow with four children, Eleanor remained at the family home in nearby Abington. Martha, having outlived her own children, felt a close bond to her grandchildren, particularly the two youngest: Wash, barely six months old, and Nelly, age four. To assist their widowed daughter-in-law, as well as to add brightness to their own home, the Washingtons invited Wash and Nelly to live at Mount Vernon, while the two older girls, Eliza and Patsy, remained with their mother at Abington. Two years later, the widow Custis married Dr. David Stuart, a prominent Alexandria physician and politician. The Stuarts, with the two daughters, remained at Abington while Wash and Nelly continued to live at Mount Vernon.[17] Although the Washingtons never formally adopted the two grandchildren, they showered them with affection; Washington referred to them as the "little folks," while Martha enjoyed watching them "prattling about." Nelly remembered her grandmother as "more than a mother to me and the president the most affectionate of fathers. I loved them more than anyone."[18]

In addition to Wash, Nelly, Eleanor, her new husband, and their two daughters, also present to celebrate the holidays in 1783 were Lund Washington and his wife Elizabeth. Lund, a distant relation (third cousin), had been Mount Vernon's overseer since 1762.[19] From outside the family, rounding out the gathering were Washington's two military aides, Humphreys and Walker.[20] They were the last in a long line of thirty-two young officers, "beardless boys," who had served the commander in chief. Born in Derby, Connecticut, David Humphreys graduated from Yale. When the Revolution broke out, he left his position as a schoolmaster and joined the Second Connecticut Militia Regiment. He proved more skillful with the pen than the sword, however, and his superiors recognized his literary talents. He became aide-de-camp to General Israel Putnam, followed by a similar post with Nathanael Greene. While serving Greene, Humphreys wrote a long (thirty-stanza) overwrought poem laced with patriotic hyperbole lavishing praise on Washington.

> His voice inspir'd, his godlike presence led.
> The Britons saw, and from his presence fled.

Keen to curry favor and advance his career, as soon as the poem was in print, in May 1780, Humphreys posted a copy to the general.[21] It worked. Washington, perhaps looking for his own Boswell, ordered Humphreys to join his staff, putting the young officer at the center of events, attached to a man who would be his patron for life. As a mark of distinction, Washington assigned Humphreys the special task of carrying the British battle flags captured at Yorktown to Philadelphia for a ceremonial presentation to Congress.

More modest, and less flamboyant, London-born Benjamin Walker arrived in New York at an early age as an employee of a London merchant. At the outbreak of the war, he joined the First New York Regiment, commanded by the city's best-known Son of Liberty, Alexander McDougall. He marched with the regiment on the ill-fated invasion of Canada, and in 1778 he joined the staff of General Friedrich von Steuben, where he remained until Washington ordered him to headquarters at Newburgh, New York, in January 1782.[22]

Among their chief duties, Washington's aides were responsible for maintaining and preserving the general's papers. Always concerned about his reputation, Washington, driven by the "spur of fame," was careful to keep good records to be sure that the truth of matters—that is, his side of the story—was preserved for posterity.[23] Keeping the collection intact through the hazards of war was a challenge. In eight years, Washington moved his headquarters (often under adverse conditions) nearly 170 times. Each move risked a loss of documents. In one case, following his hasty retreat from New York City, he stuffed his papers into "a large Box nailed up" and shipped them off to Congress "until Affairs shall be so circumscribed as to admit of their return." After their return, he kept the papers in his personal possession for the rest of the war.[24]

Security for the papers was one thing; access was another. As Washington watched the collection grow, he realized that for his documents to have historic importance, it was necessary to organize and, in some cases, copy them. To oversee these tasks, in the spring of 1781 he appointed Colonel Richard Varick as "Recording Secretary of headquarters."[25] For more than two years, at the end of every week, Washington's aides gathered up documents, bound them carefully, and delivered them to Varick and his staff at Poughkeepsie, New York, where clerks organized and copied them.

In November 1783, when Washington moved his headquarters to West Point to await final word of the British evacuation of New York, he ordered Lieutenant Bezaleel Howe, commander of his lifeguard, to "take charge of the Waggons which contain my baggage and with the escort, proceed with them to Virginia, and deliver them at my house ten miles below Alexandria." Howe was to take particular care of "six strong hair trunks well clasped and with good locks [that] contain all my papers, which are of immense value to me."[26] Under the watchful eyes of Humphreys and Walker, Howe loaded the precious cargo. Following a precise itinerary, dictated by Washington, the trunks arrived safely at Mount Vernon. In the first letter sent in his retirement (1 January 1784), Washington wrote to Varick congratulating the colonel and offering his "entire approbation of the manner in which you have executed the important duties of recording Secretary, and the satisfaction I feel in having my Papers so properly arranged and so correctly recorded. I am fully convinced that neither the present age or posterity will consider the time and labour which have been employed in accomplishing it, unprofitable spent."[27] Working in Washington's study, with the general keeping a careful watch, Humphreys and Walker unpacked and organized the papers.[28]

Despite "bad roads and frozen rivers," as Christmas Day wore on, neighbors arrived at Mount Vernon "to pay their Respects." The general, according to one visitor, "seemed very happy," and his wife, making "everything as agreeable as possible," offered hospitality.[29] At three o'clock, dinner was served. To the table liveried enslaved Africans presented the seasonal favorite—Christmas pie packed with boned chicken and turkey, steeped with numerous spices nestled under a savory crust, all having been cooked in an oven watched carefully for several hours. Glasses filled with his favorite Madeira, Washington, who "laughed and talked a good deal," offered a toast and then invited guests to propose their own salutes. He then launched his "Attack of Christmas Pyes."[30] After dinner the tablecloth was removed, more wine flowed, and conversation filled the room.[31]

Pleased to be done with war and politics, Washington wrote Gilbert du Motier, the marquis de Lafayette, in a phrase that he would repeat numerous times, "I am a private citizen on the banks of the Potomac and under the shadow of my own vine and my own fig tree, free from the bustle of camp and the busy scenes of public life."[32] Martha shared her husband's desire for privacy and escape from public duties. She wrote her friend Hannah Boudinot, wife of Elias Boudinot, former president of the Confederation Congress, that the years of lengthy absences from Mount Vernon and "long journeys have not only left me without inclination to undertake another, but almost disqualified me from doing it, as I find the fatigue is too much for me to bear."[33] To the relief of the general and his wife, the days between Christmas and New Year's were quiet moments. There were no battles to plan, no orders to give, no military reviews to organize, no reports to prepare for Congress.[34]

Shortly after New Year's Day, Washington dismissed Humphreys and Walker, thanked them for their "long and zealous services," and presented each with $100 to assist them in their journey home.[35] Walker returned to New York City; Humphreys rode directly to Annapolis to lobby for a job. From there, setting aside the "boldness of the request" and ignoring any sense of confidentiality, Humphreys revealed to Washington that, after the general had surrendered his commission, Mifflin had approached him confidentially to ask "if anything should occur to me [i.e., a job] I should communicate it to him in a letter." Untethered from reality, a puffed-up Humphreys sought to be secretary of foreign affairs. Might Washington, he asked, in his "private character and as a perpetual Memorial of your friendship and approbation," recommend him for the post?[36]

Washington replied that he would "cheerfully" support him.[37] Privately, however, he believed that his former aide's ambition exceeded his skills. On the same day he assured Humphreys of his support, he wrote Mifflin that while Humphreys might be suitable to play a supporting role, in terms of the more important posts, "Congress should think it expedient to make another appointment."[38] Congress did find a lesser post more suited to Humphreys's abilities. They elected him secretary to the Commissioners for Forming Commercial Treaties in Europe.[39]

Next to his wife and grandchildren, the most important person at Mount Vernon was Washington's cousin and longtime farm manager, Lund Washington. Before taking his post at Mount Vernon, Lund had managed the Ravensworth properties of Henry Fitzhugh, one of Virginia's largest landowners. Not long after marrying Martha, Washington, recognizing Lund's skills and trusting in a familial relationship, invited him to Mount Vernon to manage his plantation. Working for Washington—who was described as aloof, imperious, and a noted micromanager (even at a distance)—was a challenge. Lund, however, did well in this orderly world, and the master and manager developed an amicable relationship. Indeed, Lund was one of the few people Washington addressed by first name in his letters, which he then signed as an "Affectionate friend and servant." In 1775, when Washington went off to war, Lund was left in a world turned upside down. Washington had to rely on his "fidelity and industry."[40]

Although he was well versed in farm issues—planting, harvesting, management of livestock, overseeing a workforce of more than two hundred enslaved individuals—Lund had rarely entered the other parts of Washington's complicated world. Though Washington endowed Lund with authority, he could never robe his cousin with the stature and influence of the general himself. Lund could be ignored and defied.

Most perplexing to Lund was the task of organizing and keeping accurate records of Mount Vernon's tangled finances, which, under the stress of war, grew more troublesome. At first, Washington was pleased with Lund's work and expressed faith in his cousin—"do as you will as I cannot pretend to interfere at this distance."[41] Lund did not always welcome such autonomy. Having spent nearly two decades at Mount Vernon, he was well acquainted with Washington's obsessive concern with details and the general's penchant for dressing down those who failed to follow his directions. In response to Washington's grant of authority, Lund responded that he was uneasy and would "be much better satisfied if you would give positive direction in many things, rather than leave me in a state of uncertainty."[42] Martha's long absences added to Lund's difficulties. When she was away, months at a time, to be with her husband, Lund reluctantly assumed the added duties of "Housekeeper," a responsibility that he admitted he was "by no means fit for." When he married Elizabeth Foote in 1779, she came to live at the mansion and took on domestic matters, providing Lund welcome relief from this burden.[43]

Lund's "state of uncertainty" lasted through the entire war. As pressure mounted, Lund's shortcomings became increasingly apparent, causing Washington to send ever more detailed, often hectoring, instructions. Even in times of battlefield crisis, Washington could not let go of Mount Vernon. On 19 August 1776, as an overwhelming British force of 135 warships and more than thirty-two thousand soldiers prepared to assault the American positions at New York City—a moment when the fate of the Revolution was in balance—Washington took time to write a long letter to Lund with detailed instructions to plant near the mansion house "[t]rees without any order or regularity but pretty thick, as they can at any time be thinned." At the north end, he was to plant "locusts and that at the South, of all the clever kind of Trees (especially flowering ones), that can be got, such as Crab apple, Poplar, Dogwood, Sassafras, Laurel, Willow." All these plantings were to be interspersed with "ever greens such as holly, Pine, and cedar, also ivy— to these may be added the wild flowering Shrubs of the larger kind."[44] Four months later, while leading the Continental Army in their retreat across New Jersey, Washington, still on the subject of trees, instructed Lund to plant locusts along the edge of the mansion "eight or ten feet to the first limb."[45] At a distance, Washington's wishes could be difficult to fathom. Surrounded by wartime chaos he could barely influence, Washington "had created in his mind a world at home wholly amenable to his control, one where his every wish would be followed to the letter."[46] Not always consistent, or empathetic, Washington was prone to criticizing Lund for pestering him with questions that he thought his manager ought to be able to answer himself. In other instances when Lund did take the initiative, Washington overruled him.[47] While farm and financial matters bedeviled their relationship, in the spring of 1781 an affair of honor further disrupted their relationship when Lund risked Washington's most valued possession—his reputation.

In April 1781, to take pressure off British forces under Benedict Arnold operating in northern Virginia, Admiral Mariot Arbuthnot ordered Captain Thomas Graves, commander of the HMS *Savage*, to sail up the Potomac and lay waste to the area, destroying rebel farms and plantations. For three weeks, Graves wreaked havoc along the river, torching warehouses, barns, homes, and crops. His first call on his rampaging cruise was the Maryland shore opposite Mount Vernon where a landing party destroyed several buildings.[48] Graves then crossed to the west side of the river and anchored below Mount Vernon. The captain sent a message to Lund demanding that a "large supply of provisions" be sent immediately, lest Mount Vernon suffer the unhappy fate of its neighbors. Although he had no means of defense, Lund responded boldly "that when the General engaged in the contest he had put all to stake, and was well aware of the exposed situation of his house and property, in consequence he had given him orders by no means to comply with any such demands, for that would mask an unworthy compromise with the enemy, and was ready to meet the fate of his neighbors."[49] With smoke rising visibly from the smoldering ruins across the river, Graves's threat rang true. In a second message, Graves "invited" Lund to come aboard the *Savage*. Lund, recognizing the seriousness of the situation, complied and brought "with him a small present of poultry, of which he begged the captain's acceptance." Graves assured Lund that despite what he had done on the Maryland shore, not "for a moment did he entertain the idea of taking the smallest measure offensive to so illustrious a character as the General." Less than assured, Lund returned to the plantation and "instantly dispatched sheep, hogs, and an abundant supply of other articles" to Graves.[50]

What Lund did not realize was that more than provisions were on their way to the British. While he was placating Graves, seventeen of the plantation's enslaved Africans—fourteen men and three women—were making a break for freedom. Six years before, Virginia's royal governor, Lord Dunmore, had issued a proclamation promising freedom for slaves who fled their masters and sought the protection of the king. Graves's presence gave Washington's slaves the opportunity to flee. All the escapees worked on the mansion farm, among them several skilled artisans (including an overseer, Frederick; a weaver, James; and a cooper, Stephen), as well as people who worked in the household. These were only the first to escape. During the *Savage*'s cruise on the Potomac, nearly one hundred enslaved Africans from other plantations made their dash for freedom.[51]

Washington never forgave the British for these actions. At the end of the Revolution, during a meeting with general Sir Guy Carleton negotiating the British evacuation of New York City, Washington brought up the issue of his "property."[52] But as damaging as the loss of such valuable possessions was to him financially, it was Lund's abject acquiescence to Graves that troubled him most. It was a serious blemish on his reputation. At the same time that the *Savage* was making its cruise up the Potomac, to the south, Lafayette was leading troops engaged with British forces in northern Virginia. When he learned about the affair at Mount Vernon, Lafayette wrote to Washington, "You cannot conceive how unhappy I have been to hear that Mr. Lund Washington went on board the enemy's vessels and consented to give them provisions."[53] Pricked by Lafayette's notice, Washington turned his anger on his cousin: "What gives me most concern, is, that you should go on board the enemy's vessel and furnish them with refreshments. It would have been a less painful circumstance to me, to have heard, that in consequence of your noncompliance with their request, they had burnt my House and laid the Plantation in Ruins. You ought to have considered yourself as my representative and should have reflected on the bad example of communicating with the enemy and making a voluntary offer of refreshment to them with a view to prevent a conflagration."[54]

By early 1783, it was clear that the war was ending, and Washington, like the soldiers serving with him, pined to go home. What awaited him? He was in the dark. Lund had not provided a full account since 1778, giving as his excuse that the accounts were "irregular" and he had "an aversion to writing." Washington sent a blistering letter requiring an "Account of my crops together with receipts and expenditures of my money and state of my stocks and etc." He demanded "to know before I come home (as I shall come home with empty pockets whenever peace shall take place), how affairs stand with me and what my dependence is."[55] Indeed, Washington's pockets were so "empty" that, after the evacuation of New York City, 25 November 1783, he was forced to borrow money from his friend, New York's governor George Clinton, to make his way home.[56] When his distressed nephew, Fielding Lewis, asked for a loan, his uncle shot back that he had "no money."[57]

As the holiday season passed, and wintry weather discouraged others from visiting, Washington faced an "abundance of work" as he pored over his books trying to bring order to "deranged" accounts, which, according to him, were "Ten years in arrears."[58] The confused condition of these papers stood in stark contrast to Varick's twenty-eight volumes of painstakingly organized wartime papers.

For all his talents and hard work as a farm manager, Lund's dislike of travel made him ill suited to perform an essential task—collecting rents on Washington's western lands. According to Washington, settlers were "going into the western country," squatting on his land, and not paying rent. Since rents from these lands were a vital source of income, he was "suffering greatly."[59] Rents were to be paid annually, but for nearly ten years, Lund (whom Washington accused of suffering "an unconquerable aversion" to travel) went west only once, and then "partially."[60] According to Battaile Muse, Washington's rental agent in Frederick and Fauquier Counties, had the tenants paid "their rents annually they would have been in a better situation as well [as] your accounts," but facing years of accumulated rents and interest, and often "very poor," they ignored demands for payment and "looked for law before payment"—a process, Muse warned, "that had many stages to pass through."[61] Reflecting on his situation, Washington lamented that in "losing all my rents," his "private concerns do not wear the most smiling countenance."[62]

Thanks to royal grants rewarding him for service in the French and Indian War, as well as a variety of private purchases, Washington held title to more than twenty thousand acres in the region of the Ohio and

Great Kanawha Rivers.[63] In the years since, however, the upheaval of the Revolution, lack of precise surveys, and careless recordkeeping had thrown confusion over his claims. Washington confessed that, while the years had left him with an "imperfect recollection," he was nonetheless adamant that his rights were "indisputable." Strong willed, he was determined to defend them. Beginning in early February 1784, he set about looking into his "private concerns." He launched several inquiries seeking legal documentation, surveys, land office records, and warrants to verify his claims. The responses provided little satisfaction.[64] Some inquiries went simply unanswered. Among those who ignored Washington, none was more brazen and troublesome than Gilbert Simpson. Simpson's case, noted Washington, called for "louder attention."[65]

In the years before the Revolution, Simpson had been a key figure in Washington's plans to develop his western lands. With Washington's support, in the spring of 1773, Simpson had begun clearing land and planting corn on a parcel known as Washington's Bottom, a 1,644-acre tract thirty-five miles southeast of Fort Pitt on the banks of the Youghiogheny River. Simpson promised Washington that "in five years [the investment would] add something worthwhile to your fortune and a reasonable competency of good living to me."[66] However well the venture may have turned out for Simpson, for Washington it was a disaster. Since the land was to be settled by farmers who needed to grind grain, Simpson agreed to build a mill. Three years went by, the war began, and still there was no functioning mill. From his headquarters in Cambridge, Washington wrote Lund complaining about that "confounded Simpson" and asked him to investigate the matter. "I never hear of the mill without a degree of warmth and vexation at his extreme stupidity."[67] Given his distaste for travel, Lund undertook no investigation. In February 1784, during a visit to his "aged mother" who was living in Fredericksburg under the care of his younger sister Betty Lewis, Washington saw an opportunity to press Simpson.[68] His nephew John Lewis was preparing to set out for Fort Pitt on business. Hoping that a stern message delivered in person by a close relative might stir a reply, he entrusted Lewis with a letter to Simpson. He told Lewis that he would be "obliged" if, in addition to delivering the letter while he was "going by," he would observe and report on the size, & condition of his Plantation: & the condition of the Mill—& for enquiring how many Tenants he has placed on the Land, for how long a term, & upon what Rents. Whether there is any person living upon a small Tract he holds at the Great Meadows—what sort of an improvement is thereon—of whom the person took it and upon what terms—And should Mr. Lewis have a favourable opportunity, the General would be obliged to him for informing those Settlers upon his tract West of the Monongahela, on the waters of Shurtee's & Raccoon creeks, that he has a Patent for the Land, dated the 5th day of July 1774—that he will most assuredly assert his right to it—but, in consideration of their having made improvements hereon ignorantly, or under a mistaken belief, founded on false assertions, that the Land did not belong to him; he is willing that they should remain upon it as Tenants, upon a just & moderate Rent, such as he & they can agree upon. The like may be said to any Person or Persons who may be settled at a place called the Round Bottom, on the Ohio opposite Pipe Creek & a little above a Creek called Capteening, which has been surveyed by the county Surveyor of Augusta upon proper Warrants from Lord Dunmore, ever since the 14th day of July 1773.

Lewis was also to "discover by indirect means an agent in the neighborhood of Fort Pitt to charge with the seating and leasing the General's lands." All of this was to be done "as soon as possible."[69]

As was his custom when dealing with people for whom he had little respect, in his letter to Simpson carried by Lewis, Washington dosed his anger with sarcasm: "Having closed all my transactions with the public it now behooves me to investigate my own private business, no part of which seems to call for louder attention than my concerns with you. How profitable our partnership has been, you best can *tell*; and how advantageous my mill has been none can tell *so well as yourself*" (italics in original). The accusation was harsh: "you have been much more attentive to your interest than mine." Washington demanded a "full settlement of this account."[70]

When Lewis met with Simpson and delivered Washington's demands, Simpson's only answer was to recite a tedious tale of woe about the difficulties of life in a "howling wilderness"—smallpox, hostile Indians, crop failures, drought, and troublesome settlers who either failed to pay rent or simply disappeared. As for the toxic reports circulating about him, they were nothing more than the "malicious assertions of designing men." Concluding on a defiant note, Simpson declared that he was "determined never to live on a place where I am suspected as in such cases I have a spirit of resentment as well as other men and heartily wish for a settlement and a separation. I am now growing in years and rather infirm and should it happen that I cannot wait on you I should be glad you would send an attorney for you to settle our affairs."[71]

Lewis's report painted a disturbing picture. In the time he was with Simpson, he could get "no satisfactory account." Clearly things had gone awry, and he informed his uncle that "from the inquiry I made I think it would be necessary to send some person, and as soon as possible, to make inquiry into the situation of your plantation and Negro's. The information I got of some of your Negro's [slaves] is such as I chuse not to commit to paper, for fear of a miscarriage of the letter." Lewis ended his somber, enigmatic report with a fragment of good news: A few days before leaving, he "fell in with Mr. David Bradford, a gentleman of the law and a sensible man of good character." Bradford struck Lewis as being as "proper a person as you could employ." And so he hired him to "undertake" an "enquiry into the situation of your lands" and to "post" the people who might have settled on his lands of his intention of asserting his claims.[72]

For nearly a month, Bradford rode the circuit, warning the settlers of their legal jeopardy. He reported alarming news. The settlers were in a defiant mood. Having heard nothing from the general in a decade, they had been "lulled under the idea that his claim would never have made its appearance in this quarter" and were "greatly alarmed, indeed, on being acquainted of the General's intentions of asserting his claim." News from the west arrived slowly, and Bradford's report did not reach Mount Vernon until May. By that time, affairs had deteriorated to such a point that Washington had decided to make his own trip west.[73] First, however, there was a pressing matter that drew him from Mount Vernon to Philadelphia.

The winter of 1782–1783 had been the American army's winter of discontent. Following the victory at Yorktown, Washington had ordered the troops back to their encampment at Newburgh, New

York, a few miles above West Point, a key position from which they could monitor the British forces holding New York City. Rumors of peace circulated, and the soldiers sensed that the war was ending. Officers, who had not been paid in months, were uneasy. If the war ended and a bankrupt Congress sent them home, how might they ever get their pay? During these troubles, on 10 March an anonymous address circulated in the camp warning the officers that, in peace, "your voice shall sink, and your strength dissipate . . . when swords shall be taken from your sides."[74] The army was on the precipice of mutiny. The anonymous author called for a meeting of the officers on Tuesday, 11 March. Sensing rebellion, Washington canceled the meeting and instead called the officers to meet under his authority on 15 March. On that day more than three hundred officers assembled. As he stood before them, "every eye fixed upon the illustrious man." The speech was personal: "I have been a faithful friend to the army. I was among the first who embarked in the cause of our common enemy." Washington implored his listeners "to rely on the plighted faith of Congress to cause all your Accts. to be fairly liquidated."[75] According to one observer, Philip Schuyler, "The whole assembly, were in tears."[76] The meeting adjourned, and the officers returned to their regiments. Less than a month later, news of peace arrived; on 18 April 1783, Washington issued a general order announcing "a cessation of hostilities."[77] It would take several months for the final treaty to be ratified, but the war was over. The army was disbanding. For the officers, their worst fears had come to pass—peace and no pay.

Joy and despair filled the officer ranks. They longed to go home, but once they left the company of one another and scattered to their states, their influence on Congress would evaporate. Seeking a way to keep this "band of brothers" together, on 13 May 1783, a group of senior officers met at General von Steuben's headquarters, Mount Gulian, Fishkill, New York. With von Steuben presiding, they created the Society of the Cincinnati, modeling themselves on the historical Lucius Quintus Cincinnatus, the Roman general who, after defeating the enemies of the Republic, put aside his sword and returned to the plow. In their Institution (Constitution) prepared by General Henry Knox, they pledged to certain "immutable principles," including "[a]n incessant attention to preserve inviolate those exalted rights and liberties for which they have fought" and "an unalterable determination to promote and cherish the future dignity of the American Empire." Membership in the society was limited to officers with "three years' service," who would "subscribe one month's pay." To perpetuate the society, "and as testimony of affection to the memory and the offspring of such officers as have died in the service, their eldest male branches shall have the same right of becoming members as the children of the actual members of the Society" (i.e., hereditary membership). The society's Latin motto was *Omnia reliquit servare rem publicam* ("He gave up everything to serve the republic").[78]

Although Washington was not present at the creation, three weeks later, 19 June, at the society's first meeting, with patriotic emotions running high, by acclamation, the members elected Washington president general. Immediately following, Major Pierre L'Enfant, a French officer who had joined the American army in 1777, presented a design for a medal to be worn by the members. It was, he reported, "the Bald Eagle, which is unique to this continent, and is distinguished from those of other climates by its white head and tail."[79] The members approved the design, and L'Enfant was charged with preparing the medal. In this moment of euphoria, without great reflection, but moved by affection for his fellow officers, Washington consented to be placed at the head of an organization whose avowed purposes were charitable and patriotic, but at the same time it was elitist, hereditary, and national in scope, with aims that hinted at a shadowy political agenda.[80]

Through the summer of 1783, while Knox, von Steuben, and others recruited members to the society, Washington continued to oversee the army's disbanding while making plans to reoccupy New York City. He played no direct role in the affairs of the Cincinnati.

Matters took an unwonted turn on 12 September, when an unknown "friend" sent James Madison, a delegate in Congress from Virginia, a copy of the society's Institution accompanied by several "notes" describing the recent proceedings of the members as well as a description of the "medal."[81] Until this moment, although Madison and others in the Congress were aware of the society, they had little information about it and had given it scant notice. A letter to Madison from his friend Edmund Randolph, Washington's personal attorney and a former member of Congress, caused anxiety. Randolph feared the society would "keep alive the distinction between citizen and soldier."[82] The dam was about to burst. In the fall, fierce attacks on the Cincinnati appeared in newspapers in Boston, Philadelphia, and New York. Washington was taken aback. Anticipating a meeting of the society that had been called for May 1784, over which he would preside, he wrote to Henry Knox asking him to describe "in precise terms, what is expected from the President of the Cincinnati—[a]s I was never present at any of your meetings, and have never seen the proceedings of the last."[83]

Among the most virulent foes of the society was "Cassius," Judge Aedanus Burke of Charleston, South Carolina, author of *Considerations on the Society or Order of Cincinnati Proving That It Creates a Race of Hereditary Patricians or Nobility* (October 1783). The title page bellowed, "Blow ye the Trumpet of Zion." In a trenchant and piercing essay, he targeted the "Major-Generals, Brigadier-Generals and other Officers of the American Army," assailing them for conspiring to "create A Race of Hereditary Patricians." Burke was "filled with astonishment" that no one had revealed the sinister nature of this malevolent body, led by "all grasping infatuating ambition of our generals and field officers," whose aim was nothing less than "to beget, and perpetuate family grandeur in an aristocratic nobility, to terminate at last in monarchical tyranny." Congress, he declared, "winks at it." Missing from Burke's list of the accused was the president general of the society. Exhibiting a bit of imaginative thinking, Burke gave the general a pass, noting that Washington, employing "discretion, his distinguishing characteristic, appeared quite neutral."[84]

Shortly after arriving home, unaware of the rising tempest, on New Year's Day, in his capacity as president general, Washington dispatched a "Circular Letter to the State Societies of the Cincinnati," announcing "the city of Philadelphia to be the place for the general meeting of the Cincinnati on the first Monday in May next."[85] Just as the letter was making its way among the states, in Boston the *Independent Chronicle* reprinted Burke's pamphlet. Other newspapers printed excerpts; debates raged. From Boston, Benjamin Lincoln wrote that "citizens were alarmed." Knox warned that Burke's pamphlet had its "full operation" and that the Cincinnati had become "an object of jealousy." In reaction, the Massachusetts legislature had formed a committee "to consider what measures are necessary to be taken in order to prevent the Ill consequences of any Combination that are or may hereafter be formed to promote undue Distinctions among the citizens of this Free State."[86] Opposition spread. Governor Benjamin Gerard of South Carolina denounced the society's "thirst for dignities, gewgaws, and bawbles." From Paris, Benjamin Franklin opined that the founders were "too much struck with the ribbands and crosses they had seen hanging on the buttonholes of foreign officers."[87]

By spring, the onslaught had caused Washington to waver in his support for the society. He told Jonathan Trumbull that "if we cannot convince the people that their fears are ill founded, we should (at least in a degree), yield to them."[88] Anxious to get a sense of Congress, Washington asked one of Virginia's representatives, Thomas Jefferson (a person not eligible for membership in the society), to give "with frankness, and the fullest latitude of a friend, your opinion of the Institution of the Society of the Cincinnati."[89] Replying with unwonted speed, Jefferson did not mince words. He told Washington, to whom personal reputation was everything, that his "character which will be handed to future ages at the head of our revolution" might well be "compromised" by his association with the Cincinnati. The society was "against the Confederation and against the letter of some of our constitutions." Most objectionable was the right of hereditary membership. "Unfriendly" sentiment against the Cincinnati was so strong "that in all appointments of trust and honor, or profit, Congress would silently pass by all candidates of that order."[90] A New Hampshire delegate, Jonathan Blanchard, was even more blunt in his assessment: "The Cincinnati is exceedingly reprobated."[91]

To underscore his point, Jefferson enclosed a draft of the land ordinance under consideration in Congress, which he had authored, providing a temporary government for the western territory that had been recently ceded to Congress by Virginia. Included in the draft ordinance was a provision that governments in the territory "shall be in republican forms and shall admit no person to be a citizen who holds any hereditary title"—a direct slap at the Cincinnati. Three days before the final vote, by a very narrow margin, Congress eliminated the provision. The Virginia delegation, however, voted unanimously to retain it.[92]

Although the meeting was not to convene until 4 May, Washington left Mount Vernon on April 26, allowing him time to visit Congress at Annapolis.[93] According to Jefferson, who had been informed by Edmund Randolph that the general's opinion of the society was yet an "impenetrable secret," Washington "called on me at Annapolis, it was a little after candlelight, and he sat with me till after midnight, conversing almost exclusively on that subject [Cincinnati]. While he was feeling indulgent to the motives which might induce the officers to promote it, he concurred with me entirely in condemning it." Washington left Annapolis determined, Jefferson wrote, to abolish the society; "not a fiber of it ought to be left, to be an eye sore to the public."[94]

If abolition of the Cincinnati was his goal, Washington had failed. On the morning of 4 May, the meeting convened in the City Tavern, and for two weeks the members debated the future of the society. In contrast to his legendary reluctance to speak in public, Washington took the floor four times to express "warmly and in plain language" his deep reservations.[95]

On the third day of debate, 6 May, according to Winthrop Sargent, who kept a careful record of the proceedings, Washington, "[i]n a very long speech and with much warmth and agitation expressed himself on all the Parts of the Institution (deem'd exceptionable) and reiterated his Determination to vacate his place in the Society if it could not be accommodated to the feeling and pleasure of the several States."[96] At this point, it seemed that "after several days of struggle within doors and without, a general sentiment was obtained for [the Cincinnati's] entire abolition."[97] It was not to be. In a dramatic moment

arrived Major L'Enfant, who had been sent to France to procure the eagles, and to offer the order to the French officers who had served in America. He brought the king's permission to his officers to accept it, letters of solicitation from other officers to accept it, the letters of thanks of these officers accepting it, letters of solicitation from other officers to obtain it and the eagles themselves. The effect of all this on the minds of the members was to undo much of what had been done, to rekindle all the passions which had produced the institution, and silence all the dictates of prudence which had been operating for its abolition.[98]

With a fresh wind filling their sails, supporters advised that abandoning the society would be an insult to the French.[99] With abolition no longer an option, the meeting moved on to reform. On 12 May, they approved amendments to the institution that made no mention of hereditary rights to membership, leaving it to the state societies to "Judge of the qualifications of the Members."[100] Washington understood the hollowness of the measures; nonetheless, out of loyalty to his fellow officers and respect for the French, he acquiesced and accepted reelection as president general. In private, he wrote candidly to his friend Philip Schuyler that he had been "most amazingly embarrassed in the business."[101]

When the meeting adjourned, Tuesday morning (18 May), Washington left Philadelphia "immediately."[102] Since reports of his shifting conduct in Philadelphia had harmed his reputation in Congress, he hurried to Annapolis. He observed the body, as described by its secretary, Charles Thomson, in an "unsettled state" with business "at a full stand."[103] In a meeting with Jefferson, Washington found his abhorrence of the society little diminished; however, not wanting to provoke the most powerful person in America, Jefferson, in his usual elliptical fashion, confided to Washington that he did not "include him among the Samsons in the field whose hair had been cut off by the whore England."[104]

Still uneasy about his role in the society, Washington arrived home on Sunday, 23 May. Fortunately, for the moment he could put the society's matters aside, as the next meeting would not convene until May 1787.

2

THE WEST

I have come to a resolution to take a trip to the Western
Country. (GW to James Craik, 10 July 1784, in *GWP,
Conf. Series*, 1:492)

Washington's visits to Annapolis and Philadelphia had not gone
well. Although the Cincinnati had elected him their president
(what else could they do?), they had not left his leadership unchallenged.
By delegating the power to define eligibility for membership to the
state societies, they had executed a clever subterfuge, for it was widely
known that the members were much in favor of hereditary membership. Washington had been outmaneuvered.

An imposing and commanding figure, Washington was accustomed to almost always getting his way in wartime or on his plantation.
Failure to persuade his fellow officers to follow him at Philadelphia
took him by surprise. He believed that, by ignoring him, his comrades
had made a serious mistake. He shared his fears with General Arthur
St. Clair, warning that, while the "uproar" of the public was quiet for
the moment, in fact their "jealousies are rather asleep than removed."[1]

Washington's stopovers at Annapolis in May 1784 marked the
first time that he had visited Congress since resigning his commission.
Little had changed. The body was bedeviled by the same issues that had
haunted it during the war. Poverty and poor attendance, even worse
now that the exigencies of war were gone, left them ill equipped to
govern the new nation. Nonetheless, for the moment at least, he rode
away hopeful, writing to Jonathan Trumbull:

Notwithstanding the jealous and contracted temper which seems to prevail in some of the States, yet I cannot but hope and believe that the good sense of the People will *ultimately* get the better of their *prejudices* [italics in original]; and that order and sound policy will be produced from the present unsettled and deranged state of public Affairs. Indeed, I am happy to observe that the political disposition is actually meliorating every day. Everything, my dear Trumbull, will come right at last as we have often prophesied.[2]

Six months before his resignation, in June 1783, after the preliminary treaty had been signed, Washington articulated his prophecy in "A Circular Letter to States." It was his valedictory address to America. The letter, four thousand words long, began on a note of hope: "The eyes of the whole world" were turned on this new nation that had "a surer opportunity for political happiness, than any other nation has ever been favored with." The nation, however, was on "probation." Whether it would "stand or fall" rested on the action of the states. Four things, he wrote, were "essential to the existence of the United States as an independent power."

> An indissoluble Union of the States under one Federal Head.
> A sacred regard to Public Justice.
> The adoption of a proper Peace Establishment.
> The prevalence of a pacific and friendly disposition among the people of the United States, which will induce them to forget their local prejudices and policies, to make those mutual concessions which are requisite to the general prosperity, and in some instances, to sacrifice their individual advantages to the interests of the community.[3]

To his dismay, during his visits to Annapolis, Washington had discovered that in the scrum of postwar politics, his four points had been lost. Chastened by his personal defeat in Philadelphia and the lamentable situation of Congress he had witnessed in Annapolis, he recognized how disaffection, sectional rivalries, and chronic absenteeism obstructed affairs. Washington was no longer convinced that everything would "come right." His mood darkened further when, a few days after arriving home, he opened a letter from Henry Knox, the Cassandra of the North. He, too, had been in Annapolis and was now on his way home to Boston. His friend's letter did nothing to lighten his mood. He wrote Washington his glum assessment: "Things are not well and will probably be worse before they are better."[4]

At Mount Vernon visitors arrived, and with Congress having granted "free postage to all Letters and Packets to and from the late Commander in Chief," the mail poured in.[5] French officers wrote pursuing membership in the Cincinnati. Office seekers sought recommendations for positions in the government. Merchants angled to do business with Washington, including firms in France, England, and Ireland. His debtors pleaded forgiveness. The Virginia House of Delegates sent notice that to honor him they had resolved to "cause a statue to be erected of the finest marble and best workmanship." William Gordon, a Boston minister, inquired whether he might have the general's permission and cooperation to write his biography. State and local societies promoting agriculture and other good works elected Washington to membership. His friends in Congress shared with him "secret papers," keeping him fully informed on politics.[6] Nonetheless, whatever swirled in the world beyond Mount Vernon, Washington remained deeply attached to life on his plantation. He was happy to return to "the routine of his estate, completely involved with all the details of his lands and house."[7] While busily trying to catch up with a mountain of unfinished business, Washington received news that delighted him: Gilbert du Motier, the marquis de Lafayette, was returning to America.

A young man (born 1757) with little military experience, Lafayette was well connected, wealthy, idealistic, and a fierce Anglophobe (his father had died fighting the British at the Battle of Minden in 1759). Seeing an opportunity to attach French interests to the Revolution, Silas Deane, an American agent in Paris, recruited Lafayette to come to America. "Joining his colors to those of the Revolutionaries," Lafayette purchased a ship, *La Victoire*, and, with several other officers, left for America.[8] After a fifty-six-day voyage, they arrived at Georgetown, South Carolina, on 13 June 1777. Bearing flattering letters of recommendation, Lafayette arrived in Philadelphia. On 31 July, a swooning Congress, applauding the marquis's "great zeal in the cause of liberty," commissioned him a major general—without pay.[9] Later in the day Washington arrived in Philadelphia to discuss with Congress the threat of a British advance on the city. That evening at dinner, the commander in chief met, for the first time, his newest major general. Aware that the young man had access to the highest levels of French government, including the king himself, Washington, although not impressed by the marquis's military experience, understood his value as a political conduit. He also embraced Lafayette as a fellow Mason. Following dinner Washington invited the newly minted general to ride with him on an inspection of the American lines around Philadelphia. A skilled courtier, with a youthful demeanor and a flair for language, Lafayette later described this occasion as a "noble moment" when "two friends were united whose attachment and confidence were cemented by the greatest of causes."[10] So close was their relationship that Lafayette later pronounced himself Washington's "adopted son."[11] Unlike so many other foreign officers who flocked to America, Lafayette was useful. Following the victory at Yorktown (October 1781), Lafayette returned to France celebrated as "the hero of two worlds."[12]

Lafayette had intended his stay in France to be brief. Peace, however, made his return less imperative. He remained in France advocating for the interests of America, and after the formation of the Cincinnati, he assumed the role of the society's de facto representative in France.[13] Not surprisingly, the young, worldly marquis, well known for his liberal sympathies, embraced the intellectual excitement of Paris, joining Pahin de La Blancherie's Salon de la Correspondence, where scholars and artists met to embrace an emerging Romantic movement emphasizing individualism, emotion, and human progress over the cool rationality of the Enlightenment, a movement commonly referred to as "The Republic of Letters." It was "an intellectual community transcending space and time, [but] recognizing as such differences in respect to the diversity of languages, sects, and countries."[14] At its very heart was "liberty." For Lafayette, Washington, his "beloved general," was the embodiment of this international movement. He was nothing less than the "Saviour of His country, the benefactor of mankind."[15]

In 1784, Lafayette dispatched two dozen letters to Mount Vernon (Washington responded eleven times), providing detailed accounts of military and political events in Europe.[16] But no matter what news he shared with Washington, repeatedly in each letter, often in emotional terms, he expressed his deep longing to see, once again, Washington and America. "Ten times a day [I] wish myself on the other side of the Atlantic," he wrote. "[T]he years of the Revolution were the happiest in my life."[17] Washington replied with measured affection, inviting his friend to visit "with Madame la Fayette and view me in my domestic walks—I have often told you, and I repeat it again, that no man could receive you in them with more friendship & affection than I should do; in which I am sure Mrs. Washington would cordially join me."[18]

After several delays, in the spring of 1784, good news arrived from Paris. "Thank God," Lafayette heralded. "Before the month of June is over, I may be blessed with the sight of the American shore."[19] Leaving Paris without his wife, Adrienne, who remained home to care for their children—a son, Georges Washington, and two daughters, Marie Antoinette and Anastasie—Lafayette arrived in New York on 4 August. It was the height of summer and most of his friends "were in the country," escaping the city's heat. With little reason to stay and determined upon "seeing General Washington again," Lafayette, accompanied by his "traveling companion" Maurice Riquet de Caraman (a captain in the Noailles Dragoons), left the city on 7 August. After crossing the Hudson, they stopped briefly for a few hours in Brunswick, New Jersey, a time sufficient for the legislature to honor him. They stayed the night at the Jones Tavern in Clinton and in the morning set out for Philadelphia.[20]

Philadelphia was home to one of America's most distinguished learned organizations—the American Philosophical Society. Founded in 1743 by Benjamin Franklin to "promote useful knowledge," the society elected Lafayette to membership in 1781.[21] The society's interests were eclectic. Seeking to gather noted intellectuals, in much the same manner as the Paris salons, its meetings were devoted to the presentation of scholarly papers on a wide variety of topics, including "Five Thermometers," "Petrified Bones Found Near the Ohio," and "Comets Lately Discovered." Lafayette stoked interest among the members of the society when he sent a letter read at their 2 April meeting, "An Authentic Narrative of Experiments Lately Made in France with Air Balloons," in which he described the amazing moment when the Montgolfier brothers launched a hot air balloon, carrying a sheep, a duck, and a rooster, over the gardens at Versailles before an audience that included King Louis XVI and Queen Marie Antoinette.[22] Lafayette shared the news with Washington, who was skeptical. "I have only newspaper Accounts of the air balloons, to which I do not know what credence to give; as the tales related of them are marvelous, and lead us to expect that our friends in Paris, in a little time, will come flying through the air, instead ploughing the Ocean to get to America."[23] Lest America be uninformed and left behind, at the June meeting Dr. John Morgan presented his paper titled "Air Balloons" and moved that members work to encourage "an effort to send up a large air balloon."[24]

By no measure could the citizens of Philadelphia permit such a distinguished visitor as Lafayette to pass unacknowledged, nor could the society let fly an opportunity to greet an eminent member and hear in person about his most recent inquiries. As a "large cortege of former officers, militiamen and citizens" assembled to welcome him to "the beautiful city of Philadelphia," members of the society voted by "special appointment" to invite the marquis to address them.[25] Lafayette's letter of the previous April about balloons had spurred considerable discussion. The members were anxious to learn more.

On the afternoon of 12 August, twenty-two members—an unusually large gathering—met to hear the marquis. With balloons on their minds, the members were surprised as Lafayette, for two hours, said nothing about balloons but instead

> entertained them with a particular relation of the wonderful effects of a certain invisible nature, called *animal magnetism* [italics in original], lately discovered by Mr. Mesmer, a German Philosopher, and explained by him to a number of Gentlemen in Paris of which number the Marquis was himself one. By this relation it appears that persons may be so impregnated with the powers (by a process which the Marquis does not think himself at liberty yet to explain), as to exhibit many phenomena similar to those of metallic magnetism.[26]

The minutes of the meeting fail to reveal how Lafayette explained to the society a therapeutic system he did not himself understand.

Commonly called Mesmerism (named after Franz Mesmer), it asserted that there was an invisible natural magnetic force possessed of all living things that, when properly understood, could have physical effects including healing. Although dismissed by many (including Benjamin Franklin), Lafayette, a credulous romantic, embraced Mesmerism. With the unbridled enthusiasm of a zealous convert, he shared his excitement with Washington and promised that as soon as he reached Mount Vernon, he would "let him in to the secrets of Mesmer."[27] Mesmer, hoping that Lafayette would "make known in the territory of the United States, a discovery, of much importance to mankind," entrusted him with a letter to Washington. He explained that he had formed a society "for the good of humanity," suggesting that Washington, for whom he had "admiration and respect," might offer his support. Lafayette carried the letter to Mount Vernon.[28] Washington, the farmer, was a practical man who cared more about animal husbandry than animal magnetism; he put the letter aside for nearly five months and then responded in his oft-used mechanical form, thanking Mesmer for his "favorable sentiments."[29]

Leaving Philadelphia on Sunday, 15 August, crossing the country very quickly, on Tuesday morning Lafayette passed through Alexandria on his "way to his Excellency General Washington's seat Mount Vernon."[30] As usual, when Lafayette arrived, Washington had "a house full of company."[31] The general himself, however, not expecting the marquis, was away making the rounds of his farms. When he returned to the mansion, Lafayette described the moment of reunion to his wife. It was, he wrote, "very tender and our satisfaction completely mutual. I assure you that in retirement General Washington is even greater than he was during the Revolution."[32]

Life at Mount Vernon was both simple and sublime. The two soldiers rose early, shared the usual early morning hoecakes, swimming in "butter and honey." After breakfast, they spent time discussing "the past, the present and the future."[33] It was, as their friend Nathanael Greene imagined it, "a "feat of reason and flow of the soul."[34]

Not given to changing his routine, mid-morning, Washington, leaving his guest with "things to read," left to make the rounds of his farms. In the general's absence, Lafayette, accompanied by Martha, roamed about the grounds. "Nothing," he wrote Adrienne, "is so beautiful as the location of Mount Vernon. The house itself is very fine, and the countryside is delightful." To commemorate his visit and honor his hostess, he planted a magnolia tree in her garden.[35]

When not reading, walking the gardens, or enjoying the grand view of the Potomac from the piazza, Lafayette, an avid horseman, rode with Washington on fox hunts across the Virginia countryside. Disappointed at the performance of his domestic hounds, Washington asked Lafayette whether he would send him French hounds.[36] Lafayette agreed, but when he returned home and made inquiries, he confessed that it was difficult to find local hounds, since the French preferred English breeds that were faster. Finally, in May 1785, he sent seven hounds (presumably French) to Washington, along with a bundle of personal letters that he entrusted to the care of eighteen-year-old John Quincy Adams, returning home from Paris to enter Harvard.[37]

Always punctual, in the afternoon Washington returned from his circuit of the plantation. After "dressing and preparing," at three o'clock the Washingtons and their guests sat for dinner, the principal meal of the day. At table with his friends, Washington set the company at ease with his "free and affable conversation."[38] The conversation roamed beyond wartime reminiscences, farming, and discussion of politics to family and personal matters, including children. Lafayette, who in "tribute to respect and love for my dear friend" had named his own son Georges Motier de Lafayette, was taken with the "great tenderness" Washington lavished on Wash and Nelly. He found it "amusing to see the curiosity of these two little ones, who had heard me spoken of, and were very anxious to see if I looked like my portrait."[39]

Lafayette was moved deeply by the warm reception he received at Mount Vernon and the reunion with his former commander. Possessed of a "strong thirst of praise and popularity," he treasured the accolades showered on him. But as gratifying as all this adulation was to the marquis, he had not returned simply to bathe in the glory of a returning hero. He came back to America, he told James Madison, riding "Three Hobby-Horses—the alliance between France and the United States, the union of the latter and the manumission of the slaves."[40]

In Paris, Lafayette had worked tirelessly to bolster commercial relations between the United States and France. His fame and reputation gave him access to the highest councils at Versailles, including Charles Gravier, the comte de Vergennes, the astute and long-serving foreign minister who had orchestrated the Franco-American Alliance (1778) that helped win the Revolution. Only a few days before his arrival in New York, proof of Lafayette's efforts on behalf of America was announced. The king had declared Dunkirk, Bayonne, L'Orient, and Marseilles to be free ports for American ships. That news brought joy to American merchants, particularly those who were eager to find trading partners outside the British Empire. Congress wrote to the marquis to express "the high sense which Congress entertain of his important services relative to the commerce of France."[41]

As he traveled the countryside, in his usual cheerful manner, Lafayette saw America as prosperous, tranquil, and flourishing: "The houses I saw burned, I see rebuilt; abandoned lands are being occupied again, and everything I come across has an air of complete recovery."[42] The appearance of prosperity, however, could not erase Lafayette's deep concerns about the new nation. He was apprehensive about the tenuousness of the union; the political weakness of Congress; the escalating movement west that was likely to drain resources; the British, who were exerting great efforts to draw America back into their economic orbit; and the threat of the Spanish, whom the Americans "genuinely hate" for their machinations in the Mississippi Valley.[43] And then, of course, there was slavery.

During the war years in America, Lafayette had seen firsthand the brutality of slavery while witnessing the dignity and humanity of enslaved Africans. On his return to France, influenced by the rising antislavery sentiment, Lafayette's discomfort grew to revulsion. He praised the marquis de Condorcet's passionate antislavery tract, *Réflexions sur l'esclavage des negres* (1781), condemning slavery as an abomination that ought to be abolished. At the same time, however, Lafayette was uneasy with Condorcet's blunt observation that "[w]ithout the American war, Negro slavery would have been abolished within a few generations."[44] Lafayette stood in the embarrassing position of having helped establish a nation based on the principle that "all men are created equal," while in reality its economy and society were deeply rooted in slavery.

Buoyant about America but troubled by its embrace of slavery, Lafayette took as a mission an effort to persuade Washington to join him in a philanthropic venture that might show a path away from slavery. The marquis was convinced that if Washington and he led, others would follow.

Lafayette had first raised the issue of slavery with Washington more than a year before. In February 1783, he had written to him that with the Revolution nearly over, and the general about to "enjoy some ease and comfort," he hoped that Washington might join him in a plan "which might become greatly beneficial to the black part of Mankind." With the fervor of a reformer, he asked Washington to "unite in purchasing a small estate where we may try the experiment to free the Negroes." His proposal was to settle enslaved Africans as "tenants" on the estate. The details were vague. No location was given for the "estate," nor were costs mentioned. "If it be a wild scheme, I had rather be mad that way, than to be thought wise on the other tack."[45]

Washington was cautious. He spent most of his reply to Lafayette reflecting on the abyss on which the nation teetered. At this critical moment when the "true interest of this country must be measured by a Continental scale," he feared forces were at work that will "weaken the union and may ultimately break the band, which holds us together." Only at the end of his letter did Washington refer directly to Lafayette's "experiment." Although praising Lafayette's "benevolence of heart," and suggesting that he would be "happy to join [him] in so laudable a work," Washington knew that the union could wreck on the rock of slavery. Unwilling to commit himself in a letter—a medium that others might read—he suggested to his young friend that they "defer going into detail of the business, till I have the pleasure of seeing you."[46]

Washington, who according to John Adams "possessed the gift of silence," once advised his favorite nephew, Bushrod, that in public matters he ought "[r]ise but seldom [and] never be agitated by more than a decent warmth."[47] On the issue of slavery, he followed his own advice. In several letters, nonpublic, Washington did grapple with slavery, contemplating emancipation; in public, however, the financial and political hurdles, joined to the political risks, wrapped him in Adams's "silence."

The issue of slavery was ever present. In May 1782, the Virginia Assembly enacted a law, "That those persons who are disposed to emancipate their slaves are empowered to do so," but only on condition that the enslaved Africans "shall respectively be supported and maintained by the person liberating them." Even such limited action raised a furor in the countryside, and by the time Lafayette arrived at Mount Vernon, the backlash was in full swing. In the fall of 1785, petitions, eventually signed by more than twelve hundred Virginians, demanded repeal of "the subtle and daring attempt to wrest from us our slaves."[48] Silent in public, in private Washington wrote to Lafayette that he was in "despair." He held, however, to the possibility that while "[t]o set them [enslaved Africans] afloat at once would be productive of much inconvenience and mischief . . . by degrees it certainly might and assuredly ought to be affected by legislative authority."[49] Washington was being disingenuous. He knew that such action by the Virginia legislature was a forlorn hope. In the matter of slavery, Washington was no revolutionary.

Lafayette viewed slavery as an abomination that sullied America's character. The reputation of America, "the temple of liberty," that "noble cause for which as an American [he had] engaged, bled, negotiated and fought" was at risk. When others attacked America, he proclaimed himself an "American," whose "duty and inclination was to set up in the best light everything that is done by a body of Americans."[50]

Yet, while bold in his letter to Washington, as a guest at Mount Vernon Lafayette was careful to tread lightly, not wishing to cause uneasiness with his host or risk their friendship. While the two may have discussed "the detail of the business," neither made mention of such a conversation in their contemporary writings. Washington kept his silence.

Having traveled so far, it was Lafayette's intention to remain at Mount Vernon for an extended time. His late summer arrival, however, was inconvenient for his host. Convinced that the troubling situation of his western lands, particularly his deteriorating relationship with the artful Gilbert Simpson, called for personal attention, Washington had decided "to visit my Landed property west of the Appalachians." Lafayette arrived when Washington was preparing for an extended visit west.[51]

George Washington had traveled west several times. He first visited the frontier in 1748 at age sixteen as a member of a party sent to survey lands along the south branch of the Potomac River owned by the Fairfax family. Later, in 1753, as an officer in the Virginia militia, he marched on a mission to warn the French out of the Ohio Valley. When they failed to withdraw, he returned the next year, when, in a reckless move, he attacked a French party at Jumonville Glen. While the tinder had been building for some time between the English and French in North America, Washington's action, in the words of English diarist and gossip Sir Horace Walpole, "set the world on fire."[52] One year later, he rode with General Edward Braddock on his ill-fated expedition against the French at Fort Duquesne. Washington survived Braddock's disastrous defeat and went on to command the Virginia regiment assigned to protect the frontier from French and Indian raids. In 1758, he marched west again as part of General John Forbes's expedition against Fort Duquesne. After the war, in the fall of 1770, Washington made his fourth trip west in the company of his friend Dr. James Craik. He spent six weeks roving the Ohio Valley, identifying bounty lands along the Kanawha and Ohio Rivers that had been granted to him (and other soldiers of the Virginia regiment) for their service to the king.[53]

Driven by the urge to acquire good real estate, Washington did not confine his interests to the West. In the summer of 1783, while waiting at his Newburgh headquarters for the British to evacuate New York City, he took the opportunity to travel the Mohawk River with his friend Philip Schuyler, one of New York's largest landowners. The party traveled as far west as Fort Stanwix (Fort Schuyler, Rome, New York). At Stanwix, Washington could see that over a short four-mile portage, boats could reach Wood Creek, which was navigable to Lake Oswego, leading to Lake Ontario. From his observations, Washington understood that, with some energy (eventually the Erie Canal, completed in 1825), using the Mohawk River route, New York might well control access to the West, outflanking Virginia and thereby diverting trade away from a southern route to one favoring the North.

On his return, Washington visited the springs at Saratoga, where he paused long enough to visit the battlefield and take comfort from the warm mineral baths. He recommended the waters as a "remedy for rheumatism."[54] On his travels, he had seen the promise of a "new empire." Indeed, he was so "struck with the goodness of Providence, which has dealt her favors," that he partnered with New York's governor George Clinton and purchased six thousand acres along the Mohawk

River.[55] With the acquisition of the lands along the Mohawk, added to those he owned along the Potomac and in the West, Washington held title to more than 60,000 acres in at least thirty-seven locations.[56]

Planning a trip of several weeks, traveling approximately thirty miles a day, Washington estimated that by 7 September 1784 he would be at Berkeley Springs, where, he reminded his younger brother, John Augustine, he had "valuable property [that] had originally cost nothing."[57] He was chiding his brother for not following his example and buying when the time was right.[58] Three days' travel west from Berkeley would take him to his mill and plantation—and Gilbert Simpson. At Simpson's, he had a long agenda. He expected that it would take him at least five days to sort through his partner's muddled accounts, put land up for lease, meet with his current tenants (who were mostly in arrears), and warn away squatters and scofflaws who were occupying his lands illegally.[59]

After sorting out affairs at the mill, Washington intended, "if nothing unforeseen at present, happens to prevent it," to visit his property along the "Great Kanawha and on the Ohio between the two Kanawha's." Since he had no boats, and rumors of Indian unrest were circulating, Washington wrote to the commander at Fort Pitt, Lieutenant David Luckett, for assistance in traveling the rivers. While having proclaimed several times that he was "freed from the cares of public employment and the responsibility of office," the retired commander in chief did not hesitate, without consulting the Congress, to "request" that Luckett provide him with "any public boats at the post under your command [and] three or four trusty soldiers."[60]

Ready to leave, Washington invited the marquis to join him. Lafayette declined, explaining to his wife:

> It is not without anguish that I resist the general's entreaties to go on a trip that he is obliged to make toward the Appalachians. He has delayed so long for me that some of his property has become the prey of squatters. But this six-week trip would delay me too much, and in order to get the general to go there without me I had to promise to meet him again here. So, I shall leave for Philadelphia, New York, and then all New England the first of September. I shall return at the beginning of October and travel across Virginia with the general

to be in Trenton on the first days of November. There I shall see Congress reassembled and take leave of everyone.[61]

Washington suggested to Lafayette that in his tour of the North he might perform an important diplomatic function. During the Revolution, apart from the Oneida, most of the tribes of the powerful Iroquois Confederation (Seneca, Cayuga, Onondaga, Oneida, Mohawk, Tuscarora) in northern New York had supported the British. In 1778, Washington had dispatched Lafayette to the region to organize an invasion of Canada. The invasion never came off, but while there Lafayette, playing on his nationality and the six tribes' historic ties to French Canada, was able to establish a cordial relationship with several chiefs who adopted him as Kayewla (Great Warrior). After the peace, having backed the loser, the Iroquois were under great pressure by both the state of New York and the Congress to surrender vast portions of their lands.

In the spring of 1784, representatives of New York, in defiance of Congress's authority, began negotiations with the Iroquois at Fort Stanwix. However, the Iroquois, suspicious of the New Yorkers, refused to negotiate with them until they met with congressional representatives. Washington, whose own western interests would benefit from land cessions and peace on the frontier, was anxious for a settlement. At the same time, he viewed the machinations of New York as an invidious attempt to invade congressional authority and further reduce its power. Since Lafayette was traveling north, Washington suggested that he join the congressional delegation at Fort Stanwix. Lafayette's presence would comfort the chiefs, remind them of their French friends, and give legitimacy to the congressional commissioners against their New York competitors.[62] Seeing a chance of being "useful," Lafayette agreed and adjusted his itinerary to be in upstate New York at Fort Stanwix in early October.[63]

Lafayette left Mount Vernon on 4 September, arriving the next day in Baltimore, where he had a chance encounter with James Madison. A Princeton graduate who had studied under John Witherspoon, Madison had served briefly in the Virginia militia until he was elected to the Virginia House and later the Continental Congress. He returned to Virginia in 1783. Bored with plantation life and in "need of exercise after a very sedentary period," Madison had decided to go on the road and take a "ramble into the Eastern States which I have long had a curiosity to see."[64] Lafayette pressed Madison to join him.[65] Madison hesitated, explaining to his father that the marquis's itinerary "will carry me farther than I had proposed." Nonetheless, he joined the tour. What Madison did not reveal to his father, but did share in a coded message to Thomas Jefferson, was that he wanted time with Lafayette to discuss with him "the subject of the Mississippi." To the great dismay of Virginians, in July Spain had closed the river to Americans. Traveling with Lafayette would give Madison an opportunity to convince him to use his influence with the French court to persuade Spain to back down, lest there be a "rupture."[66] Joined by the French chargé d'affaires, François Barbe de Marbois, who kept a detailed journal of the trip, the three men spent nearly six weeks on an adventure that took them up the Hudson and then west on the Mohawk River toward Fort Stanwix. On their way, at Lafayette's request, they visited the Shaker Village Niskayuna near Schenectady, so that the marquis might "examine at first hand phenomena that seemed very similar to those associated with Mesmer."[67] He found little among the Shakers that linked them to Mesmerism.

The party continued up the Mohawk. On 2 October, they reached Oneida village, eighteen miles from Stanwix. From there they rode to the fort, where the Iroquois chiefs and the American commissioners sent by Congress—Arthur Lee, Oliver Wolcott, and Richard Butler—assisted by Indian missionary Samuel Kirkland, had arrived to begin negotiations. Despite the passage of more than two decades, Madison told Jefferson the Iroquois still "retained a strong predilection for the French and most of the lat[t]er an enthusiastic idea of the Marquis."[68] Indeed, Lafayette, renewing his friendship with Oneida chief Grasshopper, who had visited Philadelphia in 1781, turned out to be a sensation among the tribal representatives. That was exactly what the American commissioners had hoped, since they planned to use Lafayette as a stalking horse to gain the confidence of the Iroquois. To their chagrin, matters took a different turn. Speaking in French, Lafayette reminded them of the "great war chief Washington," who had beaten the British, and said they should now join with his representatives "around the fire." Then, in a moment that shook the commissioners, Lafayette, "with much oratory and elegance calculated to serve the interest of his king and much to promote the continental business," told the chiefs that, while they ought to trade with the Americans, "the products of France are known to you, and you are clever enough to prefer them."[69] In response, Seneca chief Corn Planter, joined by other chiefs, addressed Lafayette as "Keshena, my father," while heaping praise upon him. Madison was impressed and noted, "During this scene and even during the whole stay of the M, he was the only *conspicuous figure. The commissioners were eclipsed*" (italics in original).[70] Annoyed at being upstaged, the commissioners—particularly Arthur Lee—did all they could to promote Lafayette's early departure. The commissioners were delighted when the marquis, under the press of time, left Stanwix while negotiations were still underway.[71]

Bound east, Madison and Lafayette left Stanwix on 6 October and "descended the river Mohawk in the most beautiful weather in the world."[72] At Albany, Lafayette decided to continue his triumphal tour into New England, visiting Hartford, Portsmouth, New Hampshire, and Boston, where the French frigate *Nymph* awaited to carry him to Virginia.[73] Madison, anxious to return in time for the assembly's fall session, continued down the Hudson toward New York City.

While Madison and Lafayette were traveling through upstate New York, word spread that Washington was heading west. Several people sought to accompany him. Washington would not hear of it. Companions would be nothing but nuisances "who would soon get tired and embarrass my movements besides rendering them inconvenient." Nonetheless, he did make two exceptions. He invited Bushrod, then staying at his father's plantation, Happy Retreat near Berkeley, "to go with me," provided that his health permitted and that his absence would not interfere with his legal studies. All he would need would be a "servant and a blanket or two—everything else I shall provide."[74] The other exception was his old friend Dr. James Craik, whom he invited while warning him that the expedition would be "no entertainment."[75]

Craik, one of Washington's oldest and closest friends, was born at Dumfries, Scotland, in 1730, the illegitimate son of Robert Craik, a member of the British Parliament. He studied medicine at the University of Edinburgh. After completing his studies, Craik joined the British army and was posted to the West Indies. Resigning in 1751, he moved to Winchester, Virginia. He was with Washington at the battle of the Monongahela and ministered to the dying General Braddock. He later served in Washington's Virginia regiment. With the war over, Craik moved to Port Tobacco, Maryland, and opened a successful medical practice. In 1760, he married Marianne Ewell, a distant relative of Washington's mother.[76]

As a reward for his service in the French and Indian War, Craik, like Washington, had received bounty lands in the Ohio Valley. Craik and Washington remained close friends, and in the spring of 1777, wanting physicians in the army, Washington offered Craik the position of assistant medical director general for the Middle District.[77] Craik accepted and was with Washington during the battles around Philadelphia in the fall of that year.[78] At the Battle of Brandywine Creek (11 September 1777), Craik treated Lafayette, who had received a serious leg wound. Craik was one of the founding members of the Cincinnati, and after his discharge, at Washington's urging, he moved to Alexandria, Virginia. Craik was a frequent visitor to Mount Vernon, tending to the care of Washington, his family, and the enslaved Africans working on Washington's property. After the usual hoecake breakfast and last-minute goodbyes, on the morning of 1 September, Washington and Craik set out.[79]

3

SETTLERS

I shall use the most efficacious means to do myself justice.
(3 September 1784, in *GWP, Diaries*, 4:3)

During Washington's first "journey over the mountains" in 1748, he had endured an uncomfortable trek west traveling as a young apprentice surveyor for the Fairfax family. The expedition offered little comfort. He slept under "thread bare blankets" infested with vermin, bounced over the "worst roads that ever was trod by man or beast," and forded rivers, dangerously swollen "by reason of the great rains."[1] Despite bugs, foul weather, floods, and terrible roads, what an impressionable young man saw was a country of immense beauty and promise. In his diary the teenage Washington recorded, "The land exceedingly rich and fertile, all the way produces abundance of grain, hemp, tobacco etc.[and] beautiful groves of sugar trees."[2] Four decades later, Washington still found wonderment in the West. Beyond the barrier of the mountains was a "New Empire."[3]

This time there would be no sleeping on cold, wet ground, fending off vermin. The roads were smoother, ferries crossed dangerous rivers, and he spent evenings in the comfort of an elaborate camp (complete with an impressive marquee tent), lodging in public houses, or staying with friends and relatives, enjoying the warm surroundings of congenial company. Washington did not travel light. Aside from his own mount and those his companions rode, his party trailed six extra horses. Three servants came along to manage his "equipage," which included "two leather and one linen valises with my marquee and horsemen's tent, tent poles and pins—all my bedding—the trunk containing all that was put into it except the silver cups and spoons—canteens—two kegs of spirits—horse shoes etc." In addition to the "two kegs of spirits" (most likely whiskey) in his equipage, Washington found room for "port wine—cherry bounce, oil, mustard,—vinegar and spices of all sorts—tea and sugar in the camp kettles (a whole of white sugar, broke up, about 7 pounds weight)."[4] Cherry bounce, a powerful concoction of brandy, cherries, and spices made from a recipe kept by Martha Washington, was one of Washington's favorite drinks.[5] To prevent any untoward sampling, Washington kept the spirits, bounce, and wine "under a lock."[6] This foray west smacked more of a royal progress than a youthful trek into the wilderness.[7]

On the first day (1 September 1784), riding at his "usual travelling gait of 5 miles per hour," over roads "tolerable good," Washington made twenty-five miles, staying the night in Shepherd's Tavern at Difficult Run, a stream Washington described as "inconvenient and troublesome to cross except at the bridge."[8] Rising at five o'clock the next day, the party managed a brisk thirty-six miles and lodged at Leesburg with the Quaker Israel Thompson.

Leaving the late risers to catch up with him, Washington left Thompson's at dawn and rode off to his brother Charles's home, "Happy Retreat." Washington's youngest brother, Charles (1738–1799), had inherited land overlooking Evitts Run (Charles Town, West Virginia) from his half brother Lawrence. He moved there from Fredericksburg in 1780. Charles was the second brother to move into the area. Earlier, Samuel (1734–1781), the oldest of Washington's three younger brothers and the one most often in financial difficulty, had settled in the area and built an impressive stone house, "Harewood." A cousin, Warner Washington, also lived nearby. After Samuel's death, his fifth wife, Susannah Perrin (1734–1783), was left with four children. Thornton, the oldest, left home while the younger children (George Steptoe, Lawrence Augustine, and Harriot) remained at Harewood, living in dire straits. After Susannah's death, Washington invited Harriot to live temporarily at Mount Vernon. Charles agreed to take guardianship of the two boys and sent them to live with the Reverend David Griffith in Alexandria.[9]

At Happy Retreat, Washington began his dunning campaign. He summoned his tenants, to whom he had leased land before the war, and demanded payment on their long-overdue debts. During the Revolution, many of them had not paid anything, and those who did gave depreciated paper currency. Washington warned them that "if they did not pay and settle up their arrearages of rent very soon, I shall use the most efficacious means to do myself justice."[10] It did not go well. The tenants pleaded that they could not afford to pay the amount due. With little choice, Washington accepted what they offered and ruefully "put a close to it."[11]

Having finished the unhappy business with his delinquent tenants, shortly before noon, "many gentlemen" arrived at Happy Retreat, including Daniel Morgan, Ralph Wormeley, and Edward Snickers.[12]

Morgan, who lived in nearby Winchester, was a national icon.[13] An officer in the Virginia militia before the Revolution, Morgan, on hearing the news of Lexington and Concord and the appointment of his fellow Virginian to be commander in chief of the Continental army, assembled his company of Virginia riflemen and made a "Bee Line March" (twenty-four days, six hundred miles) to Cambridge. An unrivaled tactical commander in the Revolution, the rough-hewn soldier had returned home after the war to become one of the largest landowners in the Shenandoah Valley. For some time, Morgan had been trying (unsuccessfully) to help Washington collect his overdue debts.[14]

Also present was a summer visitor to the area—Ralph Wormeley. A wealthy planter who in the years before the war had served on the Royal Governor's Council, Wormeley, a passive Tory, survived the war by deftly navigating the roiling waters of the Revolution. His plantation, "Rosegill," was located on the Rappahannock River ten miles up from Chesapeake Bay. Attracted by the cooler weather inland, as well as the soothing nature of nearby mineral waters, however, Wormeley preferred relaxing at his lodge, "The Rocks," spending his summers away from the heat and humidity of the coastal lowlands. Wormeley and Washington were deeply involved in several land issues, including the "interesting and intricate" legal matters concerning the settlement of the complicated estate of George Mercer.[15]

Edward Snickers, "horse trader, tavern keeper, wagoner, military supplier, plantation manager for himself and land speculator," a man once accused of defrauding the American army, had a shady reputation. Washington had met Snickers when he was contracted to supply the Virginia regiment during the French and Indian War. Among his many interests, Snickers operated the ferry crossing the nearby Shenandoah River.[16]

None of the men at Happy Retreat were surprised to hear Washington lament his unhappy experience with his tenants. They, too, were heavily invested in western lands and faced the same obstacles as Washington, trying to extract rents from impoverished and insolent tenants. They had discovered that bellowing threats served little purpose. It was clearly in the interests of all—landowners and tenants—to find a practical means to access eastern markets where they might sell their produce and pay their debts. Washington was urgent on the matter, impressing on the gentlemen who had come to see him that an "object of my journey being to obtain information of the nearest and best communication between the eastern and western waters and to facilitate as much as in me lay the inland navigation of the Potomac."[17] With improved transportation, he argued, not only would the current tenants prosper, but others would come to settle as well. Tenants and landowners would both profit. It was a message he had harped on relentlessly. In his farewell to the army, delivered less than a year earlier, he had bid his comrades to seek "the extensive and fertile Regions of the West [that] will yield a most happy Asylum to those, who, fond of domestic enjoyment are seeking for personal independence."[18]

In July, when he invited James Craik to join him on his western trip, he assured the doctor, "I am not going to explore the country, nor am I in search of lands, but to secure what I have."[19] After his experience at Happy Retreat, Washington had a greater vision. He realized that securing his western lands went beyond simply upholding his claims against "land jobbers and speculators." Land ownership meant little unless these new settlements were linked. He was now on a mission to find "water transportation for all that fertile country."[20]

For the rest of his thirty-day, six-hundred-mile expedition, Washington pored over a number of maps he had brought with him, most of them inaccurate. He questioned locals about roads and rivers, and he went with them to conduct personal surveys, looking to find navigable waterways, short portages, and routes for laying out roads—all, he hoped, leading to the Potomac.

From Happy Retreat, for two days and forty-four miles through a constant drizzling rain, Washington rode to his next destination, Berkeley Springs. In scale and beauty, the countryside was impressive, its inhabitants less so. They were mostly Scots-Irish, hearty, restless, and fiercely independent. A German traveler, Johann Schoepf, described them as a "remote people who very seldom see strangers among them and do not know all that goes on in the rest of the world." Their "farms are scattered, the cabins wretched."[21] Schoepf was only partially correct. The settlers might not have been aware of the "world," but they certainly knew Washington was coming.

On the evening of 5 September, the party arrived at the Springs.[22] Known for its warm, soothing mineral waters, the town was a seasonal resort that Washington had visited several times. His first visit (1748) was during his surveying tour for Lord Fairfax. Enchanted with the "famed warm springs," he returned three years later with Lawrence, hoping that the curative waters might restore his brother's deteriorating health. They did not; Lawrence died in 1752. In the spring of 1761, suffering from a persistent, "violent cold," Washington returned to the healing waters.[23] Six years later, accompanied by Martha, the couple, in a desperate attempt to alleviate the chronic illness of their daughter, Patsy, took her to the Springs.[24]

Surrounding nearly a dozen springs, flowing from the base of the Cacapon Mountain, Berkeley Springs was a hodgepodge of "contracted, wooden cabins scattered about without any order, most of them with no glass in the windows, being only summer residences."[25] Although not as renowned as the more fashionable northern warm spring resorts in Pennsylvania and New York, by the early 1770s the Springs were welcoming a steady flow of visitors, seeking, in addition to the waters, "society and distraction."[26] In the high season, Berkeley was a lively place populated by gamblers, card sharks, land speculators, and wealthy planters, side by side with "sturdy yeomanry, and coonskin democrats." It boasted "five bathing houses, with adjacent dressing rooms; an assembly room and theatre."[27]

On this visit, Washington was more concerned with the impact that the reputation of the Springs had on the health of his real estate investments than improving his physical well-being. In fact, after several visits, none of them proving particularly effective, he was not convinced that the Springs had any healing powers. To his friend the Reverend Charles Green, the minister at Truro Parish near Mount Vernon (and sometimes medical practitioner), Washington confided that while he felt rested, "my pains grow rather worse and my sleep equally disturbed."[28] Jefferson, the keen observer of all things Virginia, was equally skeptical. In his *Notes on the State of Virginia*, he remarked that Berkeley waters were "weakly mineralized and scarcely warm. They are more visited because [they are] situated in a fertile, plentiful and populous country better provided with accommodations, always safe from Indians."[29] Despite such doubts, the Springs enjoyed a growing reputation. In 1776, a group of local boosters persuaded the Virginia legislature to rename the settlement Bath in imitation of the ancient resort in England.

Since, by his own account, he was a day ahead of schedule, Washington opted for a two-day respite, giving him a chance to meet with friends and sample entertainments other than those of the warm waters.[30] Bawdy behavior was not unknown at the Springs. When Methodist bishop Francis Asbury visited, he could only remark, "When I behold the conduct of the people who attend the Springs, particularly the gentry, I am led to thank God that I was not born to riches; I rather bless God, that I am not in hell, and that I cannot partake of pleasure with sinners."[31] Washington's diary makes no mention of any "pleasures."

Among the first to greet him was James Rumsey, the proprietor of "a very commodious boarding house for the residence of ladies and gentlemen at The Sign of the Liberty Pole and Flag."[32] Born in Cecil County, Maryland, Rumsey was a poor relation in a distinguished family. An important figure at the Springs, he was a self-taught blacksmith, millwright, carpenter, and innkeeper. His second marriage to Mary Morrow drew him west to his wife's home in Shepherdstown (West Virginia). Ambitious and restless, he was intrigued as he watched the rising volume of traffic passing before him, moving west. Shortly after the war, he joined the caravan and brought his family to Berkeley Springs.

A tinkerer, Rumsey had for some time been working secretly on a boat powered by a series of complicated mechanical devices that used the force of an opposing river current to operate pairs of poles on either side of the craft that walked on the bottom, in a crablike fashion, pushing the boat upstream. Rumsey was so certain his invention worked that at the spring session of the Virginia legislature (May 1784), he petitioned for a monopoly to operate his boat on state waters. The petition went to the Committee on Commerce, chaired by James Madison. The committee members, including Madison, heaped "ridicule" on the idea and dismissed it out of hand.[33] Washington's arrival gave Rumsey new hope.

Rumsey was aware that, aside from settling real estate matters, Washington was on a quest to find ways to establish water connections linking east and west. Suave, debonair, and "courtly in the extreme," Rumsey set out to gain Washington's patronage. Wasting little time, he invited Washington to a demonstration of his boat. Although he had "little faith" in the project, under "the injunction of secrecy" (which made the invitation even more intriguing), Washington joined Rumsey at a primitive testing tank he had constructed behind the inn where he demonstrated his invention.[34]

After watching, Washington, in a credulous moment, recorded in his diary that he had seen "the model of a boat constructed for ascending rapid current by mechanism; The principles of this were not only shown and fully explained to me but to my very great satisfaction, exhibited in practice." He was convinced that Rumsey's boat "might be turned to the greatest possible utility in inland navigation."[35] He was wrong. Rumsey's demonstration was a clever fabrication. His boat was moving across tame water, and its poles were thrusting onto a smooth, sandy bottom. In the real world, western rivers flowed through chutes and rapids with treacherous currents over uneven and rocky bottoms that would easily snap Rumsey's poles. Notwithstanding these obvious flaws, the ingenious Rumsey, an extraordinary salesperson, persuaded Washington, who was anxious to embrace any means that might help his western plans, to provide him with a public testimonial. The day following the demonstration, Washington presented Rumsey with a certificate. It was testimony from a powerful patron:

I have seen the model of Mr. Rumsey's Boats constructed to work against stream; have examined the power upon which it acts; have been an eye witness to an actual experiment in running water of some rapidity; & do give it as my opinion that he has discovered the art of propelling Boats, by mechanism & small manual assistance, against rapid currents: that the discovery is of vast importance— may be of the greatest usefulness in our inland navigation—&, if it succeeds, of which I have no doubt, that the value of it is greatly enhanced by the simplicity of the works; which when seen & explained to, might be executed by the most common Mechanic's.[36]

Rumsey charmed Washington. Before he left, in addition to presenting him with the certificate, Washington contracted with Rumsey to build an impressive (at least for Berkeley Springs) "dwelling house to be 36 feet by 24 with a gallery 7 feet on each side of the house [and] a kitchen and stable each to be 18 feet by 22 feet." Rumsey never built the main house. He did complete the kitchen and stable, but not to Washington's specifications. All three structures, according to Washington's nephew George Lewis, who visited in 1786, were "badly built and of bad timber."[37]

As they left the Springs, early on the morning of 8 September, two young men joined the party: Washington's nephew, Bushrod, and William Craik, the doctor's son. Both men, having recently completed their legal studies, were ready for a bit of adventure before settling down to practice. Bushrod had already arrived at the Springs, having come a few weeks earlier to "confirm his health."[38] After a brief detour to view his lands across the Potomac in Hampshire County, Washington rejoined the group at Oldtown, where they lodged with Colonel Thomas Cresap.

Ninety years old and blind, Cresap was a legend in the West. Initially an agent for Maryland's Lord Baltimore, Cresap had a reputation for being disputatious and violent when defending his patron's land claims along the lower Susquehanna Valley.[39] Imprisoned at least once for illegally evicting settlers, in 1741 Cresap moved west, establishing a trading post at Shawnee Old Town (simply called Oldtown), located along the Nemacolin Path, a vital route connecting the watersheds of the Potomac and Monongahela Rivers. Washington first encountered

Cresap during his 1748 survey trip. They chanced to meet again during the French and Indian War. Their last encounter had been during Washington's 1770 expedition west. A founding member of the Ohio Company (1749), Cresap, like Washington, claimed title to lands that had been ill surveyed or not surveyed at all. Shadowy claims led to disputes among Cresap, his youngest son Michael, and Washington. Cresap was, according to Washington, "extremely artful."[40] Rain kept them at Cresap's an extra day. Despite his age and blindness, Cresap's other faculties, according to Andrew Ellicott, who visited him in May, were "yet unimpaired his sense Strong and Manly and his Ideas flow with ease."[41] The two old soldiers, although cautious with one another, had much to reminisce about.

On 10 September, anxious "to proceed on to Gilbert Simpson's," Washington set off with a single servant, leaving the rest to follow with the baggage. After more than seven hours in the saddle, he arrived at Tumblestone's Tavern.[42] A weary traveler, Washington described the day's journey over various roads as "tolerably good," "tolerably bad," "indifferent," and "tedious and fatiguing." At every opportunity he inquired about the existence of navigable streams and possible routes for roads. Often, however, he noted in his diary, "I could meet with no person who seemed to have any accurate knowledge of the country." The answers that he did get "were so far from the truth" as to be useless.[43]

As he continued his journey, Washington encountered "numbers of persons and pack horses heading east loaded with ginseng." Growing in the shady environments of the Appalachians, North American ginseng was in high demand in China, where the root was an important herb. Unlike high-bulk, low-value agricultural commodities (e.g., corn, wheat), ginseng, a compact cargo, sold at a price high enough to justify costly overland transportation. For the moment, American ginseng went to China via French merchants, but that was about to change. On 22 February 1784, the American vessel *Empress of China*, laden with a cargo of ginseng, left New York bound for Canton (Guangzhou). The same day Washington was noting the shipment of ginseng coming over the mountains (12 September 1784), having sold its cargo of ginseng, the *Empress* was homeward bound with a cargo of tea, silks, and spices, launching what would become America's fabled trade with the Far East.[44]

That evening Washington arrived at the home of Gilbert Simpson (Perryopolis, Pennsylvania). Simpson's farm occupied about six hundred acres, part of a larger tract known as Washington's Bottom. The land, according to an advertisement Washington had posted in the *Virginia Journal* before his journey, consisted of meadow lands, "a good dwelling house, kitchen, barn, stable, and other necessary buildings, 110 apple trees, etc." The advertisement beggared reality, for in fact, as Washington admitted in his diary, Simpson had done little with the land or the buildings, which were "indifferently improved."[45]

The next day, he rode to his mill roughly a mile distant on Washington's Run, a small tributary to the nearby Youghiogheny River. Here he found what he had suspected for several years—a mess. There was a "mill quite destitute of water. The works and house appear to be in very bad condition. In a word, little rent, or good is to be expected from the present aspect of her."[46] The next morning, Colonel William Butler, a fellow member of the Cincinnati, best remembered for leading fierce attacks against the Six Nations during the Revolution, and Captain David Luckett, commander at Fort Pitt, paid a visit. They had come to warn Washington that, because of the "discontented temper of the Indians," it was too dangerous to proceed farther down the river. They advised him to abandon plans to visit his "Lands on the Great Kanawha, & on the Ohio between the two Kanhawas."[47] Washington agreed.

More unwelcome news arrived in the afternoon when "the people who live on my land on Millers Run came here to set forth their pretentions and to enquire into my right." The contentious meeting went on for some time as the settlers attempted, according to Washington, "to discover all the flaws they could in my Deed, &ca.; & to establish a fair and upright intention in themselves." Since not all the settlers involved were present, the parties agreed to adjourn and meet in three days' time at Millers Run, where the full body would be present to give Washington their "definitive determination."[48] The next day, Washington put the decrepit mill's lease up for auction. It proved a great disappointment: "Many People were gathered (more out of curiosity I believe than from other motives), but no great Sale made. My Mill I could obtain no bid for, altho I offered an exemption from the payment of Rent 15 Months." Matters went slightly better when he offered Simpson's plantation for lease. "Having little chance of getting a good offer in money, for rent, induced me to set it up to be bid for in wheat." Ironically, the winning (and only) offer came from Simpson himself, who in the process of bidding tried to persuade Washington to sign a one-year lease. Washington shot back that he "did not intend to go thro' the same trouble every year by making an annual bargain for it," telling Simpson "he must take it for the period on which it was offered, or not at all."[49] Ten years was the deal. Simpson agreed, albeit reluctantly. In the morning, Friday, 17 September, Washington set out for Millers Run to meet with his tenants/squatters.

Washington was in for an unwelcome surprise at Millers Run. Although during his travels he had yet to collect the full amount of rents due from his tenants, the meetings thus far had been cordial. Settlers gave due deference to the general and acknowledged his right to the land. After pleading inability to pay, they generally offered partial payment, which he accepted with considerable reluctance. At Millers Run, when Washington encountered a group of determined Scots-Irish Presbyterians, known as Seceders, led by David Reed, matters turned in an entirely different direction.[50]

In 1777, David Reed, his brother John, and brother-in-law Samuel McBride, in company with several other Scots-Irish Presbyterians, purchased land in Millers Run from an unscrupulous land speculator and constant irritant to Washington, George Croghan. Unfortunately, the land Croghan claimed was his belonged to Washington, whose title went back to a complicated set of land transactions following the French and Indian War. While he had not previously pressed his case, now, in need of money and with the land gaining value, Washington was prepared to act against the Millers Run squatters.

Washington left Simpson's on 18 September and lodged that evening with "Colo. Cannons on the Waters of Shurtees Creek—a kind hospitable Man; & sensible."[51] The following morning, he arrived at Millers Run; however, "being Sunday, and the People living on my Land, apparently very religious, it was thought best to postpone going among them till tomorrow."[52] Lest anyone doubt his stature and determination, in the early hours before the meeting, in a grand theatrical gesture, Washington, "having obtained a pilot," rode across the disputed tracts accompanied by Cannons, Colonel Presley Nevitt, and Captain Van Swearingen, the high sheriff of the county. Washington found a scene quite unlike the rundown sorry sights he had encountered at the Springs or Simpson's. He inspected fourteen properties (thirteen owners) over his 2,813 acres. In only one instance (that of David Reed) did he find a dwelling house "in bad order." The other thirteen properties—dwellings, barns, and fences—were all in reasonable condition. The land, although hilly, was arable and much of it fenced. Clearly the Scots-Irish settlers had been good stewards. It was, he concluded, "a valuable tract."[53]

Thirteen men gathered at David Reed's, "a good, logged dwelling with a bad roof," to meet Washington.[54] Three—Duncan McGeehan, David Reed, and John Glen—were veterans of Washington's army. McGeehan's brother Brice was also a veteran—he had served in the British army during the Revolution and deserted to join the rebel cause.

After dining, the meeting began. Unimpressed by the general and his entourage, the settlers made their case. Matters did not go well. James Scott spoke first, describing the "hardships they had endured, the improvements made, and the increased value of the lands by reason of their labor."[55] David Reed stood to offer a compromise. "Tho they did not conceive they could be disposed, yet to avoid contention, they would buy, if the terms were moderate." Washington, not accustomed to being challenged, and unwilling to take less than he believed he deserved, with a dramatic flourish "replied with dignity and some warmth asserting that they had been forewarned by his agent, and the nature of his claim fully made known; that there could be no doubt of its validity, and rising from his seat and taking a red silk handkerchief by one corner, he said 'Gentlemen, I will have this land just as surely as I now have this handkerchief.'"[56] Although he had "no inclination to sell . . . after hearing a great deal of their hardships, their religious principles (which had brought them together as seceders) and unwillingness to separate or remove; I told them I would make them a last offer and this was the whole tract at 25/.pr acre, the money to be paid out at three annual payments with interest; or to become tenants upon leases of 999 years, at the annual rent of ten pounds per acre pr. Ct pr Ann."[57] To avoid the curse of depreciating paper currency, prices were fixed in specie.

Washington's terms for sale were intentionally onerous. Convinced that his lands would increase in value as settlers moved west, he was loath to surrender his future fortune at current bargain prices.[58]

The settlers withdrew for "a long consultation." When they returned, Scott asked Washington whether he would sell at a "longer credit, without interest." Washington refused, leaving them with no choice but to rent, which, given their claim to ownership, they opposed vehemently. They dismissed the offer. To divide their ranks, Washington demanded that Scott poll the settlers one by one. He did and they were of a single voice—no. They were determined "to stand suit and abide the issue of the law."[59] Hearing this defiant answer, according to one local source, Washington let out an "oath."[60]

Back at Cannons's, the gentlemen, Washington recorded, "promised to hunt up the evidences which could prove my possession & improvement of the Land before any of the present Occupiers ever saw it."[61] Traveling to Simpson's the next morning, Washington made preparations for the journey home, but not before he "met with & engaged Mr. Thos. Smith to bring Ejectments, & to prosecute my Suit for the Land in Washington County, on which those, whose names are herein inserted, are settled."[62] Smith, a familiar figure on the western court circuit, had considerable experience in ejectments. He entered Washington's case in the Washington County Court, Pennsylvania, in December 1784.[63] In March 1785, however, concerned that a local justice might be too sympathetic to the settlers, Smith petitioned to move the case to the state supreme court. His petition was granted. He then asked for a postponement, which the "obliging" Chief Justice Thomas McKean granted. Additional time went by as the court rode circuit. Standing for the defendants was the popular Pittsburgh lawyer, writer, and politician Hugh Henry Brackenridge, who had gained a reputation for successfully defending settlers in eviction cases. Smith and Brackenridge's procedural haggling pushed the trial date to October 1786.

Although Washington was determined to "oust" these troublesome tenants, more was at stake than simply the property of the families at Millers Run. Given the rising spirit of resistance in the West to eastern domination, which Washington saw firsthand, he and the other landowners feared that a victory for the Millers Run families might lead to a torrent of challenges sweeping against them. With so much at risk, Washington devoted considerable time and energy to "hunting up evidence," searching court documents, examining land records, and seeking out testimony to support his claim. That he, the most revered man in America, should be challenged by a group of squatters, who accused him of being "a monopolizer or land jobber," angered him. His forbearance turned to vengeance against these "wilfull and obstinate sinners."[64] In addition to ejectment, he wanted them charged with trespass. Smith, the local lawyer, alert to community sentiment, cautioned his client against taking too hard a stand in front of a local jury that might view the "defendants rather unfortunate than blameable" and count Washington an overbearing, absentee landlord.[65] Smith was convinced that this was the strategy Brackenridge was likely to take to swing a jury.[66]

In October 1786, McKean opened the trial. Brackenridge asked immediately that the cases be tried separately. It was a clever ploy that would have prolonged the proceedings, giving Brackenridge ample time to pillory Washington (whose name would draw great attention) and other greedy speculators, accusing them of exploiting poor western settlers. McKean, a veteran of the Revolution who had served with Washington, would have none of it. He ordered the cases tried together. Smith entered the court well armed. In July, Washington had sent him a long brief providing a full history (although sometimes vague and convoluted) tracing his ownership back to the aftermath of the French and Indian War.[67] After some initial skirmishing over jury selection, the proceedings commenced. The submission of documents and testimony began in the afternoon of Tuesday, 24 October, with Brackenridge arguing that Washington's purchases had been illegal and that the settlers' improvements on the land gave them title. Testimony continued for a full day on Wednesday. Thursday morning the jury brought in their verdict in favor of Washington. The quick decision "left a lasting antagonism in western counties toward the court."[68] Smith, however, saw it as a signal victory. Congratulating himself, he wrote to Washington that appearing on his behalf he had managed to surmount "strong prejudices, artfully fomented," and a "jury [that] wished it had been in their power to have given verdicts for the defendants."[69]

With the good news, Smith offered Washington some personal advice. He believed that these families had acted out of "misfortune," and now, "reduced to indigence," he thought that they would be willing to accept Washington's original offer. He reminded Washington that the improvements they had made on his land, at their own expense, far exceeded the costs of the ejectments.[70] Smith was suggesting to his client that it might be wise to be generous toward the current tenants, in the expectation that they would remain on the land, rather than going to the considerable expense of evicting them and taking on the trouble of seeking new tenants or buyers.

Smith's advice fell on deaf ears. Washington had lost his patience and was unwilling to bend. "My lands in Pennsylvania have been so unproductive of everything but vexation and trouble." He was determined to extract his due. Despite protestations that it was not his "wish or intention to distress them," Washington was clear: "Those people have little right to look to me for favor or indulgence." He might forgive them back rent, which they could never afford to pay in any case, but he offered them no allowance for the improvements they had made. They could remain on the land as tenants, at a rent of twenty-five shillings per acre, a price they had rejected two years before.[71] If Washington thought he could bend these Scots-Irish to his will, he miscalculated. By the spring of 1787, leaving behind their homes and barns and carting away as much as they could carry, twelve families left. Only the McGeehans remained. Destitute and unable to pay his rent, in the fall of 1788 Brice McGeehan pleaded with Washington to make him a gift of the land. Washington made no response. The McGeehans moved on.[72]

Having abandoned plans to proceed toward his lands on the Kanawha and the Ohio, on the morning of 22 September, Washington turned homeward. Leaving behind most of his baggage, including kettles, trunks, canteens, and other equipment, all to be brought home by Craik and the rest of the party, he and Bushrod, traveling light, took a longer route via "Turkey foot road," so that they might make "minute enquiry into the Navigation of the Yohiggany waters."[73]

For nearly two weeks, Washington and his nephew traveled east, taking careful notice of the land, paying particular attention to identifying navigable streams that might provide access to the West. Finally, on 4 October, Washington recorded in his diary, "Reached home before sundown having travelled on the same horses since the first day of September by the computed distances 680 Miles."[74] Not counting long stopovers, taking refuge to avoid severe weather, or lingering to conduct business, on average Washington rode more than twenty-five miles per day—quite a contrast to thirty years before when Braddock's cumbersome force made barely two miles per day. Three decades of western movement had created a considerable difference. No longer a contested wilderness (at least not by Europeans), lands beyond the mountains stood at the edge of a rising American empire. Well-cared-for farms, working mills, inns filled with traveling strangers, pack trains carrying ginseng east for markets in China, were promising signs of an expanding nation. Although he was still smarting from his unhappy encounter at Millers Run, and disappointed that he had not been able to visit his lands "upon the Ohio and Great Kanawha and to take measures for rescuing them from the hands of land jobbers and speculators," Washington was "well pleased with my journey, as it has been the means of my obtaining a knowledge of facts—coming at the temper and disposition of the western inhabitants and making reflections thereon, which, otherwise, must have been as wild, incoherent, and perhaps as foreign from the truth, as the inconsistencies of the reports which I had received even from those to whom most credit seemed due."[75]

Anxious to record and share his experiences, Washington remained ensconced in his library collating and organizing the mass of information he had collected on his trip. On 4 October, writing in his diary, he reflected on his experience. He was preparing an important report. Promising "to examine matters impartially, and endeavor to state facts," he began with his conclusion: "The more the navigation of the Potomack is investigated, and duly considered, the greater the advantages arising from them appear." A visionary with a surveyor's sharp eye, Washington laid out what he had learned from personal observation and careful inquiry. Harkening back to a military metaphor, Washington warned that "with the Spaniards on their right [and] Great Britain on their left . . . the western settlers stand as it were on a pivot—the touch of a feather would incline them any way." Looking west and south, they might easily glide "gently down the stream [Mississippi]" toward

Spanish New Orleans "because they have no other means of coming to it but by a long land transportation and unimproved roads." Or they might follow the waterways northward toward the Great Lakes and Canada, where the British, in defiance of the Treaty of 1783, still held Detroit, Oswego, and Michilimackinac. There was a third challenge as well—Pennsylvania.[76]

Pennsylvania and Virginia had a long history vying for hegemony over western territory. In 1758, as an officer in the Virginia militia, Washington, a fervent defender of his colony's claims, had nearly lost his commission in a fiery confrontation with General John Forbes. When organizing his expedition against Fort Duquesne, Forbes faced a choice for a route of advance. He could either take the existing road that had been slashed through the wilderness by Braddock three years earlier or carve an entirely new and shorter route along a more northerly line of advance. For sound military reasons, Forbes and his engineers selected the latter route, which ran entirely through Pennsylvania and would clearly, in a postwar world, provide Philadelphia with a critical east-west link, much to Virginia's disadvantage. Learning of the decision, Washington, the Virginian, threw aside military decorum and complained bitterly to Forbes's subordinate, Lieutenant Colonel Henry Bouquet. Taken aback by Washington's forceful objections, the colonel dismissed the untoward outburst as simply the product of blind prejudice. Washington was incensed, and, in an unusually emotional letter, he complained to his friend Major Francis Halkett, "all is lost!—All is lost by Heavens!"[77] Thirty years later, once again, Pennsylvania's interests threatened Virginia.

In his report, Washington laid out a water route beginning on the Ohio River below Pittsburgh at the Little Kanawha River to Bull Town. "Thence there is a portage of 9½ miles to the west folk of the Monongahela. Thence along the same to the mouth of the Cheat River, and up it to the Dunker bottom, from whence a portage may be had to the North Branch of the Potomack."[78] It may have been no coincidence that Washington would benefit greatly from this route. He owned nearly twenty-five thousand acres in the Kanawha Valley, as well as twenty-five lots in Alexandria, which, under this plan, was likely to become a thriving port.[79] Despite his surveying expertise, Washington's enthusiasm for promoting his route from the Ohio to the Potomac led him to underestimate the difficulties in clearing the way.[80] He tended to overlook the time and cost of building portage roads as well as the immense effort required to improve navigation, bypassing falls and removing river obstructions. He was also prone to dismiss the difficulties of moving boats against the current. To the critics who asked how he planned to haul boats upstream, he pointed them to the plan he had endorsed at the Springs—"Rumsey's discovery of working boats against the stream by mechanical powers."[81]

Whatever its drawbacks, Washington's proposed route had the supreme advantage of being almost entirely within Virginia, except a part of the Potomac the state shared with Maryland. That, however, would prove no problem since "Maryland stands on similar ground with Virginia." However, Washington worried that Pennsylvania would not agree to any scheme linking its rivers with those flowing toward the Potomac since "it would be the inevitable means of withdrawing from Philadelphia all the trade of that part of its western territory." This issue would mean a significant loss of commerce not only with the Great Lakes but also with "the new states contemplated by Congress."[82]

Having stacked his ammunition, Washington was ready to fire a salvo. On Sunday, 10 October, he sent a "private" letter to Virginia's governor, Benjamin Harrison: "I shall take the liberty now, my dear sir, to suggest a matter, which would (if I am not too short sighted a politician) mark your administration as an important era in the Annals of this Country, if it should be recommended by you, and adopted by the Assembly."[83] With this report, Washington, the "politician," had returned. After repeating to Harrison many of the detailed descriptions from his diary, he pushed the governor to act. He proposed two major river/canal projects on the Potomac and James Rivers. The James, he thought, since it ran close to the Great Kanawha, might be more convenient for Virginia south of the Potomac. It would also draw support from those who might view the Potomac project as not in their interests. To provide accurate information, he called for "[c]ommissioners to make an actual survey of the James River and Potomac from the tide water to their respective sources." Finally, for those who worried about "the fatigues of the voyage back again," he put in a plug for "Rumsey's discovery for working boats against the stream."[84]

Washington did not confine his lobbying to Virginia. Two weeks after writing to Harrison, he sent a nearly identical letter to George Plater, president of the Maryland senate. He reminded Plater that Maryland and Virginia had a common interest in the Potomac. He also, not so subtly, warned Plater that Pennsylvania had a plan to improve navigation on the Susquehanna River and build connecting roads in the West, all of which would lead to Philadelphia. He admitted that their plan was costly and difficult, but "a people possessed of the spirit of Commerce—who see—and who will resolve to pursue advantages, may achieve almost any thing."[85] He wrote to others expressing his views on the importance of the Potomac, and while hosting a dinner at Mount Vernon, he invited his guests to share a toast to the Potomac.[86] It was a strategy that he shared in a private letter to his former comrade in arms Henry Knox:

> I am now endeavoring to stimulate my Countrymen to the extension of the inland navigation of the rivers Potomac and James—thereby, & a short land transportation, to connect the Western Territory by strong commercial bands with this—I hope I shall succeed, more on account of its political importance—than the commercial advantages which would result from it, altho' the latter is an immense object: for if this Country, which will settle faster than any other ever did (and chiefly by foreigners who can have no particular predilection for us), cannot, by an easy communication be drawn this way, but are suffered to form commercial intercourses (which lead we all know to others) with the Spaniards on their right & rear, or the British on their left, they will become a distinct people from us—have different views—different interests, & instead of adding strength to the Union, may in case of a rupture with either of those powers, be a formidable & dangerous neighbour.[87]

After fifteen years of service in the Virginia legislature and eight years as commander in chief reporting to Congress, Washington was well acquainted with legislative behavior—the inclination to receive reports, consign them to committee, and then, although not always, return them for floor debate, at which time action was often delayed or not taken at all. It was a slow, deliberative process. Unless extraordinary action was taken, his letter of 10 October was likely to fall into a legislative void. His report needed a champion. Only he could fill that role, which left him in a dilemma. How often had he written extoling the virtues of being a private citizen sitting under a fig tree, free from all public responsibilities? He was "retired." Should he gallop off to Richmond, it would be a reversal of all that he had said. He would be stepping down from Mount Olympus. As he pondered his dilemma, Gilbert du Motier, the marquis de Lafayette, provided an answer.

A few days after dispatching his letter to Governor Harrison, Washington received a letter from Lafayette. The marquis had completed his northern tour and was heading back to Mount Vernon but with a slight detour—Richmond, where he anticipated a grand welcome from citizens who remembered his defense of the state in the Revolution. He was a hero in Virginia. The legislature was anxious to honor him. Never one to avoid admiring crowds, Lafayette, recognizing that the general "had rather not go to Richmond," apologized for the delay in arriving at Mount Vernon.[88] Lafayette need not have been concerned. Washington was coming to Richmond.

4

POTOMAC COMPANY

It is now near 12 at night, and I am writing with an Aching head. (GW to JM, 28 December 1784, in *GWP, Conf.
Series*, 2:231)

Richmond had been Virginia's capital since 1780 when Governor
Thomas Jefferson, noting that Williamsburg was vulnerable to
British attack, persuaded the legislature to transfer the government to a
safer, inland location. Reluctantly abandoning the comfort of Williamsburg, the members moved sixty miles west to the rustic surroundings of
Richmond on the banks of the James River. Jefferson's concern about
Williamsburg proved prescient, as it was sacked in 1781. Unfortunately,
Richmond proved equally vulnerable and was plundered by the enemy
under the apostate general, Benedict Arnold. He burned so much of
the city that when the legislature convened on 18 October 1784 for
the fall/winter session, there was no regular chamber available in which
they could meet. Instead of the refined quarters of Williamsburg, the
representatives assembled in the William Cunningham House, a building so poorly built and common that Arnold had not troubled to burn
it during his rampage through the city.

Speaker of the House John Tyler called the session to order. He
looked out at the delegates and observed, as was often the case in the
first days of a session, that "the number present were not sufficient to
proceed to business." Two weeks elapsed until enough tardy members arrived to provide a proper quorum. The first days of the session
were filled with the customary humdrum items—reviewing petitions,

receiving committee reports, approving pensions, denying pensions, authorizing land surveys, reviewing reports from the West, and authorizing the establishment of new towns. In the evenings, members retired to nearby taverns and members' homes, where conversation often turned toward Washington's "private" letter to Governor Harrison and what his proposals meant for the future of Virginia. Adding to the flurry of interest was the news that the general and Gilbert du Motier, the marquis de Lafayette, were coming to Richmond.

Washington might more conveniently have waited at Mount Vernon to welcome Lafayette, but the opportunity to meet the marquis in Richmond—and the attention the event would draw—was an opportunity too important to miss. Washington's financial prospects were inextricably linked to orderly development in the West, which depended on river transport, better roads, settlement of conflicting land claims, and the establishment of the regular process of law. He felt it was urgent for the legislature to act on pending measures favorable to him. He needed to be cautious, however. It would be unseemly for him to appear in the capital lobbying for measures from which he stood to benefit. He was riding to Richmond, he claimed, not to press his own interests but to celebrate a hero of the Revolution—Lafayette.

Although it was a Sunday, 14 November 1784, Richmond turned out to welcome "our worthy and beloved late Commander in Chief." His entrance was "announced by the discharge of cannon, as citizens, wishing to show every mark of respect to so illustrious a character, illuminated their houses in a most elegant manner."[1]

The next morning, a committee led by Patrick Henry (including James Madison) waited "upon him, with the respectful regards of this house." Washington, who had been a member of the House for fifteen years before the Revolution, repeated that he "lamented the want of those powers, which would enable me to do justice to my feelings." Nonetheless, there was one feeling he wanted to share. Repeating what he had written to Governor Harrison, he took the moment to remind his visitors that at this moment great "advantages of commerce are not only offered but are soliciting our acceptance." He warned them "it must be our own fault indeed if we do not make them productive of a rich & plenteous harvest—and of that National honor & glory, which should be characteristic of a young, & rising Empire."[2] For the next three days, Washington held numerous "conversations" with Madison and other members of the house to impress on them "the magnitude of the object" before them.[3]

Only thirty-three, Madison was a key member of the House. He served on the Committee of Commerce and chaired the Committee on the Courts of Justice.[4] At the time a firm nationalist, he feared that the states aimed to undermine the Confederation. He was alarmed by what he had witnessed at the Fort Stanwix conference, where the New York delegates, by negotiating directly with the Iroquois, had tried to circumvent the authority of Congress. Their behavior, Madison wrote to his fellow Virginian James Monroe, had given "umbrage" to Congress by violating "both duty and decorum." Unfortunately, Congress was "too impotent to punish such offenses."[5]

Even though Washington and Madison shared a common concern about the future of the Confederation, they were barely acquainted personally. Prior to this occasion they had exchanged two letters, both perfunctory, and had met in person only briefly during the winter of 1781–1782, when Washington visited Congress following Yorktown.[6] Now, in the hurly-burly of Virginia politics, fired by a growing concern over national affairs, James Madison and George Washington were allies. At this critical moment, what mattered most was that Madison, a brilliant political strategist, shared Washington's passion to link the West to the rest of the country. Washington needed Madison's political skills in the House to guide legislation favorable to his interests.[7]

Celebrations continued, and on Wednesday evening, to honor Washington, renowned for his dancing prowess, a ball was held in the "common hall." The next day, Richmond welcomed a second hero when "the Marquis de Lafayette, attended by two French Gentlemen of distinction," arrived. "His services," announced the *Virginia Journal*, "in the late revolution, and particularly in this State, are too well known to need encomiums."[8]

That evening Washington and Lafayette were guests of honor at a "sumptuous dinner, given in Mr. Trower's tavern. Also present were Members of the General Assembly, the Governor, Members of the Council of State and the principal Gentlemen of the city."[9] Affairs were going well. With Madison at the helm, Washington scored his first legislative victory on behalf of his Berkeley Springs acquaintance, the indefatigable James Rumsey.

At the previous May session, Rumsey had tried to secure a state monopoly for his boat that could move upstream. The House had dismissed him with contempt. How things had changed. Learning that Washington was to be in Richmond, with the certificate he had received from the general, Rumsey hurried to the capital. Since Washington's trip west, his letter to Governor Harrison, and now his presence in Richmond, a fervor had gripped the General Assembly in which almost any measure that sought to link the West (particularly those supported by Washington) cascaded forward. Washington's endorsement of Rumsey's project "opened the ears of the Assembly."[10] They quickly enacted a law granting him "the sole and exclusive right and Privilege of constructing and navigating Boats upon his model in each & every River, Creek, Bay, Inlet or Harbour within this Commonwealth."[11] With affairs moving well, on Saturday, 20 November, leaving Madison in charge of managing his agenda, Washington, accompanied by Lafayette, left for Mount Vernon.

Washington's confidence in Madison was well placed. As a member of the Committee on Commerce, charged with reviewing matters "relative to the trade, manufactures and commerce of this Commonwealth," Madison held a key position. Writing to Thomas Jefferson, Edmund Randolph, Virginia's attorney general, described Madison as ready "to step into the heat of battle."[12] Unlike Washington's imposing physical stature, Madison was slightly built, standing barely five feet four, with a manner more reserved and cerebral than most of his often boisterous legislative colleagues. In a body known for tumult, where formal debate often took second place to "talk of horse-races, runaway Negroes, yesterday's play, [and] politics," Madison was the consummate lawmaker.[13] For the remainder of the session, he floor managed several pieces of legislation, authorizing roads, canals, and river improvements, all aimed at providing links to the West. Among the bills he submitted was a proposal for "opening and extending the navigation of the river Potomac."[14]

Washington and Lafayette's stay at Mount Vernon was brief. Four days after arriving, they left for Annapolis. Before departing, Washington sent Madison a petition delivered to him at Mount Vernon while he had been away at Richmond.[15] The petition, accompanied by a draft bill for creating a Potomac River Company, had been drawn up at a meeting held at John Lomax's Tavern in Alexandria, where

> sundry inhabitants of the State of Maryland, and also of this State [i.e., Virginia], set forth, that they conceive it would greatly contribute to the extension of commerce, and the improvement of agriculture, if the river Potomac was made navigable from the falls, and a communication opened by that means with the western country; and praying that an act may pass establishing a company, to be invested with full powers for that purpose.[16]

Seeing this proposal as valuable ammunition for Madison to use in the assembly, Washington set aside his packing and hurriedly forwarded copies of the petition and the draft bill to him, explaining that he was making "no apology for giving you the trouble of the enclosed," for the matter was so important that he "could not think of withholding these Papers until my return."[17] After posting the documents, he and Lafayette left for Annapolis.

Having been separated from his wife, Adrienne, and their three young children for more than six months, Lafayette was anxious to return home. The French frigate *Nymphe* was waiting in New York to transport him to France.[18] Washington planned to ride with the marquis as far as Baltimore, making a brief stop at Annapolis. There, Washington met with "some of the leading members of the Maryland Assembly" to discuss the Potomac bill being considered in the Virginia Assembly. The Marylanders made it clear that Virginia's unilateral action made them "discontent." They told Washington that the measures drawn up in Alexandria had "too great a leaning to local advantages on one part, and too much compliance on the other part." Wisely, Washington backed away, explaining that the draft "came to my hands at a moment when I could not read, much less consider it."[19] Coming from a person knowledgeable, and consumed with the issues at hand, Washington's excuse appears disingenuous; nonetheless, it was vital to prevent the Virginia Assembly from enacting a bill that the Marylanders opposed. Such action would give Baltimore merchants, already suspicious of their

Virginia neighbors, ample ammunition to sink the proposal, which they deemed harmful to their port.

It was imperative that the two states come to an agreement. Both legislatures were approaching adjournment of their fall sessions. Neither would reconvene until spring 1785. Seeing that he was needed at home, Washington cut short his trip. He offered his apologies to Lafayette for leaving him to travel on alone while alerting Madison to the danger and suggesting that a joint committee composed of representatives from both states be formed quickly

> to meet at some intermediate place, and agree, (first knowing the sentiments of the assemblies), upon an adequate bill to be adopted by both States[.] This would prevent dissimilar proceedings, as un- productive as no bill—save time—and bring matters at once to a point. A measure of this kind is consonant, I know, with the ideas of some of the leading members of the Maryland Assembly, who requested me to suggest it to my friends in our assembly and inform them of the result.[20]

The Virginia house "lent a ready ear." On the day before Madison's bill was scheduled for a vote, 14 December, it was dropped from the calendar; instead, the delegates, recognizing the importance of "opening and improving the navigation of the river Potomac, from the tide water, up the said river as far as the same can be carried," agreed that "acts passed without previous communications between the two states, may be dissimilar and productive of much delay." To coordinate efforts, the assembly appointed three commissioners, "George Washington, Horatio Gates and Thomas Blackburne, to meet such persons as may be appointed by the State of Maryland, and to concert with them the regulations under which a company ought to be established."[21] With adjournment less than a month away, time was of the essence. Complicating matters, Blackburne declined to join the committee, explaining that family affairs kept him home, leaving the business to Washington and Gates.[22]

George Washington was no friend to Horatio Gates. The two men had an unhappy relationship dating back to their service in the Revolution. After Major General Gates's victory over the British at

Saratoga (19 September–7 October 1777), his reputation was riding high, while Washington, in contrast, had suffered a series of setbacks. General Sir William Howe had defeated him at Brandywine Creek (11 September 1777), taken Philadelphia (26 September 1777), and inflicted a second defeat on the Americans at Germantown (4 October 1777). Comparing their records, some officers in the army, friends of Gates, and several members of Congress speculated that perhaps Gates, not Washington, should be commander in chief. Although the so-called Conway Cabal—named after General Thomas Conway, one of the officers anxious to thrust Washington aside and elevate Gates—remained only gossip, Washington, aware of these machinations, never again trusted Gates.[23]

Despite the well-known animosity between the two, in August 1782, without consulting Washington, Congress posted Gates to the Continental army encampment at Newburgh, New York, to "duty as the Commander in Chief shall direct."[24] It was at Newburgh that Gates, surrounded by young officers who blamed Washington for Congress's neglect of the army, gave tacit encouragement to those who conspired to undermine the authority of the commander in chief. When alerted to Gates's conniving, Washington, remembering the Conway Cabal, could only remark that "old leven [Gates] is again, beginning to work, under a mask of the most perfect dissimulation."[25] When the scheme collapsed, the officers involved scurried for cover while Gates artfully deflected responsibility.[26]

To Henry Knox, who knew and detested the wily Gates, Washington wrote sarcastically that he was on his way to Annapolis "with my bosom friend Genl G—tes, who being at Richmond contrived to edge himself into the Commission."[27] Washington need not have worried. On Christmas Eve, Gates, pleading ill health, decided it was best for him to "go to bed instead of going to Mann's" tavern for the meeting.[28] In the meantime, the Maryland House of Delegates, having received "the petition for opening and extending the navigation of the Potomac, and the resolution of the general assembly of Virginia on that subject, to be of great importance and worthy the immediate consideration of this government," appointed a conference committee (House and Senate) to meet with the Virginia representatives. Absent

Blackburne and Gates, Virginia was represented by a committee of one—Washington. Virginian or not, the ten members from the Maryland House and Senate elected Washington to preside. It was an unusual situation and a testament to Washington's stature that, although he was not a member of either legislature, the Marylanders turned to him to help fashion the bill. Five days later, meeting over the Christmas holiday, the "joint committee" made its report, presenting draft legislation for "establishing a company for opening and extending the navigation of the Potomac."[29]

Washington wrote to Madison reporting the results at Annapolis: "It is now near 12 at night, and I am writing with an Aching head, having been constantly employed in this business since the 22d without assistance from my colleagues—Genl Gates having been sick the whole time, and Colo Blackburn[e] not attending." The result was not all that he had wished. "Matters might perhaps have been better digested if more time had been taken, but the fear of not getting the report to Richmond before the Assembly would have risen, occasioned more hurry than accuracy—or even real dispatch. But to alter the Act now, further than to accommodate it to circumstances where it is essential; or to remedy an obvious error if any should be discovered will not do." Maryland had played its hand well.[30]

Washington was tired. Since 1 September he had been away from home more than six weeks, traveling hundreds of miles. In his absence, Lund, even if not always to his employer's exacting standards, had managed the estate. But much else had been left undone. Affairs in the West remained in turmoil, and piles of paper crowded his desk. "Applications, which oftentimes cannot be complied with. Enquiries, which would employ the pen of a historian to satisfy. Letters of compliment, as unmeaning perhaps as they are troublesome, but which must be attended to. And the commonplace business, which employs my pen & my time; often disagreeably."[31] Since the departure of Walker and Humphreys, Washington had been without assistance. The weight of work and the constant arrival of company sat heavily on him.[32] "I already begin to feel the effect. Heavy, & painful oppressions of the head, and other disagreeable sensations, often trouble me. I am determined therefore to employ some person who shall ease me of the drudgery of this business."[33] The search failed until, finally, 26 July, when William Shaw, his new "book-keeper and secretary," arrived to undertake his duties. In the meantime, Washington bore the "drudgery."[34]

Unaware of the details of the discussions in Annapolis, Madison had continued to push forward in Richmond. To garner support in the house for the Potomac project, which clearly favored Alexandria, he had prepared a similar measure providing funds for a James River canal that would serve the interests of Richmond and Norfolk.[35] Madison's plan, submitted on 18 December, called for the incorporation of a com-pany, with trustees appointed by the governor who would solicit sub-scriptions, oversee construction, and pay a fixed 10 percent interest rate, which the state "inviolably pledged for both principal and interest."[36] The measure passed and was only awaiting final approval when the Maryland bill arrived.

Madison had little room to maneuver. Dropping his own bill, he endorsed "a bill & Resolutions corresponding with those of Maryland."[37] The measure provided for an

> incorporated body [issuing] 500 shares amounting to about 220,000 dollars, of which the states of Virginia and Maryland are each to take 50 shares, that the tolls shall be collected at three por-tions at the three principal falls, and with the works vested as real estate in the members of the Company, and the works shall be begun within one year, and finished within ten years under penalty of entire forfeiture.[38]

Seeing "the only danger of miscarriage arising from the impatience of the members to depart, & the bare competency of the present num-ber," Madison oversaw several days of hectic politicking between the House and the Senate until, on 4 January, the bill passed precisely on the model transmitted from Maryland.[39] Also included was a modified, more modest bill, which did not need Maryland's participation, provid-ing improvements on the James River. One last detail remained: To complete the package, linking the Potomac to the Ohio, the legislature approved funds for the construction and repair "of a convenient Road from such part of the Waters of the Potowmack, to such part of the River Cheat or of the River Monongahela."[40]

Madison was pleased with his accomplishments, but the work had been done, he noted to Jefferson, in a hurry with "all the precipitancy which marks the concluding stages of a session which abound I fear with inaccuracies."[41] He was correct. The organization of companies to clear navigation on the James and particularly the Potomac raised some old issues.[42] In 1776, by a piece of careless legislation, Virginia had ceded to Maryland jurisdiction over the river, reserving only the right of free navigation.[43] In the new circumstances, the error needed correction, but with no time left in the session, the House appointed three commissioners (George Mason, Alexander Henderson, and James Madison) "to concert with Commissioners on the part of Maryland, regulations touching the navigation and jurisdiction of the Potomac."[44] A letter from Madison carrying the good news from Richmond arrived at Mount Vernon on 17 January 1785.[45]

Retirement! Hardly. George Washington had returned to the fray. In the last few months of 1784, he had demonstrated extraordinary energy and political influence. He had journeyed west, surveying his property, firing incompetent managers, dunning unruly tenants, and gathering information for a wide-ranging plan of internal improvements that would open "free and easy access communication with the western territory (thereby binding them to us by interest), the only knot which will hold."[46] He returned to Mount Vernon and made his report to the governor, but then, realizing his report might not be sufficient, he rode to Richmond, descended dramatically on the legislature, enlisted Madison to press his case, and, in a grand public celebration, rendezvoused with Lafayette.

It was by the sheer force of his personality, Benjamin Harrison wrote, that "works under your patronage and protection will advance more rapidly than they would otherwise do." Washington brought two states, more accustomed to squabbling than cooperating, into alignment.[47] It was a phenomenal achievement, thrusting him into the character of the consummate political deal maker in a fractious republic, while also ensuring Virginia's ascendency over the West. His efforts, he reported to Lafayette, "had not been employed in vain."[48]

While savoring his triumph, Washington confided to Lafayette that he was troubled by an unexpected act of the House "which has been productive of infinitely more embarrassment than pleasure."[49] After enacting nearly all the measures he had advocated, to "demonstrate the grateful wishes of his country," by unanimous vote the House voted to vest "in George Washington, Esq. a certain interest in the companies established for opening and extending the navigation of Potomac and James rivers."[50]

Washington had long guarded his Cincinnatus-like image as a statesman, seeking only the public good. Such was his motive when he had declined a salary during the war. He likened this gift of stock "in the same light as a pension." Washington was worried. Once the "gratuity" was made public, the purity of his motives would be compromised. The fact that he owned stock in the companies, as well as extensive real estate in the West and Alexandria, meant that he would benefit from these improvements. Such revelations would provide ample fodder to feed critics assailing him of being no better than other greedy speculators using corrupt means to fill their pockets. Washington was aware of his vulnerability. In a moment of candor, he confessed to Jefferson that in the matter of western lands, he was not "disinterested."[51]

Calling the stock gift the greatest embarrassment "since I left the walks of public life," Washington cast about for advice. To Lafayette he wrote, "It is not my wish, nor is it my intention, to accept this gratuitous gift; but how to decline it without appearing to slight the favors of my Country—committing an act of disrespect to the Legislature—or having motives of pride, or an ostentatious display of disinterestedness ascribed to me, I am at a loss."[52] Lafayette sympathized and suggested that, instead of refusing the gift outright, it should "[b]e gently turned towards some public popular establishment."[53]

Washington pressed the new governor, Patrick Henry, and others to repeal the act granting him stock. In October 1785, the House responded and agreed that Washington's "shares with the tolls and profits hereafter accruing therefrom, shall stand appropriated to such objects of a public nature, in such manner, and under such distributions, as the said George Washington, esq. by deed during his life, or by his last will and testament, shall direct and appoint."[54] Washington held the stock until his death (1799), when he willed the Potomac shares "towards the endowment of a UNIVERSITY to be established within the limits of the District of Columbia" and the James River shares "to benefit of Liberty-Hall Academy, in the County of Rockbridge, in the Common-wealth of Virginia."[55]

In the spring, the Potomac Company opened subscription books at locations in Richmond, Alexandria, and Winchester, Virginia, and in Annapolis, Frederick, and Georgetown, Maryland. Advertisements appeared in local newspapers announcing that "laudable subscriptions so essentially necessary to accomplish a work fraught with such universal advantages are now opened."[56] Five hundred shares were offered at $400 each, raising a capital of $200,000. However, until the paid-up subscribers met, after 10 May, the company had no established governance. Although Washington was uncertain "of whom the company may consist," no one doubted that as the "godfather" of the enterprise, the general was in charge.[57]

Acutely aware that the company needed to attract investors, Washington launched a personal public relations campaign promoting the project to friends and allies, among them Richard Henry Lee, president of the Congress; William Paca, governor of Maryland; the Revolution's "Financier," Robert Morris; and his comrade in arms, Henry Knox in Boston.[58] Washington was relentless in his advocacy. In mid-January 1785, when Elkanah Watson, traveler, businessman, and writer, visited Mount Vernon ("the two richest days of my life"), he found Washington "absorbed" by the Potomac project. It "was his constant and favorite theme." Watson confessed that Washington had "completely infected me with the canal mania and enkindled my enthusiasm."[59] He had become, in the view of one historian, "a Potomac navigation bore."[60]

While Washington rallied support among his friends, visitors, and allies, Virginia and Maryland had yet to resolve the nagging issues of navigation left over from the 1776 agreement. To address this question, in the previous June session (1784), Virginia had appointed four commissioners—Alexander Henderson, James Madison, George Mason, and Edmund Randolph—to meet with their Maryland counterparts. For reasons unknown, the commissioners never met. Considering the new circumstances, however, late in December, amid the flurry of activity surrounding Potomac navigation, the House acted to reaffirm their commitment "to concert with commissioners on the part of Maryland, touching navigation and jurisdiction of the Potomac."[61]

In accordance with the agreement, Governor Paca wrote to Virginia's governor, Patrick Henry, setting 21 March as the date for a joint meeting in Alexandria. Henry made no reply, nor did he inform the Virginia commissioners that Paca had set a date for the meeting. Assuming, on little ground, that no response from Richmond meant that all was in order and the time and place were acceptable, the Maryland delegates (Daniel St. Thomas Jennifer, Thomas Stone, and Samuel Chase), traveling through a late winter storm, arrived in Alexandria on 21 March.

Washington, who from a Maryland source had learned of the meeting only the day before (20 March), was appalled at Governor Henry's blunder.[62] Concerned that without Virginia represented the meeting would collapse, putting the Potomac project in jeopardy, he sent messages urging Mason and Henderson, both of whom lived nearby, to ride to Alexandria. Taking no chances, on the same day he learned of the meeting, Washington sent his carriage to Mason's home, Gunston Hall, to carry him to Alexandria. Henderson arrived on his own. The two commissioners, making excuses for their absent colleagues, Madison and Randolph, asked for a two-day pause to await their arrival. When the two Virginians did not appear, discussions began without them. To monitor the situation and prevent any unraveling, Washington rode to Alexandria and joined the commissioners for dinner, during which, to relieve the tension induced by the nonappearance of Madison and Randolph, he invited them to adjourn to the greater comfort of Mount Vernon.[63] They agreed. Mason arrived at Mount Vernon early on Thursday to brief Washington. The next day, the remaining commissioners joined them. Washington's gracious (astute) act relieved the uneasiness caused by Governor Henry's "forgetfulness."[64] It also allowed him, even though he was not a member of the delegation, to influence the proceedings. There was little disagreement. Favored with good food and fine wine, after four days of amicable discussion the delegates came to an agreement outlined in thirteen articles. Article 1 captured the spirit of the compact by setting forth that the Potomac River and Chesapeake Bay would be "ever considered as a common highway free for the use and navigation" of both states.[65]

Maryland quickly approved the compact, and the Virginia House, under the skillful guidance of Madison, did the same.[66] The momentum that had secured a bilateral agreement buoyed nationalist sentiments. Sensing the moment was right to draw all the states into a broad agreement on commerce and trade, the Virginia House voted to invite all of them to send "commissioners at a time and place to be agreed on, to take into consideration the trade of the United States to examine the relative situations and trade of the United States, to consider how far an uniform system in their commercial relations may be necessary to their common interest and perfect harmony."[67] The House named James Madison, Edmund Randolph, Walter Jones, St. George Tucker, Meriwether Smith, David Ross, William Ronald, and George Mason as its representatives. Madison was skeptical and thought the effort would "probably miscarry"; nonetheless, it was "better than nothing."[68] In March, the Virginia delegates, believing it "prudent to avoid the neighborhood of Congress, and the large Commercial towns, in order to disarm the adversaries," announced that the meeting would be held at Annapolis on the "first Monday in September next."[69]

Like Madison, Washington thought little would come of the Annapolis meeting. For the moment, his attention was on selling subscriptions to the Potomac project and planning the inaugural meeting of the company scheduled for 17 May. That morning Washington rode to Alexandria. Of the ninety subscribers, fifty-six gathered in Lomax's Tavern on the corner of Princess and Water Streets. Some familiar faces were on hand, including Lund Washington, Horatio Gates, and Nelly's husband David Stuart.[70]

"After a mid-day banquet," the chairman, Daniel Carroll, president of the Maryland Senate, called the meeting to order. Although the subscription drive had secured only 403 shares out of the 500 offered (the majority held by Virginians), the subscribers present decided that the number was "more than sufficient to constitute the Company under the Act."[71] To no one's surprise, they elected Washington as president along with four directors: two from Maryland (former governor Thomas Sim Lee and the current governor Thomas Johnson) and two Virginians (George Gilpin and John Fitzgerald, both Alexandria merchants).[72] After setting the time for the next general meeting, 1 August at Georgetown, the meeting adjourned.[73]

The enabling legislation stipulated, "That in case the said company shall not begin the said work within one year after the said company shall be formed or shall not compleat the same within ten years thereafter, then shall all the interest of the said company, and all preference in their favor as to the navigation and tolls aforesaid, be forfeited, and cease."[74] With a deadline certain, it was imperative to move as quickly as possible. Acting as president, Washington wasted no time. The day following the meeting in Alexandria, he notified his fellow directors that as "the season begins to advance we should have a meeting as soon as it can be." He set the date for 30 May.[75]

On that day, Washington dined with the directors at the City Hotel in Alexandria, where, with his usual astuteness and grace, he invited them to join him the next morning in the more relaxing environment of Mount Vernon. At the meeting, after electing William Hartshorne treasurer and John Potts secretary, the directors spent two days settling on a plan that divided the work on the river into two segments: one "from the Great Falls to Payne's Falls (Harpers Ferry) and the other from the upper part of Shenandoah Falls to the highest place practicable on the North Branch."[76] Each section would have a crew "of fifty men to be under the general direction of one skillful person who shall have a proper assistant, as well as three overseers with each party."[77] Critical to the project was finding a competent manager, with sufficient technical skill to oversee a complicated project. Since "no engineer in America had ever seen a canal lock, [and] few understood anything of the mechanical principles involved," the local talent pool was shallow.[78] Remembering the French engineers who had served with him during the Revolution, Washington asked Lafayette for assistance.

> The nature of our work, will be first, at the principal falls of the river to let Vessels down by means of Locks—or, if Rumsey's plan should succeed, by regular or gradual slopes—in either case, the bad effect of Ice & drift wood in floods, are to be guarded against—2d As the Canals at these places will pass thro' rocky ground, to be able to remove these with skill & facility, & to secure the Canals when

made. 3dly—in other parts of the river, the water will require to be deepened, & in these places the bottom generally is either rock under water, or loose stone of different sizes; for it rarely happens that Sand or Mud is to be found in any of the shallow parts of the river. I mention these things because it is not the Man who may be best skilled in Dikes: who knows best how to conduct water upon a level—or who can carry it thro' hills or over Mountains, that would be most useful to us.

In a nod to his friend, and to avoid any offense, Washington added that, while he might "prefer to go to France for an engineer, the majority may incline to send to England whilst others may turn their eyes toward Holland." Ever the promoter, he concluded his letter with a postscript: "Do you think that there are persons of your acquaintance in France who might incline to become adventurers in it? I give it as my decided opinion to you that both are practicable beyond all manner of doubt; & that men who can afford to lay a little while out of their money, are laying the foundation of the greatest returns of any speculation I know of in the world."[79]

The search began with a series of newspaper advertisements appearing in Alexandria, Baltimore, and Philadelphia seeking a "Skillful Person." The deadline for applications was set as 1 July 1785.[80] On 2 July, the directors met to review applications. There were none, either from the United States or from abroad. With only six months left to begin the project, lest the company forfeit its rights, the directors were desperate, at which point in the meeting Washington "took the liberty" of mentioning James Rumsey. Some members, having only a "superficial acquaintance" with Rumsey, were hesitant. To placate them, Washington offered to invite Rumsey to an interview. They agreed. Washington summoned Rumsey to Alexandria, advising him that it would be well if he brought "some letters or other credential of your industry &c.—& if these were to come from members of the Company, they would have the greater weight."[81] With Washington by his side, Rumsey, the only candidate, got the job.

Although the purpose of the company was to provide a navigable waterway to the headwaters of the Potomac at Cumberland, Maryland (nearly two hundred miles), for the initial phase the directors laid out a more modest plan taking the project only as far as Harpers Ferry (approximately sixty miles). The directors ordered Rumsey to begin work with a crew of fifty men at three locations along the river, commencing at Great Falls above Georgetown, from there to Seneca Falls, and ending at Shenandoah Falls (Harpers Ferry).

As planned, on 1 August, the company directors gathered at Shutters Tavern in Georgetown for their annual meeting.[82] Decisions were made

> respecting rations to be allowed the Workmen—the mode of payment—manner of keeping an acct. of their work &ca. &ca&ca. &ca. and to a determination of proceeding first to the Seneca Falls and next to those at the Mouth of Shenandoah for the purpose of investigation & to direct the operations thereat adjourned Sine Die.[83]

The next morning, with the weather "clear and warm," and accompanied by Rumsey, the party set off, "except Govr. Lee who went to Mellwood to visit Mr. Igns. Digges (his father-in-Law) who lay at the point of death."[84] News that Washington was coming set off excitement. At the confluence of the Monocacy and Potomac (Frederick, Maryland), local citizens, sounding bells and firing cannon, greeted the party. Enthusiastic townspeople invited Washington to stay for a public dinner, but, anxious to get to Harpers Ferry, he declined the honor. Traveling by horseback and canoe, the party reached Harpers Ferry on Saturday evening, 6 August. The next morning, they set out to explore the falls. To get a closer look, Washington decided to run the white water in a "canoe with two skillful hands." After a perilous dash, he reported that the passage was too risky for regular use. A better route was a shallow "swash" on the far side of the river through which "navigation must be conducted."[85] That evening the directors met and concluded that by "easily removing" some of the rocks, Washington's route offered a safe channel eliminating the need for locks, thus providing a clear passage upstream to Cumberland. Downstream was more difficult, but by dredging, constructing retaining walls, and blasting away large rocks, combined with digging skirting canals around rapids, shallow draft flatboats could move safely. At Little Falls and Great Falls, where the river dropped more than one hundred combined feet, such simple solutions did not suffice. Left with no alternative, the directors agreed to construct locks at those locations. Unfortunately, neither Washington nor the directors, nor Rumsey, had any serious understanding of the principles of hydrology or experience in lock construction.

Unimpeded by any lack of knowledge, Director Thomas Johnson took a personal interest and presented a plan for the locks. Having "only my own ideas to guide me," in a somewhat incoherent letter, he wrote to Washington to share his notion "of the situation of the Great Falls for locks and manner of constructing them." He admitted that he was "puzzled about the lateral pressure of the water" and was unable to calculate the required strength of the locks to oppose the flow of water. As to his sources of information, "I have no books of my own nor am I in a favourable place to borrow books on the subject," which meant that his calculations "may probably be so far from accurate as to be entirely wrong for I have no learning in this way[;] the only merit or rather the excuse I can claim is intention."[86]

Taken aback by Johnson's brass, Washington took more than a month to reply. Since Johnson was too important to annoy, Washington was polite in his response, thanking him for his calculations, adding, "This in particular, is a new work—stands in need of all the information we can obtain, and is much indebted to you for many estimates, and ideas which have been very useful." Lacking proper information, the Potomac Company forged ahead, guided only "by common sense and trial and error."[87]

Despite the challenges, Washington could not curb his enthusiasm. His plan to link the West was underway. In high spirits, he wrote to William Grayson, a former aide-de-camp, "We have got the Potomack Navigation in hand—Workmen are employed, and the best Manager and assistants we could obtain."[88]

Washington continued to lead the company. Despite his optimism, the company's affairs did not go well. Trying to tame an unruly river proved beyond the company's capacity. Unlike its serene appearance seen from the piazza at Mount Vernon, the upper Potomac was narrow, winding, fast moving, and dangerous. Seasonal droughts and floods made the river unpredictable—low water in summer grounded boats, and high water in winter and spring washed away walls and riverbanks. Vexing labor problems and dwindling finances added to the project's woes.

Workers were difficult to recruit. Free white labor was scarce. Company representatives stood on the docks in Philadelphia and Baltimore recruiting and purchasing indentured servants and redemptioners, most of whom were unskilled and unreliable and took the first opportunity to run away. To identify captured fugitives and prevent further escapes, the company ordered their eyebrows and heads shaved every week. Regulations called for ample rations, but delivery of supplies to the remote camps was problematic. Pay, too, was uncertain—dense wooded paths and unaccompanied couriers were prime targets for robbers.

Unable to attract or keep white workers, the company, at Washington's suggestion, resorted to renting enslaved Africans at £20 per month Virginia currency. Owners, however, learning of the considerable number of workers killed on the job, were reluctant to risk their property. Housed in these rough camps, this mixture of "disorderly fellows," free whites, contracted whites, and enslaved Africans lived up to their reputation. It was a volatile mix.[89]

Although Washington continued to have faith in Rumsey's boat project, as problems mounted he called into question Rumsey's effectiveness managing the company's project. Frustrated at delays in construction and rising costs, in January 1786 Washington sent Rumsey a copy of a magazine from Scotland "containing the estimates of the expense of a canal" built in that country.[90] Rumsey rightly saw this unsolicited advice as a rebuke to his management. In the spring, he was further irritated when the directors hired James Brindley, nephew of England's celebrated canal builder (also named James Brindley), to examine the works along the Potomac. While generally positive, Brindley heaped criticism on the nature of the locks at Great Falls. It was all too much for Rumsey. On 4 July (no one mentioned the date), the directors met at Seneca Falls. Rumsey was present. Pricked by the criticism and unhappy about his pay, "Mr. Rumsey having signified his disinclination to serve the Company any longer for the pay and emoluments which had been allowed him, and the Directors not inclining to increase them, they parted."[91]

Rumsey did not go quietly. Shortly after he "parted," when the directors appointed his former assistant, Richardson Stewart, to succeed him, Rumsey let fly a barrage of formal complaints, accusing the directors of "incompetence, hiring other incompetents, deceit, disobedience, cruelty to subordinates, encouraging workers to ignore property owners' rights and obstructing company efforts."[92] Washington summoned the directors to a special meeting at Great Falls to examine Rumsey's charges. For two days, they listened to testimony and then dismissed Rumsey's accusations, Washington calling them "malignant, envious, and trifling."[93] Unfortunately, Rumsey's dramatic departure brought no respite. Stewart proved even more incompetent. They fired him in June 1788.[94]

Construction labored on. Unable to meet the looming legislative deadlines set for them, the company petitioned for an extension. It was granted.[95] Other extensions would come as the project inched its way along the river. Although he complained about "lingering," Washington remained intensively interested in the company and continued his role as president until his election as president of the United States (1789) required him, by his own standards, to step down.[96] At his death, still believing in the enterprise and the value of the shares, he willed his interest to support the establishment of a university in the newly created District of Columbia.[97]

Work on the canal ground ahead until 1828, when, facing failure, the Potomac Company conveyed its rights and assets to the newly incorporated Chesapeake and Ohio Canal Company.[98] The C and O reached Cumberland in 1850, at which point it ended. In the same year, the Baltimore and Ohio Railroad arrived at Cumberland. Not stopping there, the line pushed on, reaching Wheeling (present-day West Virginia), its terminus on the Ohio River, in 1853.[99] Washington's dream was finally realized, but by a technology that doomed his canal.

5

FAMILY

In my absence I had a very sickly family. (GW to William
Gordon, 3 November 1784, in *GWP, Conf. Series*, 2:116)

Against the centrifugal forces of politics, land speculation, and internal improvements, which pulled Washington away from Mount
Vernon to Richmond, Annapolis, and distant western river valleys,
the centripetal tug of farm and family drew him home. These were
the centers of his life, and during his long absences they had not fared
well. Early in November 1784, shortly after his return from the West,
Washington wrote to historian Reverend William Gordon of Roxbury,
Massachusetts, that "in my absence I had a very sickly family. Mrs.
Washington has been very unwell—Miss Custis extremely ill—and your
friend Tub a good deal reduced by a diarrhea—he has got perfectly well
& is as fat & saucy as ever. Mrs. Washington is well recovered, but Miss
Custis remains in a puny state."[1] As the holidays approached, Washington's spirits revived with the news that his family was to increase by
one—Martha's niece, eighteen-year-old Fanny Bassett, was coming to
live at Mount Vernon.[2]

Frances ("Fanny") was the daughter of Anna Maria Dandridge,
Martha Washington's younger sister, married to Burwell Bassett. The
family lived at Eltham Plantation, Kent County, a few miles from Williamsburg on the Pamunkey River. In the fall of 1777, when smallpox
ravaged the county, Martha, concerned about the health of Anna's
three children (John, Burwell, and Fanny), had invited her sister to

send them to Mount Vernon, where they might be inoculated safely. The Bassetts sent the older boys, Burwell and John, but kept Fanny, barely ten, at Eltham.

At Mount Vernon, under Martha's careful eye, the boys took the pox "light" and recovered within two weeks.[3] After they returned home, Martha reported to her sister that Burwell and John "have been exceedingly good boys, indeed, and I shall hope you will let them come to see me whenever they can spend so much time from school." Barely two weeks after the boys returned to Eltham, Martha was taken aback by the news that her sister Anna had died, most probably from smallpox. Worried that Fanny, left alone with two older brothers and her father, lacked appropriate female company, Martha wrote to her widowed brother-in-law that "my dear sister in her life time often mentioned my taking my dear Fanny if she should be taken away before she grew up—If you will let her come to live with me, I will with the greatest pleasure take her and be a parent and mother to her as long as I live."[4] At that moment, the idea was impossible, for at the same time Martha was writing, her husband was leading a battered Continental army into their winter encampment at Valley Forge. As was Martha's custom, when the army went into winter quarters, she was preparing to leave Mount Vernon to join her husband. Believing it better that Fanny remain at Eltham with her family than be left at Mount Vernon without Martha (or, worse, living in an army camp), Bassett declined the offer. For the remainder of the war, Fanny remained at Eltham in the company of her brothers and father.[5]

For teenage Fanny, compared to the excitement of Mount Vernon, Eltham was dull. In late fall 1784, Fanny, stricken with "fall fever," became "unwell."[6] With the war over and Martha permanently ensconced at Mount Vernon, Bassett agreed that his daughter might go to live with her aunt, where "the change of air & exercise will soon give her health." Fanny quickly became, Martha told her friend Elizabeth Powel, like "a child to me."[7] The general likewise took pleasure in having the "little folks" around.[8]

In the spring, another relation arrived—Washington's twenty-two-year-old nephew, George Augustine Washington, son of his youngest brother, Charles.[9] While serving as a wartime aide to Gilbert du Motier, the marquis de Lafayette, George Augustine had contracted a chronic "fever and pain in the breast," most likely tuberculosis. As the disease progressed, like his late uncle Lawrence, George Augustine sought a cure in warmer climes. His first stop was Bermuda, then the Bahamas, and finally South Carolina, where he stayed with his distant cousin, William Washington, at his plantation Sandy Hill, twenty-five miles west of Charleston, hoping that the "mildness of a southern winter would perfectly" restore him. It did not. He wrote to his uncle that the "pain in my breast attended with giddiness and pain in my head" persisted.[10] Haunted by the memory of his brother Lawrence, with whom he had traveled to Barbados thirty years before on a similar failed pilgrimage seeking to restore his health, Washington was pessimistic. He found no comfort in watching George Augustine "travelling about in pursuit of health, which, it is to be feared he will never obtain."[11] Washington's fears were confirmed when his cousin wrote that George Augustine's "disorder is too inflexible to be removed by a mere change of climate."[12] Filled with sympathy, and aware that his brother Charles was too straitened to assist, Washington paid his nephew's medical bills and was pleased when this "very amiable young man for whom I have an entire affection and regard" left Charleston to come live at Mount Vernon, where Washington observed to Fanny's father that George Augustine was "much amended in his health, but not free from the disorder in his side."[13]

Only a few days after arriving at Mount Vernon, George Augustine surprised his uncle—he and Fanny planned to marry.[14] Although they had known one another since childhood, in recent years they had been apart. It was either an epistolary courtship or else a very sudden one. Lest Burwell Bassett think ill of him for concealing the love affair, which had been going on right under his nose, Washington explained to him that "neither directly, nor indirectly have I ever said a syllable to Fanny, or George, upon the subject of their intended connection." Whatever his misgivings, however, Washington noted that "the sooner [the marriage] is consummated the better," and he insisted that the couple "should live at Mount Vernon."[15] For his part, Bassett, recognizing the advantages of the match to his daughter and his family, assured Washington "from my long acquaintance with him I have no reason to alter the good opinion

I ever entertain of him."[16] Martha extended an "invitation" to Fanny for the couple to live at Mount Vernon. Washington also spoke directly to George Augustine. With matters arranged, one detail remained: Fanny Bassett was underage. To obtain a marriage license, her father had to give consent in person to a magistrate or provide a document to the same effect, signed by two witnesses. On the day before the wedding, Washington and Bassett's oldest son (also named Burwell) rode to Alexandria to present the father's signed consent.[17] On Saturday evening, 15 October, "after the candles were lighted," the couple married in a ceremony presided over by the local Anglican minister, Reverend Spence Grayson, and attended only by close family, including Lund and Elizabeth Washington.[18]

While affection was Martha's motive for wanting the newlyweds to join the extended family at Mount Vernon, her husband had an additional purpose in mind. The marriage offered him an opportunity to solve a problem that had bedeviled him for some months: Lund was retiring.[19]

For more than twenty years, Lund had tended to the plantation. Under trying conditions—war, weather, financial pressure, and a hectoring boss—he had successfully managed affairs during Washington's long absences, and when the general was home, he stood by him as his right-hand man. Lund was an essential part of what Washington valued most—farm and family. In 1779, Lund had married his cousin Elizabeth, and for the next five years the couple lived at Mount Vernon. By 1784, as their family grew, Lund and Elizabeth decided to build their own home, Hayfield, about five miles south of Alexandria on land gifted to them by Washington. After moving to Hayfield, Lund made it known to Washington that he wished to retire. At the time, Washington, caught by surprise, told Lund that "it will take some time to digest my own thoughts." Now he had an answer.[20] Even though he lacked practical experience and suffered ill health, George Augustine was a person Washington could trust. Shortly after the wedding, George Augustine took on the duties of farm manager.

Aside from brief trips tending to business in Alexandria or inspecting work on the Potomac River project, until his departure for the Constitutional Convention in the spring of 1787, Washington stayed close to home, giving particular attention to matters on the farm and keeping a careful record, "Notes and Observations" of nearly every agricultural activity.[21] Unlike Lund, who was often on his own, George Augustine worked under the gimlet eye of his uncle. Washington, who bore down heavily on Lund, was easier on his nephew. Since they were together so often, the documentary record, unlike the numerous letters between Washington and Lund, is thin.[22] In late March 1789, as Washington was preparing to leave for New York and the presidency, he did write, in the fashion he often used with Lund, a long letter to George Augustine instructing him about manure, tobacco, grain, oyster shells, and dozens of other matters. Unlike his brusque letters to Lund, however, this letter concluded with warm sentiments:

> The general superintendence of my Affairs is all I require of you, for it is neither my desire nor wish that you should become a drudge to it—or, that you should refrain from any amusements, or visiting which may be agreeable either to Fanny or yourself to make or receive. Nor is it my wish that you should live in too parsimonious and niggardly a manner. Frugality & economy are undoubtedly commendable and all that is required.

In a moment of sentimentality, Washington signed his letter "I am ever your warm friend and Affectionate uncle."[23]

Wash, Nelly, George Augustine, and Fanny brought spirit and lightness to Mount Vernon. There were others in the family, though, who regrettably brought Washington more worry than pleasure—among them were his late brother Samuel's orphaned children: five sons (Thornton, Ferdinand, George Steptoe, Lawrence Augustine, and John) and a daughter, Harriot.[24]

After spending a life in "indolence and inattention," Samuel had died in 1781, followed two years later by the death of his fifth wife, Susannah Perrin.[25] Samuel left his accounts in a mess and the family close to financial ruin. He did well, however, to appoint his surviving brothers George, Charles, and John Augustine, in company with James Nourse, a neighbor, as executors of his estate.[26] Since they lived the closest, Charles and Nourse took the burden. Charles, however (who, his brother George complained, had a "natural indolence" and lived a life "spent in intoxication"), played little role managing his late brother's affairs.[27] To extract the children from such an unwholesome environment, Nourse, with financial help from Washington, arranged for George Steptoe and Lawrence Augustine to live in Alexandria and study with David Griffith, minister of Fairfax Parish. Of the three left at home, John, the youngest, died at age four. Thornton, the oldest, remained at Berkeley, dying in 1787. Ferdinand died of consumption in 1788, and although only twenty-one, he had, in his short life, managed to accumulate significant debts. Seeking to recover their money, his creditors came knocking at Washington's door. He refused their demands and informed them "that I have repeatedly refused and am determined not to have anything to do in the settlement of his affairs; for his conduct, while living, was such as I totally disapproved of. His extravagance could not be unknown to those who had dealings with him."[28] Daughter Harriot moved around, living with various family members. During her lifetime, Washington provided her "such reasonable and proper necessaries as she may stand in need of."[29]

Since Nourse lived at a distance, Washington, who saw promise in George Steptoe and Lawrence Augustine, was willing to pay "attention to those boys who are in my neighborhood," but that was as far as he was willing to go. "I cannot," he told Nourse, "concern myself in the smallest degree with the management of their estates." Swamped with trying to disentangle his own affairs, he wrote to Bushrod, "It would be undertaking a trust which I cannot discharge properly."[30] To Washington's relief, the boys settled in and matters went well. Griffith assured Washington that "the whole of Mr. Nourse's conduct towards his wards seems friendly and affectionate—manifests a disposition to do them all the justice in his power, and an earnest solicitude for their improvement in morals and manners and learning."[31] After the boys spent nearly three years with Griffith, however, Washington, without consulting Nourse (who had moved to Annapolis), thought it was time for them to leave Alexandria and begin their formal education.[32] Following the advice of his friend, Colonel William Fitzhugh, with whom he served on the vestry of Pohick Church, Washington decided that "the Academy at Georgetown is upon a good establishment [and] is a desirable place to fix my nephews."[33] The "Academy" was under the direction of the Reverend Stephen Bloomer Balch.

Born in Maryland, at an early age Balch moved with his family to Mecklenburg, North Carolina. After graduating from the College of New Jersey (Princeton) in 1774, Balch became principal of the Lower Marlborough Academy in Calvert County, Maryland. Called to the ministry, licensed to preach in 1779, he returned to North Carolina and spent several months as an itinerant minister. In 1780, he traveled north to Georgetown, where he helped establish the First Presbyterian Church.[34] While serving as minister, Balch, to augment his salary, took on the duties of headmaster at the recently formed Columbian Academy (1781), where "Latin, Greek, mathematics, science, surveying and navigation" fitted up the curriculum.[35]

George Steptoe and Lawrence Augustine were to begin their studies in 1785, boarding with Balch and his wife, Elizabeth Beall, daughter of Georgetown's founder Colonel George Beall, in their home on Duck Lane (Thirty-Third Street). Washington approved of the school's curriculum, particularly surveying, but he was also concerned that these young Virginia aristocrats "be introduced into life with those qualifications which are deemed necessary." Washington, who had a reputation for being a fine dancer (a skill he probably acquired at Fairfax manor during his teenage years), instructed Balch to enroll his nephews in "the Dancing School in Georgetown kept by Mr. Tatterson." Conscious of his own educational deficiencies, he also asked that the boys be taught French. For these lessons, their uncle would pay, "cheerfully." He insisted that they be kept close to their studies, but he did "not desire that they should be deprived of necessary and proper amusements."[36]

The boys embraced an expansive definition of their uncle's meaning of the word *necessary*, particularly in clothes, on which they spent lavishly. Faced with mounting bills from his nephews, who were "apt to want too much" and unable to "restrain the profuse and improper advances of goods for them at a distance," Washington wrote to Balch that he had decided "to bring them to Alexandria, where I shall be witness to their wants."[37]

On the same day that he wrote to Balch, Washington instructed his secretary, William Shaw, to proceed immediately to "Alexandria, to agree for the Schooling & Board of my Nephews George & Lawrence Washington now at the Academy at George Town & thence to the latter place to conduct them to the former for the purpose of going to School at the Alexandria Academy."[38] Two days later, with the boys in tow, Shaw returned to Alexandria.[39] In the meantime, Washington had written to William Brown, president of the Board of Trustees of the newly established Alexandria Academy. More than a month before, Brown had solicited him for a contribution to the academy's new building. Like so many solicitations Washington received, he had ignored it. However, with his nephews now enrolled in the school, he saw matters differently, and on 24 November, just as Shaw was picking up the boys in Georgetown, Washington wrote to Brown apologizing for not responding to the earlier solicitation, explaining that the request "among many other letters got buried." He assured him that "nothing is of more importance than the education of youth," lauding "the association which is formed in Alexandria to effect this desirable purpose."[40]

Although he was now willing to "give it support," first, he told Brown "there is a matter which I will take some other opportunity of bringing before the Trustees for their consideration." Aware from his own family experience of the unhappy conditions orphaned children often encountered, Washington asked the trustees to agree that his gift would be used "for the purpose of educating orphan children who have no other resource—or the children of such indigent parents as are unable to give it." Six months later, he expanded his largesse to include "girls who may Fitly share the benefits of the institution, in a ratio not to exceed one girl for four boys."[41] In recognition of Washington's generosity and his announced interest in education, the board elected him a trustee. Washington's interest in the academy boosted fund-raising. When completed, the new building featured three stories: "[T]he first floor held the English School that taught grammar, writing, arithmetic, and physical sciences to paying students. The second floor held the Learned Language School, which taught classical Latin and Greek. The Free School was on the third floor, where similar skills were taught as on the first floor."[42] Under the leadership of the academy's headmaster, Reverend William McWhir, a Presbyterian minister recently arrived from Belfast, the boys followed a curriculum nearly identical to the one at Georgetown.

In their first year, George Steptoe and Lawrence Augustine boarded with the elderly widow Parthenia Dade, the aunt of Washington's neighbor Robert Alexander, brother-in-law to his nephew Fielding Lewis Jr. The boys remained with her until January 1787, when they moved to the home of Samuel Hanson, an Alexandria merchant, a trustee of the academy, and a fox-hunting companion of Washington's. A stickler for detail and discipline, Hanson, who had been warned of the boys' unpleasant habits, promised Washington "to promote your views relative to their frugality, and endeavour to check any inclinations they may discover of a contrary tendency." Hanson laid out "the terms upon which I propose taking Young Gentlemen as Boarders":

1st The Expence of Board & Washing & mending 35£.

2d One fourth of the above sum to be advanced at the beginning of Each Quarter.

3d The Boys to find their own Beds.

4th The Boys to be informed by their Parents or Guardians that they are to be accountable to me for their Conduct out of School, and to be impressed with a conviction that in Case of Misbehaviour & Complaint made in Consequence thereof, to the Teacher at the Academy, reproof or Chastisement will ensue.

This regulation I hope will be thought necessary not only with respect to the preservation of Decorum in my family, but with regard to the morals of the Boys themselves, who, without such a restriction, would, I apprehend, be apt to keep bad hours, & get into improper Company especially on the Sabbath, when I should think it incumbent on me to see that they attended some place of publick religious Worship.[43]

Washington accepted Hanson's terms, and for the moment, Lawrence Augustine and George Steptoe seemed well settled.

Although Washington's name adorned the membership lists of many institutions, he rarely did more than accept the honor. Except for his donation, such was the situation with the academy, where he kept away from giving opinions, particularly about curriculum issues. "I have never taken any part in the management of the Academy."[44]

Under McWhir's guidance, the boys did well. To tout the school's accomplishments, at the end of the fall term of 1787, McWhir organized a "public examination" at which the students "delivered public orations before a large and respectable audience." Washington came to see his nephews. He could not have been more pleased. Although his younger brother Lawrence Augustine was not mentioned, George Steptoe won a prize in Latin and ancient geography. Returning late to his lodgings, Washington confided to his diary that the event "was well executed."[45]

What had gone well at the academy with Mr. McWhir took a decidedly different turn at Samuel Hanson's home, where the boys boarded. Away at the Philadelphia Convention (8 May 1787–22 September 1787), Washington learned from his wife, who kept him informed of family affairs, that Hanson—described by Washington's secretary, Tobias Lear, as "a very clever fellow"—had submitted his bill for the nephews' boarding and expenses directly to Thomas Porter, Washington's agent in Alexandria, who managed the boys' financial affairs.[46] That Porter answered the call (which Washington thought was excessive) and drew the money from his account incensed him, since he expected that his brother Samuel's estate would be footing the bills. Hanson, he told George Augustine, must "never do the like again." Whatever the method of payment, however, Washington understood that Samuel's estate was far too little to pay the mounting bills for George Steptoe and Lawrence Augustine. He admitted that, as soon as he returned home from Philadelphia, he "expected to be saluted" by his nephews' creditors.[47] Hanson, desperate to placate Washington, apologized quickly and "endeavoured to explain to your Satisfaction a part of my Conduct which, I have good reason to apprehend, has (from misrepresentation, I trust) incurred your displeasure."[48] Accepting Hanson's apology, Washington told him that he continued to feel satisfaction "from the consideration of [his nephews] being under the eye of a gentleman so capable as you are of advising and exacting a proper conduct from them."[49]

The problem, however, was that Hanson could not exact "proper conduct" from George Steptoe and Lawrence Augustine. Barely two months later, Hanson dropped a surprise on Washington: He wanted to be rid of the boys. His excuse was that he had taken in some "[g]entlemen to dine with me." Since the new guests dined late and the boys early, Hanson had to prepare two seatings. It was troublesome and expensive. More to the point, however, life with two willful teenagers was unpleasant. His nephews, Hanson reported to Washington, "arrogate to themselves no Small degree of self-estimation from those high and distinguished offices to which you have been appointed." The brothers simply refused to be governed by Hanson's rules. They were of "an obstinate habit, they have contracted of keeping company with servants; so that I could never keep them out of the kitchen—going out, without my permission, to dine with their school mates. Wearing their best clothes upon common occasions and staying out late of evenings and sometimes the whole night." Laying the blame on their teacher McWhir, "an enemy to corporal punishment," Hanson concluded that "tenderness and forbearance" only encouraged the boys to engage in worse behavior.[50]

Chastened by the continuing ill behavior of his nephews, Washington replied to Hanson that he was "sorry it is not convenient for you to board my Nephews any longer—Mr. Lear is desired to see what can be done with them—For the advice you have given them I feel myself obliged & wish they had sense & prudence enough to be governed by it." Lear arranged for the boys to board with McWhir.[51]

The boys brought their bad habits with them. Three months was all McWhir could endure. Often absent, he put the boys in the care of his servants. Given their history of flaunting authority, and being left in the hands of servants for whom they had no regard, the "boys will do as they please." His house, McWhir told an exasperated Washington, "neither suits them nor me."[52]

For Samuel Hanson, the eviction was providential. His gentlemen boarders had "quitted; one on account of marriage; the other, to make an unexpected voyage to the West Indies." Hanson, needing paying guests, reversed his previous position, asking Washington "to let me have them again."[53] Washington had his doubts about Hanson, particularly his stiff conditions. In addition to raising his charges for boarding the boys, due in advance, he insisted on "not only nominal, but an actual authority, over them," adding that "it will be impossible for me to restrain, without the power to punish, them." Lawrence

Augustine was a particular problem. "George," by contrast, was "of an obliging disposition."[54] Uneasy, but keen to put the matter aside, Washington agreed.[55]

Life with Samuel Hanson proved tumultuous. Soon George Steptoe, of the "obliging disposition," proved to be as troublesome as his brother, while Lawrence Augustine, in a remarkable turnaround from a "perverse, insolent, unmannerly boy," morphed into an "exceptionable" young man.[56]

Thinking he might have a bit of leverage, in June 1788, as it was certain that Washington would be president, Hanson wrote to him inquiring about an "appointment under the new government." Washington responded, dismissing Hanson's request as "altogether untimely and improper."[57] One month later, Hanson wrote again, this time asking Washington to support his application for appointment as assistant teacher at Alexandria Academy. Washington made no response. Angered by first being rejected by Washington and then ignored by him, Hanson changed tack; his behavior toward the nephews took a downward turn.

On Monday, 4 August 1788, Washington "went up to Alexandria to a meeting of the Potomack Company." That, however, was not the sole reason for his visit. Lawrence Augustine's behavior had gone sour again. The "great sloven," as Hanson called him, refused to abide by Hanson's house rules. He needed "chastisement." Matters had come to such a state that Hanson asked Washington's approval "to flog him." Washington told him "he was authorized to administer [chastisement] whensoever he should deserve it."[58] To avoid any accusation that he "acted from any impulse of passion," Hanson waited twenty-four hours before the whipping. On the morning of 5 August, after George Steptoe left for school, Hanson took a whip to Lawrence Augustine. His older brother, hearing the screams, rushed back to the house, where he found Lawrence Augustine "on the floor with Col. Hanson on the top of him and a cowhide laying on the table, alarmed at this unexpected sight, I interposed, without thinking on what I was about to do, and even then offered no insult to Col. Hanson, but hindered my brother from being beat with an instrument which I deemed improper to inflict a punishment for so small a crime. I was driven to it by brotherly affection."[59]

While George Steptoe and Hanson confronted one another, Lawrence Augustine fled. Somehow, he found the means to reach Mount Vernon, where, later in the afternoon, having been away checking on the progress of work at Muddy Hole, Washington returned home to find his disheveled and emotionally distraught nephew. Even when Lawrence showed him the "bruises," Washington was unsympathetic. Since he had approved the "chastisement," he could hardly side with Lawrence Augustine. Indeed, he even planned "to correct him" himself, but he relented after Lawrence Augustine promised "that there should be no cause of complaint against him for the future." He sent him back to Hanson. George Steptoe, too, incurred his uncle's displeasure by his "unjustifiable behaviour in rescuing his brother from that chastisement which was due to his improper conduct."[60] Contrite, George Steptoe assured his uncle, "I will make any concession to Col. Hanson, and as what is done cannot be undone, I shall persue that only method of atonement for folly, to be sorry for it, and do so no more."[61]

"Chastisement" does not appear to have taken place again, but relations with Hanson never recovered. The boys continued to defy him—sleeping to 9:00 a.m. and defying a 10:00 p.m. curfew. When confronted by Hanson, they threatened to leave. Seeking to be relieved "from a grievous burden," Hanson suggested that the boys move elsewhere. Washington thought it was a good suggestion, and in the spring of 1789, as he was preparing to leave for New York to assume the presidency, he asked his old friend James Craik to take them in.[62]

Lawrence Augustine and George Steptoe stayed with the Craiks for a little over a year.[63] It may well have been the happiest time of their youth. The boys did well, and Washington was relieved. The boys finished their studies in Alexandria, and Washington thought them ready for college. In the fall of 1790, he sent Lear to check out the University of Pennsylvania.[64] Accepted, they entered the university with, as usual, Washington bearing the expense.[65] He remembered those tuition bills in his will. After providing for his "dearly beloved wife Martha" and several relations, he noted that the "loans" he had made to George Steptoe and Lawrence Augustine for their education, "near five thousand dollars," had never been repaid. For their inheritance, it was sufficient to simply forgive them. The accounts, he wrote, "stand balanced."[66]

While his errant nephews were a persistent bedevilment to Washington, other family members were no less burdensome. In February 1787, John Augustine Washington ("Jack"), his favorite brother and Bushrod's father, died. Washington grieved the death of his "much loved brother who was the intimate companion of my youth and the most affectionate friend of my ripened age."[67] Aside from himself, of the immediate family only "three of us remain," he wrote—brother Charles, his widowed sister Betty Lewis, and his mother, Mary Ball Washington.

A widow for more than forty years, Mary Ball Washington had raised five of her own children (a sixth died in infancy) and three stepchildren.[68] Despite her vital role in raising her oldest son, George, little is known of Mary Ball.[69] Even her birth date is uncertain. Born at Epping Forest, the home of her father Joseph Ball and her mother Mary Johnson, sometime between 1707 and 1709, she lost both parents before she was twelve. Her uncle, Colonel George Eskridge, took her as his legal ward. In 1731, she married widower Augustine Washington, who, with his deceased wife, had four children. One of them, Butler, died in infancy, and a daughter, Jane, died in 1735. Two brothers, Lawrence (1718–1752) and John Augustine (1720–1762), survived. The new couple's firstborn, George, was born in 1732, followed in quick succession by five others, all of whom, apart from the infant Mildred, lived to adulthood. In 1738, the family moved to Ferry Farm on the banks of the Rappahannock River opposite Fredericksburg. Five years later, Augustine died, leaving his widow with five children at home ages five to eleven. Although Augustine left his property to his and Mary's oldest son, George, it remained under the mother's control until he turned twenty-one.

Perhaps it was the presence of five young children—Lawrence and John Augustine had married—that dissuaded suitors from courting the young widow, or it may have been Mary's strong, prickly personality that kept them away. Regardless, Mary Ball Washington never remarried. She held a firm hand, managing the farm and raising her children in a simple one-and-a-half-story wood frame building, four rooms down and four rooms up. Jealous of any authority over the children and wary of any interference, when her oldest stepson Lawrence and his father-in-law, William Fairfax, conjured a plan to enlist George as a midshipman in the Royal Navy, she intervened with a decided no.[70]

Even though his work as a surveyor for the Fairfaxes and service in the Virginia militia kept him away a good deal of the time, Ferry Farm remained Washington's home until 1754, when he moved forty miles away to Mount Vernon.

In accordance with his father's will, at twenty-one Washington came into full possession of Ferry Farm. As each of his siblings married, Washington saw little need for his mother to remain alone at the farm. In 1772, he bought her a house in Fredericksburg next door to her married daughter Betty Lewis. Two years later, he sold Ferry Farm to Hugh Mercer.[71]

While the rest of America heaped praise on Washington, Mary Ball, like many mothers, cast a more critical eye on her son. Indeed, the few accounts that survive portray her, in later life, as a demanding and unhappy person given to grumbling that her relatives, particularly her son George, ignored. So loud were her complaints that in 1781 a sympathetic Virginia legislature, hearing of her "condition," moved to grant her a pension. Seeing the likely embarrassment, Washington's friend, Governor Benjamin Harrison, told him that he "took the liberty to put a stop to this supposing you would be displeased at such an application, I make no doubt but the assembly would readily grant the request, and it now only rests with you to [say] whether it shall be made or no."[72] In a long letter to Harrison, in which he described all that he had done for his mother and maintaining that "she has an ample income of her own," Washington finished by instructing Harrison, "in pointed terms if the matter is now in agitation in your assembly, that all proceedings on it may be stopped—or in case of a decision in her favor, that it may be done away, & repealed at my request."[73] The proposal was dropped. However, Mary's complaints continued. Giving up on her oldest son, early in 1787, she wrote George Augustine that "it be time I am borrowing a Little corn no corn in the corn hous I Never Lived soe pore in my Life was it not for Mrs french [probably Anne Brayne Benger French of Fredericksburg] & your sister [Betty Washington] Lewis I should be almost starvd butt I am Like an old almanack quit out of date."[74] George Augustine shared her complaint with Washington. Recognizing his mother's age (nearly eighty) and declining health, Washington suggested that she sell what she owned, "break up housekeeping, hire out all the rest of your servants [slaves] except a man and a maid and live with one of your children." Mary's logical choice, of course, might well have been to move in with her son at Mount Vernon; after all, he was one of the richest men in Virginia, possessed of a large house that could easily accommodate her, and was renowned for his hospitality. Mount Vernon, she thought, would suit her well. Washington quickly disabused her of any notion of coming to live with him and Martha.[75] Mount Vernon was not the place for her. He let her know that his home was constantly filled with "strangers who are going from north to south, or from south to north." With company always bustling about, she would be forced to be constantly "dressing to appear in company" or show up "dishabille." If, as likely, she did not conform, she would be "a prisoner in [her] own chamber."[76] To Washington, a distinguished personage who placed a high value on civility and proper appearance, his mother—sickly, poorly educated, and known to be cranky—would not fit well at fashionable Mount Vernon.[77] Furthermore, Martha, accustomed to rule in the domestic sphere, may not have been anxious to have her mother-in-law in residence.

Seemingly slighted by George and unwilling to live with indolent Charles or her daughter Betty, Mary Ball opted to remain in her home in Fredericksburg, where Betty, living nearby, cared for her. Her last years were difficult. After diagnosing Mary with breast cancer, her physicians, Charles Mortimer and Elisha Hall, seeking the best medical advice, wrote to America's most renowned doctor, Benjamin Rush in Philadelphia. Rush's response was discouraging: "The respectable age and character of your venerable patient lead me to regret that it is not in my power to suggest a remedy for the cure of the disorder in her breast."[78]

Her health continued to decline. On 25 August 1789, Burgess Ball, husband of Washington's niece Frances (Charles's daughter), wrote the newly inaugurated president with the sad news: "[Y]our Mother departed this Life abt 3 o'clock today. The Cause of her desolution was the Cancer on her Breast, but for abt 15 days she has been deprived of her speech, and for the five last days she has remain'd in a Sleep."[79] Washington wrote his sister, "Awful, and affecting as the death of a Parent is, there is consolation in knowing that Heaven has spared ours to an age, beyond which few attain, and favored her with the full enjoyment of her mental faculties, and as much bodily strength as usually falls to the lot of four score." President Washington ordered "mourning Cockades and Ribbon" to be worn in his household.[80]

Washington's mother, brothers, sister, stepchildren, and step-grandchildren—along with multiple nieces and nephews—tested him.[81] Charles's failures, Jack and Samuel's early deaths, Betty's widowhood, George Augustine's persistent ill health, tracking and supporting George Steptoe and Lawrence Augustine, raising Wash and Nelly, and managing his mother's affairs consumed much of his private life. "I am so much involved in, & so perplexed with other people's affairs," he wrote to Bushrod, "that my own are very much unattended to."[82] To Benjamin Franklin, the only other American who shared as much fame and attention, he lamented, "Retirement from the public walks of life has not been so productive of the leisure and ease as might have been expected."[83] In a poignant personal moment on Thursday, 30 June 1785, at the end of four days during which he and Martha entertained eighteen visitors (five remaining overnight), Washington recorded in his diary, "dined with only Mrs. Washington which I believe is the first instance of it since my retirement from public life."[84]

Although Washington complained about visitors, as a wealthy Virginia gentleman, granting hospitality to guests was hardly new. Before the Revolution, those at his table were mostly family, neighbors, fox-hunting companions, local politicians, and business partners. The Revolution altered his world. Now that he was a legendary figure, visitors from all over America, as well as Europe, found their way to Mount Vernon. Between Christmas Eve 1783 and the day he left to assume the presidency, 16 April 1789, nearly six hundred people arrived on his doorstep (often unannounced).

Providing for guests was time consuming and expensive; however, despite the burden—borne mostly by his wife, steward Richard Burnet, and the household's enslaved Africans—there were few things Washington enjoyed more. He may not have dominated gatherings with repartee or small talk, but there was no doubt that when he spoke, guests gave attention. He was inquisitive and eager to hear the news from other parts of America and abroad.

Among those coming to visit were a dentist, an artist, a writer, and a sculptor—people who were on their way to Mount Vernon to pay their respects to "the great hero of the western world."[85]

6

VISITORS

In for a penny, in for a pound. (GW to Francis Hopkinson, 16 May 1785, in *GWP, Conf. Series*, 2:561)

He was not a diplomat or a statesman, nor had he ever written, painted, or sculpted anything of note; nonetheless, Jean Pierre Le Mayeur was especially welcomed at Mount Vernon. He was a dentist.

George Washington had his first tooth pulled when he was twenty-four. That was the beginning of a lifetime of dental torment. As early as 1760, George Mercer, an officer who had served with Washington in the Virginia regiment, provided a detailed physical description of Washington, noting that "[h]is mouth is large and generally firmly closed, but which from time to time discloses some defective teeth."[1] In the fall of 1773, as the problem grew worse, Washington sought help from "Mr. Baker Surgeon Dentist" in Williamsburg.[2] Subsequent to that visit, years of army food and primitive dental care worsened the pain. In 1781, he consulted with Baker again, asking whether he might supply "a pair of Pincers to fasten the wire of my teeth [and] scrapers, as my teeth stand in need of cleaning."[3] Although little worked, Washington was unwilling to give up, and in May 1783 a chance encounter offered new hope.

With preliminary peace secured, on 6 May the British commander in chief, Sir Guy Carleton, sailed up the Hudson River to Tappan, where he and Washington met to discuss the evacuation of New York City. Samuel Fraunces, New York's best-known tavern keeper and an alleged spy for the Americans, catered the meeting. Aware of Washington's dental issues, Fraunces mentioned that Jean Pierre Le Mayeur, a "Dentist of whose skill much has been said, was applying to leave New York."[4] Washington seized the moment and wrote immediately to Lieutenant Colonel William Stephens Smith, his representative in New York:

> The other day at Orange Town, Mr. Fraunces informed me, that, this applicant was the Dentist of whose skill much has been said; and that he was very uneasy at not being able to get out. Having some Teeth which are very troublesome to me at times, and of wch I wish to be eased, provided I could substitute others (not by transplantation, for of this I have no idea, even with young people, and sure I am it cannot succeed with old) and Gums which might be relieved by a Man of skill—I would thank you for making a private investigation of this Man's character & knowledge in his profession and if you find them such as I can derive any benefit from encourage him to come out, and to take this in his way to whatever post, or place he may be bound. At any rate if he really is skilful, I should be glad to see him with his apparatus—I would not wish that this matter should be made a parade of, & therefore give you the trouble of arranging it—I cannot (having forgot it) give you this Man's name, but Mr. Fraunces can point you to him—I think he told me he lodged at a Mr Lispenards where he had exhibited some proofs of his skill.[5]

After several inquiries, Smith replied that Le Mayeur "is a man of polished Manners of Strict Integrity, at the Head of his Profession—and a friend to this Country—the assertions are founded upon the sentiment of the most respectable Characters of the Circle in which he has moved since his arrival here."[6] Within a few days, the British granted Le Mayeur a pass. He went directly to Washington's headquarters at Newburgh and attended the general with some success.[7]

A few months later, after the British had evacuated the city, Le Mayeur returned to New York, where he reported to Washington that his practice was flourishing:

> I have had the pleasure of gratifying to Ladies and to Gentleman who I believe have the honor of being personally known to your Excellency by furnishing them with good living teeth in the Room of those which were broken or otherwise decayed. Miss Ried of

New Jersey—daughter of General Ried of the British army and Miss Shaw the sister of lady Wheate and a Relation of Colo. Varick lately a secretary to your Excellency have been furnished with to each and Colo. Varick himself has four fronts and one Eye tooth, th[r]ee of which were transplanted in [D]ecember and are at this day perfectly secure and two others which have been transplanted some days since are in a promising state and will be perfectly ferm at the period of my departure from this place.[8]

Although Washington's problems persisted, Le Mayeur's attendance had brought him comfort. Hoping for further relief, in the spring he invited Le Mayeur to visit Mount Vernon. In April 1784, the *Virginia Journal and Alexandria Advertiser* announced that "Dr. Lamayner, Dentist, from New-York, who transplants Teeth, is now in this Town, and may be spoke with by calling at Mr. Perrin's Store."[9] After treating patients in Alexandria, Le Mayeur rode to Mount Vernon.

Le Mayeur was a genial guest. He became a favorite of Washington's grandson, Wash, playing games with him and buying him a toy red pony "just big Enough for the little house which master George and myself built on the side of the hill."[10] No path to Washington's favor was surer than one that connected to his stepgrandson. Le Mayeur left Mount Vernon bound for Richmond carrying letters of introduction to the Speaker of the House, the attorney general, Governor Patrick Henry, and other prominent figures.[11] On arriving, he advertised that he would perform "operations on the teeth, hitherto performed in Europe, such as transplanting, &c., &c., &c." Le Mayeur also offered "any person that will dispose of their front teeth (slaves excepted) two guineas for each."[12] From Richmond, Le Mayeur brought his traveling dental practice to Charleston, South Carolina, and to Havana, Cuba. Six months later he returned north, staying some time in Washington's house in Bath and visiting Mount Vernon.[13] Le Mayeur's dental skills may not have given his patient the relief he sought; nonetheless, any association with Washington was sure to enhance his reputation.

In this new nation of loosely connected states, there were only two truly "national figures"—Benjamin Franklin and George Washington. Both were famous, not only in America but in Europe as well. Franklin took precedence. Wearing simple garb and presenting himself as a rustic American, Franklin—scientist, diplomat, intellectual, habitue of the Paris salons—swirled through French society charming all those he met. When Franklin returned to Philadelphia, Thomas Jefferson, writing from Paris, remarked that "it seemed as if the village had lost its patriarch."[14] Washington, by contrast, never visited Europe, but in an age that embraced neoclassicism—all things Roman and Greek—in contrast to the homespun Franklin, he conformed perfectly to the image of the ancient hero. He was Cincinnatus, a farmer called from the fields to defend his country, victorious in battle, devoid of vainglory, a defender of republicanism, who returned home to a pastoral scene, retiring under his own vine and fig tree. Among the foreign guests arriving at Mount Vernon to visit this classic hero were English painter Robert Edge Pine, writer Catharine Sawbridge Macaulay Graham, and French sculptor Jean-Antoine Houdon.

A painter and political polemicist, Pine, whose work largely featured historical scenes and portraits, was a radical Whig who championed the American cause.[15] His career leaped forward in 1760, when at age thirty he won first prize from the Society for the Encouragement of the Arts for his *Surrender of Calais to Edward III*. With his new fame, Pine became a regular exhibitor in London, but his contrary politics estranged him from established society. His Whiggish reputation was such that when he sought permission to paint a portrait of George II, the king refused a sitting. Undeterred, Pine went ahead, without the king's permission or presence, painting an unflattering, full-length portrait. Pine's talents shone brighter when he painted those with whom he agreed politically. He executed a portrait of the Tory establishment's bête noire, John Wilkes. Adding to his reputation as a Whig portraitist, in 1771 he gained access to the Tower of London, where he painted portraits of Richard Oliver and Brass Crosby, imprisoned for supporting the publication of parliamentary debates.[16] Unlike dour King George, these portraits presented vibrant, handsome men.

Shunned by the London establishment, and with commissions drying up, Pine retreated to Bath, where he found congenial company among a community supporting the American cause. In 1778, he took a particularly sharp jab at Parliament and the ministry with his allegorical painting *America Lamenting*. Aimed at expressing "the great oppressions and calamities of America," Pine's allegory depicted a female America kneeling at the foot of a monument to fallen American generals. Above her the "figure of peace, holding an olive branch, appears from the clouds." A later engraving by Joseph Strutt gained wide circulation. Among those at Bath who admired Pine's work was Washington's former neighbor George William Fairfax.[17]

Under press of business in England, Fairfax had left Virginia in 1773 and settled in Bath. Since his departure, Washington had kept up a business and personal correspondence with him and acted as Fairfax's legal agent in Virginia. Sympathetic to the American cause, in 1784 Fairfax sent Washington a copy of *America Lamenting*, describing Pine as a gentleman who "lived very near us and did Mrs. Fairfax & self the favor, to consult us oft in designing it."[18]

While Pine found support from his Whig friends in Bath, they did not supply enough commissions to fill his purse. Unable to find work in England, he decided to emigrate to America. Fairfax introduced him to Washington:

> Poor Mr. Pine is as true a "Son of Liberty["] as any Man can be, ever openly declared it, which with the great crime of publishing the Piece, lost him business, and made so many Enemies in this selfish Nation, that he is compelled to go to America to seek bread in his profession, tho he is certainly one of the first Artists in this Isle. Give me leave to assure you Sir, that there is not a Person in England that merits a better reception in America than the unfortunate Gentn whose only fault was his good wishes to our Country. Therefore, shall be [greatly] obliged to your Excellency, to honor Mr. Pine with your Notice and if you will be so good to recommend him to your friends if he goes to Virginia, or continues in Philadelphia, it will be doing great Charity, for he has a very amiable Wife and six Daughters, women grown, a very heavy expence to a Man that has lost his great business through party zeal.[19]

Pine arrived in Philadelphia in the summer of 1784. With America's most celebrated painters, John Singleton Copley and Gilbert Stuart, in England, Pine had an open field.[20] Having brought along with him, in addition to his large family, several of his unsold paintings, he set up a gallery in a house at the corner of High and Sixth Streets, selling his work and taking commissions.

Highly productive from his arrival until his death in 1788, Pine worked on more than ninety paintings, including several portraits of well-known Americans and an uncompleted historical series on the Revolution. No commission, however, was more important than the one he sought from Washington. Since he had no connection to him, Pine began to court several men well known to Washington, including writer and composer Francis Hopkinson; Thomas McKean, lawyer and signer of the Declaration of Independence; Charles Thomson, secretary to the Congress; his friend Robert Morris; and Thomas Mifflin, former president of the Confederation Congress. While each wrote to Washington acknowledging Pine as an "eminent artist," they knew such praise hardly differentiated him from many others who sought to paint the great general. However, Pine, they argued, was different. He was, as Hopkinson wrote, a friend to America, a person whose "zeal for the American cause that brought him over from England to secure, whilst it is yet possible, faithful Representations of some of the most interesting Events of the late War—not ideal Pictures, but real Portraits of the Persons and Places concerned."[21]

Having been painted several times, Washington had little interest in sitting again in the "painters chair."[22] Pine, however, offered something additional. His association with prominent radical Whigs, supporters of America, made him a potential fount of knowledge about politics in England. Washington was eager to query him. Furthermore, how could he refuse to meet a person coming to paint for "posterity the many glorious acts which honours the name of an American"?[23] He was "an Artist of acknowledged eminence, one who had discovered a friendly disposition towards this Country—for which, it seems, he had been marked." Washington, "in for a penny, in for a pound," agreed to sit for Pine.[24]

In his diary for 28 April 1785, Washington noted that "Mr. Pine a pretty eminent Portrait, & Historian Painter arrived in order to take my picture from the life & to place it in the Historical pieces he was about to draw."[25] Since Washington's diary entries, at least regarding people, tend to lack much physical description, it is not surprising that he omitted mentioning what might have been the first thing he noticed when the artist stepped from his carriage. Pine, according to a recollection of Francis Hopkinson's son Joseph, was such a "small man" that he looked as if he came from a "family of pygmies." The contrast with the six-foot-plus Washington was dramatic.[26]

The day after Pine arrived, Washington was off to Richmond. With his principal subject gone, Pine had time on his hands. At Martha's request, he turned his attention to painting portraits of the grand-children—Elizabeth Parke Custis, George Washington Parke Custis, Eleanor Parke Custis, and Martha Parke Custis—and Martha's niece, Fanny Bassett.[27] He did not paint Martha. After an absence of eight days, Washington returned, and Pine began to work on his portrait. Unlike previous painters intent on idealizing Washington, Pine's characterization gives Washington a subdued, not heroic, appearance. There is no drama and no hint of battle, and his uniform lacks color. In his right hand he holds a cane rather than a sword. The sitter has a certain drawn look. The face is expressionless.

Like most contemporary painters working away from their studio with limited time, Pine did as much and as quickly as he could on site. "His custom was, on small, thin pieces of canvas, to paint the heads of his sitters, making on paper pencil sketches of their figures, so that on his return home, having pasted his heads on larger canvases he, with the assistance of his two daughters rapidly finished them."[28]

In a makeshift studio, Washington and Pine talked of politics and old friends—particularly the Fairfaxes, whom Washington had not seen in more than a decade. He was particularly curious about what Pine knew of a visitor on her way from Boston to Mount Vernon, "the celebrated Mrs. Macaulay Graham."[29] Pine knew her well. In 1775, during the opening scenes of the American Revolution, he had painted her in a full-length portrait as a true Republican heroine: posed in front of classical ruins, dressed as a Roman matron with the distinctive purple sash of a Roman senator draped across her shoulder. Her right arm rested on a stack of books, the most prominent being her own *History of England*.[30]

One of the most famous (to some, infamous) women in England, Macaulay, when barely two years old, had lost her mother, leaving her to be raised in the cold embrace of a widowed, absent father who, in grief, isolated himself from society. Macaulay, in her blunt manner, recounted her early years to Benjamin Rush, telling him she was "a thoughtless girl till she was twenty, at which time she contracted a taste for books and knowledge by reading an odd volume of some history, which she picked up in a window of her father's house." Greek and Roman history inspired her to become a historian and an enthusiastic advocate of republicanism.[31]

A member of the Bluestocking Circle, a loose gathering of privileged women interested in education, by her early thirties Macaulay was recognized as a writer of "inexhaustible" knowledge, a characteristic in women not often appreciated in eighteenth-century English society. On meeting her at Canterbury, Elizabeth Carter, the poet and writer who had translated Epicurus, described her as a "very sensible and agreeable woman, and much more deeply learned than becomes a fine lady; but between the Spartan laws, the Roman politics, the philosophy of Epicurus, and the wit of St. Evremond, she seems to have formed a most extraordinary system."[32]

In neither her politics nor personal life did everyone account Macaulay as "sensible." After her first husband, Scottish physician George Macaulay, fifteen years her senior, died (1766), she moved to Bath and lived with the Reverend Thomas Wilson, a man twenty-eight years her senior, in a relationship that engendered considerable gossip. She gave further ammunition to wagging tongues when, following Wilson's death, she married William Graham, a surgeon's mate, a man far beneath her social status and twenty-five years her junior. "Her passions were too strong for her reason," clucked one observer.[33] Her American friend and political sympathizer, the outspoken Mercy Otis Warren, wrote to John Adams that "Macaulay's Independency of spirit led her to suppose she might associate for the remainder of her life with an inoffensive obliging youth with the same impunity a gentleman of threescore and ten might marry a damsel of fifteen."[34]

Macaulay's politics were equally controversial. In her magisterial eight volumes, *The History of England from the Accession of James I to that of the Brunswick Line* (1763–1783), she skewered "the Stuarts with a vigorous Whiggish slant."[35] Her republican sympathies were anathema to Tory conservatives such as Edmund Burke, who denounced her as "our republican Virago."[36] In America, Macaulay's works won warm praise, particularly her attack on Thomas Hobbes and her letter to the Corsican patriot, Pasquale Paoli, defending republican government, wherein she hinted at the right of revolution should a monarch break his contract with the people.[37] Benjamin Franklin thought highly of her work. John Adams, after reading the early volumes of *The History of England*, shared her disgust at the decline of virtue and morality in public life. He wrote to thank her for "strip[ping] off the Gilding and false Lustre from worthless Princes and Nobles, and to bestow the Reward of Virtue, Praise upon the generous and worthy only."[38] She in turn admired Adams's essay *A Dissertation on the Canon and Feudal Laws* (1765), published in London by ardent Whig Thomas Hollis. In addition to Franklin and Adams, Macaulay forged links with several other prominent Americans, including Richard Henry Lee, Arthur Lee, Josiah Quincy Jr., Samuel Adams, and Abigail Adams.[39] In 1784, anxious to visit "the empire of freemen on the other side of the Atlantic," Macaulay and her husband set sail for Boston, arriving on 15 July 1784.

Unlike England, where critics assailed her for her scandalous private life, in the new republic Macaulay drew an admiring audience. Boston's *American Herald* celebrated her arrival by reprinting her *Address to the People of England, Ireland, and Scotland* (1775), in which she accused a corrupt ministry in a "steady progress of despotism to have attempted to wrest from our American colonies every privilege necessary to freemen—privileges which they hold from the authority of their charters, and the principles of the constitution."[40]

During her visit, Samuel Adams introduced her to Mercy Otis Warren, who had been waging her own war against "dissipation and extravagance." Her target was the commonwealth's governor, John Hancock, whose profligate lifestyle, she wrote, undermined "the well-being of society." Warren described Macaulay as "not only a learned but a virtuous worthy character with much sensibility of heart and Dignity of Manners. Indeed, when I contemplate the superiority of her Genius I blush for the imperfections of human Nature, and when I consider her as my Friend, I draw a veil over the Foibles of the Women."[41]

Having spent the winter in Boston, in the spring Macaulay left New England armed with letters of introduction from Henry Knox,

Benjamin Lincoln, and Mercy Otis Warren. She headed south, passing "thro Newport to N. York, thence to Philad and so on to G. Washington's Seat at Mt. Vernon in Virginia."[42]

In New York City, she met Richard Henry Lee, president of the Congress. Lee provided her with a lavish letter of introduction. Flattering both Macaulay and Washington, he wrote

> to introduce to you Mr. Graham, and his Lady the justly celebrated Mrs. Macaulay Graham, whose reputation in the learned world and among the friends to the rights of human nature is very high indeed. Her merit as an Historian is very great, and places her as an Author in the foremost rank of writers. I am well pleased to find that she, as well as all other judicious foreigners, think themselves when in America, however distant from Mount Vernon, obliged to pay their respects to you. I believe that this has been her only motive for going so far South as Virginia.[43]

On Saturday, 4 June 1785, a "very warm" day, Washington noted in his diary, the "celebrated Mrs. Macaulay Graham & Mr. Graham arrived here."[44] He "received them with usual hospitality and the delicate attentions due to a woman of literary distinction." For the next ten days, Washington, breaking from his daily routine, rode out to his farms only once, preferring to spend his time with the Macaulays. Every day was special. During their stay, more than two dozen guests came to dine and meet a "Lady whose principles are so much and justly admired by the friends of liberty and mankind."[45] Macaulay, the historian, was curious, and, confessing to Washington that she was giving some thought to writing about the "late glorious revolution," she asked him whether she might see his papers. Since returning home, aside from his secretaries, Washington had allowed only one other person, the Reverend William Gordon of Roxbury, to examine his papers, but, even then, only after Congress had granted him permission.[46] Mrs. Macaulay was special. Congressional permission was not required. On a rainy Wednesday, confined to the mansion by harsh weather, Washington opened his archives "for her perusal & amusement."[47] Unfortunately, whatever her intention, ill health prevented her from writing about the Revolution, leaving it to her friend Mercy Otis Warren to become the first woman to write a history of the Revolution: *History of the Rise, Progress, and Termination of the American Revolution* (3 vols., 1805).

Macaulay charmed Washington. She was the historian he knew best. He listened to her opinions. Devoted to republicanism, Macaulay voiced a strongly held opinion that "men grow mad with unregulated power." Only "a democratical republic was capable of preserving dominion and freedom to the people." To survive, however, a republic depended on the virtue of its citizens. Macaulay took a dim view of her nation's recent past. Reflecting on the history of England since the Glorious Revolution, she saw corruption that had seeped in and "poisoned every part of the constitution."[48] She feared that "Americans had too much of the leaven of their ancestors in them."[49] As the new nation prospered, she worried that it would likely "copy all the excesses of the Mother Country, and vye with her citizens in all the deceitful pleasures of a vicious dissipation." Sitting amid the splendor of Mount Vernon, served by enslaved Africans, Washington might have felt her barbs, even if unintended, but it had never been Macaulay's purpose to embarrass her host. Like many English radicals, Macaulay agreed with Thomas Paine that America had the "power to begin the world over again."[50] Nevertheless, her disappointment was palpable, lamenting that a weak, fumbling Congress had left the nation adrift. Shortly after she left, Washington wrote to Richard Henry Lee, thanking him "for introducing a lady to me whose reputation among the literati is so high, and whose principles are so much and so justly admired by the friends to liberty and of mankind. It gave me pleasure to find that her sentiments respecting the inadequacy of the powers of Congress coincided with my own."[51] What the nation needed, Macaulay argued, was a powerful assembly balanced by a chief magistrate whose virtue and moral excellence would stand above all. It is unlikely that she was brazen enough to tell her host that in her estimation he, the "first character in the world," was that person.[52] The day after the Macaulays departed, Washington returned to his normal routine: "Rid to my Plantations at Muddy hole, Ferry, and Dogue run. Also, to the Mill."[53]

For the rest of the summer, aside from day trips to Alexandria—one "with Mrs. Washington, who wanted to get some clothing for little Washington Custis"—and two trips to survey progress on the Potomac project (1 August–12 August; 20 September–23 September), Washington remained at Mount Vernon.[54] He and Martha entertained the usual parade of guests, while on his daily inspection rides he oversaw harvesting wheat, planting Chinese seeds in his "botanical garden," and cutting down cherry trees, and he lamented a summer drought that threatened his crops.[55] Even as Washington saw to his life as a farmer, he was aware that another distinguished foreign visitor, French sculptor Jean-Antoine Houdon, was en route to Mount Vernon to memorialize him not in the medium of paint or written histories but in marble.

A year before, 22 June 1784, the Virginia House, "[t]o devise the most proper measure of perpetuating to posterity the gratitude and affection which this country bears to General Washington," resolved "[t]hat the Executive, [Governor Benjamin Harrison] be requested to take measures for procuring a statue of General Washington, to be of the finest marble and best workmanship."[56] One month later, Harrison wrote to Thomas Jefferson, the newly appointed American minister to France, that "we have unanimously fixed on you and my friend Doctor Franklin who we all know are fully competent to the task and therefore most earnestly request the favor of you to undertake it."[57] After consulting Franklin, Jefferson responded, "There could be no question raised as to the Sculptor who should be employed, the reputation of Monsr. [Jean-Antoine] Houdon of this city being unrivalled in Europe."[58] Indeed, Houdon had already executed celebrated busts of Franklin (1778) and John Paul Jones (1780), as well as French Enlightenment figures Diderot (1771), Voltaire (1778), Rousseau (1778), and Molière (1781).

To avoid the considerable expense of bringing Houdon to America, the Virginia Assembly commissioned Charles Willson Peale to paint a full-length portrait, *Washington at Yorktown* (1784), to be shipped to Paris as a model for his work. However, when the canvas arrived in Paris, Houdon dismissed the painting as "unsuitable." He must work from life. As a result, Jefferson informed Governor Harrison:

> Doctr. Franklin and I became satisfied that no statue could be executed to obtain the approbation of those to whom the figure of the original is known, but on an actual view by the artist. Of course, no statue of Genl. Washington, which might be true evidence of his figure to posterity could be made from his picture. Statues are

made every day from portraits but if the person be living, they are always condemned by those who know him for a want of resemblance, and this furnishes a conclusive presumption that similar representations of the dead are equally unfaithful. Monsr. Houdon whose reputation is such as to make it his principal object, was so anxious to be the person who should hand down the figure of the General to future ages, that without hesitating a moment he offered to abandon his business here, to leave the statues of kings unfinished, and to go to America to take the true figure by actual inspection and mensuration.[59]

On 20 July, embarking on the same vessel carrying Franklin home, Houdon left for America. Landing at Philadelphia on 14 September, Franklin informed Washington, "He is here, but the Materials and Instruments he sent down the Seine from Paris, not being arrived at Havre when we sail'd, he was obliged to leave them, and is now busied in supplying himself here. As soon as that is done, he proposes to wait on you in Virginia, as he understands there is no Prospect of your coming hither."[60] Though he had "no agency in the matter," but feeling "under a great obligation for [Houdon's] quitting France, & the pressing calls of the Great Ones to make a Bust of me, from the life," as soon as Washington heard from Franklin that Houdon had arrived, he wrote to the artist, "It will give me pleasure Sir, to welcome you to this seat of my retirement: and whatever I have, or can procure that is necessary to your purposes, or convenient & agreeable to your wishes; you must freely command."[61]

Although conventionally religious, Washington did not attend church on a regular basis; however, on Sunday, 2 October, a warm fall day, he "went with Fanny Bassett, Burwell Bassett, Doctr. Stuart, G. A. Washington, Mr. Shaw & Nelly Custis to Pohick Church; to hear a Mr. Thompson preach." In the afternoon they returned for dinner. Later in the evening, after they had retired, the house was unexpectedly awakened by the arrival of "Mr. Houdon, sent from Paris by Doctr. Franklin and Mr. Jefferson to take my Bust, on behalf of the State of Virginia, with three young men assistants, introduced by a Mr. Perrin, a French Gentleman of Alexandria, arrived here by water from the latter place."[62] Houdon was about to undertake his most famous commission.

At Mount Vernon, Houdon planned to take a facial image of Washington, as well as careful measurements of his entire body; from these he planned to execute plaster busts. Bringing these back to Paris, in the comfortable surroundings of his own studio, he could sculpt a full marble statue. Houdon and his assistants remained at Mount Vernon for more than two weeks. Perrin, who acted as interpreter, however, remained for only three days. Since the artist did not speak English and Washington did not speak French, Perrin's departure complicated matters.[63] Although there was little in the way of conversation, Washington admired Houdon's work and invited him to accompany him to the funeral of his neighbor, Sarah Harrison Manley. He had also invited him to be a guest at Fanny's wedding.[64]

On Thursday, 6 October, when it rained "all day," Washington remained at home and "sat for Mr. Houdon to form my Bust." The next day the weather turned "clear, warm, & pleasant." Washington sat in the morning for Houdon but spent the afternoon plowing "up the Cowpen in order to sow the ground with Orchard Grass Seeds."[65]

For Houdon, observing Washington outside the formal studio pose was critical to gaining an understanding of his subject. He followed him about, observing his moods, posture, and facial expressions. Houdon sought to capture Washington's physical features, his head, neck, and chest as well as the contours of his face, while at the same time trying to probe the inner character of his subject. Although he took careful measurements and fashioned two terra-cotta busts, in order to ensure that he had all the physical data necessary, Houdon asked permission to make a life mask. Washington agreed.

This was not the first time Washington had posed for a life mask. In August 1783, while meeting with Congress in Princeton, artist Joseph Wright had laid him "upon a cot" and daubed his "face with plaster." Washington remembered the scene with some humor:

> Whilst in this ludicrous attitude, Mrs. Washington entered the room; and seeing my face thus overspread with the plaster, involuntarily exclaimed. Her cry excited in me a disposition to smile, which gave my mouth a slight twist, or compression of the lips that is now observable in the bust which Wright afterward made.[66]

Always keen to understand the mechanics of things, Washington was as interested in the process as he was in the finished product. With careful detail, he recorded Houdon's method "for preparing the Plaster of Paris & mixing of it." Houdon's assistant first broke the plaster of Paris into pieces "the size of pullet egges" and baked them in an oven "hotter than it is usually heated for bread." And then, after leaving the mixture to cool overnight, it was "pulverized (in an iron Mortar) & sifted for use through a fine lawn sieve & kept from wet." The powdery plaster was then put into a

> Bason, or other Vessel with water; sifted through the fingers, 'till the Water is made as thick as Loblolly or very thick cream. As soon as the plaster is thus put into the Water, it is beat with an Iron spoon (almost flat) until it is well Mixed, and must be immediately applied to the purpose for which it is intended with a Brush, or whatever else best answers, as it begins to turn hard in four or five minutes, and in Seven or ten cannot be used, & is fit for no purpose after-wards as it will not bear wetting a second time. For this reason, no more must be mixed at a time than can be used within the space just mentioned.[67]

After preparing his face with grease and covering his eyes and in-serting straws in his nostrils so that he might breathe, Houdon brushed plaster "as thick as Loblolly or very thick cream" over his entire face. Within minutes, the plaster became firm. Six-year-old Nelly stumbled onto the scene. She later described it to her brother, Wash:

> I was passing the white servants Hall & saw as I thought the Corpse of one I consider'd my Father. I went in, & found the General extended on his back on a large table, a sheet over him, except his face, on which Houdon was engaged in putting on plaster to form a cast. Quills were in the nostrills [sic]. I was very much alarmed until I was told that it was a bust, a likeness of the General & would not injure him.[68]

On Monday, 17 October, Washington recorded in his diary, "Mr. Houdon having finished the business which brot. him hither, went up with his People, work, and impliments in my Barge, to Alexandria, to take a Passage in the Stage for Philadelphia the next Morning."[69] Before he left, Houdon presented Washington with one of the plaster busts.[70] The other he took with him to display at Congress in New York.[71] By Christmas, Houdon was back in Paris, carrying "with him face mask only, having left the other parts of his work, with his workmen to come by some other conveyance."[72]

With the life mask, detailed calculations, and the bust (which arrived separately), Houdon had all the materials at hand to begin a full statue.[73] One key decision remained: What would be "the costume of the statue"? Houdon queried Jefferson, who, offering no suggestions himself, deferred to Washington and asked "whether there is any particular dress, or any particular attitude which you would rather wish to be adopted. I shall take singular pleasure in having your own idea executed if you will be so good as to make it known to me."[74] As the American "Cincinnatus," Washington's conventional answer might have been to ask to be portrayed in a classical pose draped in a toga suitable for the Roman Forum. Washington understood, however, that, unlike his many portraits, housed in private homes or elite galleries where few people were likely to view them, Houdon's statue was intended to be a public monument featured prominently in the rotunda of the Virginia state capitol, where it would stand as a memorial to him and a symbol of the new nation. What message to convey? Washington was uncertain, and so was Houdon. Washington consulted with his friends. Houdon sought advice from Benjamin West.

Born in Pennsylvania, Benjamin West moved to London in 1763. An accomplished history painter, he enjoyed a high reputation in London circles. In 1770, he completed his most famous painting, *The Death of General Wolfe*. In a moment of great drama, with vivid colors, West depicted the gallant General Wolfe dying in the arms of his adjutant after defeating the French on the Plains of Abraham. Eschewing convention, West dared to paint his hero in contemporary dress rather than in Greek or Roman togas. The painting was an enormous success. An engraving of it by William Woollett became a best-seller. Faced with the challenge of how to present another hero, Houdon naturally turned to West for advice. West's answer came via

David Humphreys, who had returned recently to America from Paris. Humphreys was well acquainted with Houdon, Jefferson, and their conversation about heroic dress. West, Humphreys told Washington, advised Houdon that he was much "in favor of the modern custom," adding that "this taste, which has been introduced in painting, is received with applause and prevails extensively."[75]

It had been eight months since Jefferson's original query about the dress. Less than a week after receiving Humphreys's report, Washington wrote to him, "perhaps a servile adherence to the garb of antiquity might not be altogether so expedient as some little deviation in favor of the modern custom."[76] Jefferson fully approved.

> I was happy to find by the letter of Aug. 1. 1786. which you did me the honour to write me, that the modern dress for your statue would meet your approbation. I found it strongly the sentiment of West, Copley, Trumbull, and Brown in London, after which it would be ridiculous to add that it was my own. I think a modern in an antique dress as just an object of ridicule as a Hercules or Marius with a periwig and chapeau bras.[77]

Interrupted by the French Revolution, late payments, and delayed construction of the new Virginia capitol, Houdon did not deliver the statue until 1796.[78] Chief Justice John Marshall described the final product, carved from Carrara marble and standing six feet two, as "a very exact representation of Washington."[79] James Madison gave testimony as well, noting that Houdon's work was "an exact likeness; portraying well the characteristic features stamped on the countenance of the Original."[80] On the front of the statue's base, Houdon inscribed the words *George Washington*. On the side adjacent, he proclaimed "fait par Houdon Citoyen Français, 1788." Weighing several tons, the statue was unveiled on 14 May 1796.

Houdon was "servile" to neither antiquity nor modern custom. He began the statue when Washington was "living under his vine and fig tree," as a private citizen. By the time Houdon finished, Washington was president of the United States. Houdon's statue is a synthesis of Washington's life. Ramrod straight, head slightly angled to the left but looking forward, with the left leg slightly bent as if in motion, there is no question of the decisiveness and character of the subject. Houdon presented Washington the soldier wearing a military uniform but in a subtle fashion—no hat, no gorget, no sash—sword detached and discreetly behind him, epaulets on the shoulder subdued. Behind him, Houdon placed a plow. Washington's right hand holds a walking stick; his left rests on the fasces, a Roman symbol of political power composed of a symbolic thirteen rods.[81]

7

FARMER

I think with you that the life of a Husbandman of All others, is the most delectable. (GW to Alexander Spotswood, 13 February 1788, in *GWP, Conf. Series*, 6:110)

Apart from New Hampshire, Georgia, and the Carolinas, during the war years Washington had headquartered in every state. Except for those days when he pitched his grand marquee tent in the field with his troops, he billeted in refined homes. During the siege of Boston, he commandeered two of Massachusetts's most elegant mansions, both in Cambridge: Wadsworth House and Vassall House.[1] While defending New York City, he and his staff lodged at the elegant home of William Smith on Pearl Street, and he later resided at Richmond Hill, overlooking the Hudson River. In Philadelphia, he stayed at the fashionable homes of Henry Laurens and Robert Morris. Impressed by what he had seen on his eight-year house tour, Washington returned to Mount Vernon, his mind filled with plans to continue the never-ending improvements for the mansion and grounds.

Chief among these projects was the ongoing work to complete the last and most impressive addition to the mansion house: the "new room," conceived before the Revolution. Construction had limped along during the war years and cost a good deal more than Washington anticipated. Nonetheless, the result was, according to Samuel Powel, a close friend and a frequent visitor to Mount Vernon, a "magnificent Room Sixteen feet high perhaps thirty-Seven by Twenty-Eight feet. . . . The Chimney piece is of Italian Marble with Columns of Sienna

Marble & very handsome bas relief Tablets of white marble relative to rural Affairs. . . . The Room is the whole height of the House. The Ceiling is coved & richly ornamented in a light pleasing Taste."[2] No part of Mount Vernon was dearer to Washington than his "new room." Indeed, it was by his own instruction that his body lay in this room three days before final entombment, 18 December 1799.

While skilled hands (free and enslaved) crafted the room, Washington had designed it. He saw to it that the space reflected the unifying theme of his career, not as a soldier or politician, but rather as a farmer. "The life of a Husbandman of all others," he wrote Alexander Spotswood, "is the most delectable."[3] To Arthur Young, the English farmer, journalist, and agricultural writer, he reflected that in no other part of his life did he "find so great satisfaction, as in those innocent & useful pursuits. In indulging these feelings, I am led to reflect how much more delightful to an undebauched mind is the task of making improvements on the earth."[4]

Since agriculture was the bedrock of his life, he engaged John Rawlins, an English stucco artist, paying him more than he thought his due to mold in the ceiling of the room images of the farmer's tools—the scythe, the rake, the hoe, and the sickle. Similar stucco decoration appeared above the doorways and even along the edges of the grandiose marble chimney piece. The room signified Washington's love of the land and Mount Vernon.[5]

Washington had come into ownership of Mount Vernon on his brother Lawrence's death in 1752. Through his own industry, tied with Fairfax family connections, Lawrence had acquired considerable property. To his wife, Ann, he left "all my lands on Little Hunting and Doegs Creek [Dogue Run] in the county of Truro and County of Fairfax with all the houses and edifices thereon during her natural life." After leaving "one hundred and fifty pounds" to his sister Elizabeth (Betty), he bequeathed his brothers Samuel, John, Charles, and Augustine other properties. Lawrence, however, gave special attention to his "loving brother George Washington," to whom Ann's property would pass on her death.[6]

Ann's mourning was brief. Five months after Lawrence's death, she married George Lee and moved with her daughter to Lee's plantation,

Mount Pleasant in Westmoreland County. Retaining legal ownership, in December 1754, Ann leased her inherited property—twenty-one hundred acres—to her brother-in-law.[7] For Washington, the Mount Vernon lease ended what had been a very trying year. In January, Virginia governor Robert Dinwiddie had commissioned him a major in the militia and dispatched him, along with a force of three hundred men, to the forks of the Ohio with orders to evict the French, who were, in Dinwiddie's judgment, trespassing on the king's lands.[8]

Young, inexperienced, brash, and prone to action, early in the morning on 23 May at Jumonville Glen, about fifty miles east of the forks, Washington launched an unprovoked attack on a sleeping French party. After the engagement, Washington withdrew to an open field, Great Meadows, and built Fort Necessity, a ramshackle stockade where he boasted that "with my small numbers I shall not fear the attack of 500 men."[9] While waiting for the French counterattack, Washington learned that, as the result of the death of Colonel Joshua Fry, commander of the Virginia regiment, the governor had promoted him to lieutenant colonel. The news of his promotion arrived just before a large French force appeared, surrounding the fort and forcing its surrender on 4 July. Offered generous terms, Washington and his men marched home. Recounting events, he wrote his brother Augustine, "I can with truth assure you I heard bullets whistle and believe me there was something charming in the sound."[10]

In response to the French advance, the next year (1755), General Edward Braddock arrived in Virginia with orders to march his army west and dislodge the French from the Ohio. Washington accompanied Braddock on what turned out to be a colossal disaster. He survived the rout, and on his return Governor Dinwiddie posted him to command of the Virginia regiment with orders to defend the colony's western flank. It was an unhappy posting. Tasked with commanding an unruly Virginia militia, he also endured contempt from regular British officers, who dismissed him as a mere colonial. Relief from the tedium of garrison duty arrived in 1758, when he was ordered to join General John Forbes on a second advance to the Ohio. When Forbes announced, however, that he planned not to follow the road cut by Braddock's army three years before, which ran across Virginia, but rather to take a more direct route through Pennsylvania, Washington, the Virginian, was furious. He saw Forbes's plan as a plot to weaken Virginia's ties to the West, while awarding Pennsylvania direct access to the Ohio. In two long, vigorous (impolitic) letters to colonels Henry Bouquet and Francis Halkett, he claimed that should this route be followed, "all is lost! All is lost by Heavens!"[11] Despite Washington's objections, Forbes persevered. As his army hacked its way through the wilderness, the French garrison, hopelessly outnumbered, abandoned Fort Duquesne. When the British arrived on 25 November, smoldering ruins welcomed them.

Having endured a testy relationship with his civilian and military superiors, and seeing little prospect of glory, in December Washington rode to Williamsburg and resigned his commission. He had finally decided that, as his friend Robert Orme once advised him, Mount Vernon was his true "Happiness."[12] He was about to share that happiness with his new bride, the widow Custis.

Martha Dandridge Custis was one of the richest widows in Virginia. Washington's union with her, giving him access to her considerable fortune, lifted him up several rungs in Virginia's social hierarchy.[13] After their marriage on 6 January 1759, at Martha's home in New Kent County, the Washingtons spent several weeks visiting friends and relatives. Recently elected to the Virginia House of Burgesses, early in February Washington moved with his new bride to Williamsburg, where they remained until 2 April, when the General Assembly gave him "leave to be absent from the service of this house."[14] Four days later, after stopping "to get the key from Colo. Fairfax's," the Washingtons, including Martha's children John Parke Custis (Jacky) and Martha Parke Custis (Patsy), arrived at Mount Vernon.[15]

For nearly four years Washington had been away, on the "cold and barren frontiers," protecting Virginia "from the cruel incursions of a crafty savage enemy." During his long absences, his older brother John Augustine and his wife, Hannah Bushrod, had managed the estate, leaving him, as he admitted readily, "little acquainted with the business relative to my private affairs." But now, having "quit a military life" and finding an "agreeable partner," Washington settled happily into the place that would be his home for the remainder of his life.[16]

When he and Martha moved to Mount Vernon, in accordance with Lawrence's will, the property was still in the hands of Ann and her husband. Nonetheless, certain that it would come to him in time, and to remove any doubt about his authority, Washington wrote to Robert Cary, a London merchant who for many years had served Martha's deceased husband Daniel Parke Custis.[17] He instructed Cary that "for the future please to address all your Letters which relate to the Affairs of the late Daniel Parke Custis Esqr. to me, as by Marriage I am entitled to a third part of that Estate and Invested likewise with the care of the other two thirds by a Decree of our Genl Court."[18] In the same letter, Washington gave unmistakable signs of his ambitions and Martha's influence. "Handsome," "genteel," "fashionable," and "newest" were the words he used to describe the syllabub glasses, desert glasses, spermaceti candles, candlesticks, carpets, and a lengthy list of personal items, mostly stylish items of dress, he bought for himself and his wife. What had previously been a little-lived-in bachelor's home was becoming a fashionable residence.

His first few years at Mount Vernon were difficult. In a slam at John Augustine, Washington complained that during his absence the estate had fallen under "terrible management." To support his family, he used his wife's money to "purchase lands and negroes and provisions of all kinds." But even Martha's money was not enough. Like most other Virginia planters, Washington was in debt.[19] Tobacco was the chief culprit. From the very first days of the colony, tobacco had been Virginia's mainstay. It was a fickle dependence. Prices fluctuated wildly, and the crop exhausted the soil. In 1759, however, prices were high, and Washington brought in a crop of more than thirty-four thousand pounds. The next four years were even better, but then the market collapsed in 1764.

The uncertainty of tobacco cultivation pushed Washington to inquire more deeply into what was called in England the "new agriculture," a movement employing science and practical improvements, transforming traditional agriculture into a modern market-oriented enterprise.[20] Only a few months after settling in at Mount Vernon, he asked Cary to send him *A New System of Agriculture; or, A Plain, Easy and Demonstrative Method of Speedily Growing Rich by a Country*

Gentleman (1755). The anonymous "Country Gentleman's" book was both a tirade against antiquated English farming practices—"Tis a very great misfortune to England, that the cultivation of her lands is in the meanest of her people"—and a clarion call for new practices by which "[b]arren land by good husbandry may be made very fruitful and profitable."[21] Along with *A New System of Agriculture*, Washington requested two other volumes: Batty Langley's *New Principles of Gardening; or, The Laying Out and Planting Parterres, Groves, Wildernesses, Labyrinths, Avenues, Parks, &C. after a More Grand and Rural Manner, Than Has Been Done Before* (1728) and William Gibson's *A New Treatise on the Diseases of Horses* (2 vols., 1751).[22] Not long after receiving these books, Washington began experimenting. He tried new methods of plowing, and in April 1760 he concocted and spread over his wheat, oats, and barley a compost mixing earth, horse manure, Potomac mud, marl, and sheep dung.[23] By 1767, Washington had left the world of the tobacco planter, dependent on a single staple crop that exhausted the land, to become a farmer planting a variety of food crops on land cultivated and renewed by intelligent husbandry.[24]

Being a farmer was at the center of Washington's life. When he bid farewell to the army, 2 November 1783, he shared his vision for the nation with his "patriotic band of brothers." He urged them to see ahead their "enlarged prospect of happiness" as they retired "victorious from the Field of War to the Field of Agriculture." With the burden of war behind them, they were free to pursue "commerce and cultivation of the soil."[25] For himself, after "nine years total inattention," he was eager to return to his land. He was keen to acquaint himself with agricultural reforms, "the new husbandry," that had been sweeping England during his long absence from Mount Vernon. Washington sought "to explore the latest practices in animal and crop husbandry and examine updates in farm technology."[26] Condemning the practices of his Chesapeake neighbors, whose system of agriculture was "unproductive "and "ruinous," he laid plans "to pursue a course of husbandry which is altogether different and new to the gazing multitude."[27] In the way of a careful general, Washington laid out a strategic plan for improvement. He began by tallying his assets. Through inheritance and purchase, he held nearly eight thousand acres at Mount Vernon, which he divided into four working farms: River, Ferry, Muddy Hole, and Dogue. A fifth, the mansion house farm, with five hundred acres, was devoted principally to domestic pursuits and decorative gardens in the style of an English country estate.[28] More than three hundred enslaved Africans labored on his farms, each farm a small community unto itself. When affairs at the mansion allowed and the weather permitted, every day, usually in the morning, Washington rode circuit touring his fields.

In his "Notes and Observations," Washington recorded practices that he condemned as "exceedingly unprofitable and destructive."[29] Reading volumes taken from his own close-packed shelves of books on agriculture, which made up approximately 14 percent of his entire library, Washington realized that to improve his farms, he needed someone more skilled than himself to organize "a complete course of husbandry." Although there had been progress in improving American agriculture, there was no one in the new nation to whom Washington could turn. Lund had managed well, but he was hardly an innovator, and besides, he was retiring. Lund's successor—Washington's nephew, George Augustine—was likewise competent to manage, always under Washington's careful eye, but the young man knew little about modern scientific farming. Washington concluded that what he needed was a "thorough bred practical English farmer, from a part of England where husbandry seems to be best understood and is most advantageously practiced." To recruit a candidate, he turned to his friend William Fairfax in Bath.[30]

Fairfax consulted with Edmund Rack, secretary to the Bath Agriculture Society. Rack recommended James Bloxham. For fifteen years, Bloxham had worked for William Peacey, a well-known farmer in Gloucestershire. In a letter enclosing a recommendation from Peacey, Fairfax promised Washington that Bloxham "will answer any Persons purpose, as a hard-working Servant, capable of Ploughing, Sowing, Hedging, Ditching, Shearing, Mulling and Brewing for a family, particularly attentive to Stock, and not inferior to any Man he knows in Thatching of Houses and Barns. [I]n a word, he is in his degree the best I have heard of."[31]

Washington agreed to Bloxham's steep terms: fifty guineas a year, house, food, and money to bring "his wife and family to this

Country."[32] On a rainy afternoon, 21 April 1786, Bloxham arrived at Mount Vernon. Not all went well. Three months after arriving, Bloxham wrote Peacey that the land was not level and the enslaved Africans who worked the fields had "no notion of making of a plow to turn the work well." The country "is very poor and there is no chance for anybody to do any good." Not accustomed to slavery, and exhibiting common racist sentiments, he was particularly distressed at having to associate with "Black people" and viewed the enslaved farm hands as "stupet" in their work.[33] Bloxham, of course, was encountering one of the chief obstacles that thwarted improvement. No matter what new methods or tools might be introduced, enslaved workers, managed by incompetent overseers, had little incentive to work harder or better.[34] Fortunately, as the summer heat lessened, Bloxham mellowed.[35] Peacey explained to Washington that Bloxham's intemperate letter was written "in bad spirits on account of being at so great a distance from his family." When his family finally arrived in 1788, Bloxham's spirits recovered, and he remained with Washington until the early 1790s.[36]

The new nation was turning swords into plowshares. Even John Adams, hardly known as a farmer, celebrated America's growing interest, noting to his friend James Warren, "The Enthusiasm for Agriculture like Virtue will be its own Reward. [M]ay it run and be glorified."[37]

Newly formed agricultural societies were one of the chief agents driving interest in new methods of husbandry. Inspired by institutions established in England promoting scientific and practical improvements, in the winter of 1784–1785, twenty-three prominent Philadelphians organized the Philadelphia Society for Promoting Agriculture.[38] Recognizing Washington, the farmer, the new society elected him their first honorary member.[39] Of all the honors he received, this was among the ones Washington prized most. To James Warren he wrote, "I wish most sincerely that every State in the Union would institute similar ones; and that these Societies would correspond fully, & freely with each other; & communicate all useful discoveries founded on practice, with a due attention [to] climate, Soil, and Seasons, to the public."[40] A few weeks later, the newly formed "South Carolina Society for promoting & improving agriculture & other rural concerns" elected him to honorary membership as well.[41] Such progress so pleased Washington that he boasted to Gilbert du Motier, the marquis de Lafayette, that America "shall become a storehouse and granary for the world."[42]

While improving the quality and quantity of crop yields brought Washington recognition, it did not necessarily mark him far above his correspondents. Anxious to cast himself as more than simply a skilled farmer, and to secure his place in the company of elite pioneers of agricultural reform and experimentation, Washington decided to build an impressive greenhouse.[43] He began construction near the upper garden in the spring of 1784. By the summer, however, he decided that his plan was drawn "upon too contracted a scale."[44] It was not impressive enough. For advice on how to build a larger greenhouse, he turned to Margaret Tilghman Carroll, sister-in-law of his former aide-de-camp, Tench Tilghman. The widow of the barrister Charles Carroll, Margaret watched over a finely manicured eight-hundred-acre estate, Mount Clare in Baltimore, overlooking the Patapsco River. On a visit to the estate, John Adams described the main house as "elegant and splendid. It stands fronting looking down the River, into the Harbour. It is one Mile from the Water. There is a most beautiful Walk from the House down to the Water. There is a descent, not far from the House. You have a fine Garden—then you descend a few Steps and have another fine Garden—you go down a few more and have another."[45] Carroll was an accomplished horticulturist, known widely for her collection of ornamental plants, which she cultivated in an impressive orangery attached to her house.

Popular among the rich and fashionable, the orangery was a large, heated indoor area in which the proprietor grew exotic, tropical fruits such as lemons, limes, and pineapples, as well as delicate shrubs and trees. Louis XIV's "Orangerie," designed by Jules Hardouin-Mansart, housed three thousand orange trees. Carroll's orangery, according to Tilghman, was twenty-four feet by twelve feet, with a flat ceiling and a heated floor. The heated floor was of particular importance since the trees had to be "kept warm at the roots."[46]

The greenhouse was the last of the major construction projects that Washington undertook at Mount Vernon, and work on the structure proceeded slowly. Not until 1787 was the roof completed.[47] Built of brick in the popular Georgian fashion, and standing on the north side of the upper garden, aside from the mansion house, it was one of the largest structures on the plantation. An impressive Palladian window dominated the south-facing front, with smaller windows on each side. Shutters, tucked inside, could be closed to preserve heat. Windows on the east side caught the morning sun, but on the west, to shield the room from the harsh afternoon rays, a large door was installed. In the cooler months, heat was generated by a large fireplace at the back, with the warm air distributed by a series of flues concealed under the floor. If it was meant to impress, it certainly did its job. One visitor described it, with a bit of exaggeration, as "a complete Greenhouse which at this season is a vast, a great source of pleasure. Plants from every part of the world seem to flourish in the neatly furnished apartments and from the arrangement of the whole, I conclude that it is managed by a skilful hand."[48]

Prominent in the membership lists of the various agricultural societies, corresponding with the most notable agriculturists in his world, and building his own greenhouse, Washington, the distant provincial, entered the fashionable world of English agricultural improvement. This movement drew "the attention of the court, the nobility and clergy, and the intellectual and scientific men of the day including King George III, 'Farmer George.'" Most important, Washington made a close friend, in an epistolary sense, of Arthur Young.[49]

A prolific author and careful observer of farming practices in England, Ireland, and France, Young was best known as the editor of the *Annals of Agriculture and Other Useful Arts* (1784–1815). Taking direction from Washington's letter of 30 June 1785 seeking a farm manager, Fairfax had consulted with Young.[50] In January 1786, although he had no recommendation for a manager, Young, anxious to begin a direct correspondence with a "brother farmer" whom he described as being "as great a farmer as a general," sent Washington four volumes of his *Annals of Agriculture*, inscribing volume 1, "To General Washington in testimony of the Veneration I feel for so great and good a character."[51] Washington responded to Young, assuring his newfound mentor:

> Agriculture has ever been amongst the most favorite amusements of my life, though I never possessed much skill in the art; and nine years total inattention to it, has added nothing to a knowledge which

is best understood from practice. But with the means you have been so obliging to furnish me I shall return to it (though rather late in the day) with hope and confidence.

The system of agriculture, if the epithet of system can be applied to it, which is in use in this part of the United States, is as unproductive to the practitioners as it is ruinous to the landholders. Yet is pertinaciously adhered to. To forsake it, to pursue a course of husbandry, which is altogether different and new to the gazing multitude, ever adverse to novelty in matters of this sort, and much attached to their old customs, requires resolution; and without a good practical guide, may be dangerous; because of the many volumes which have been written on this subject, few of them are founded on experimental knowledge—are verbose, contradictory and bewildering. Your Annals shall be this guide. The plan on which they are published, gives them a reputation which inspires confidence; and the favour of sending them to me, I pray you to accept my very best acknowledgments. To continue them, will add much to the obligation.[52]

Washington concluded his letter by ordering thirty-six bushels of various seeds and asking advice for laying out a "most complete and useful farmyard, for a farm of about five hundred acres."

For the next decade, Young and Washington engaged in lively correspondence, exchanging more than a dozen letters.[53] Washington, the practical farmer with an interest in science, described conditions at Mount Vernon while offering observations (often critical) concerning the farming practices in America. From his years of travel and experience, Young had much to share with his American friend. He sent his *Annals* and books that he thought might interest Washington to Mount Vernon on a regular basis, as well as "implements of husbandry, seeds, etc." Young asked Washington's permission to publish the letters of his celebrated correspondent. As usual, when it came to public acknowledgments, Washington was conflicted: "On one hand it seems scarcely generous or proper, that any farmer, who received benefit from the facts contained in such publications should hold his mite of information from the general stock. On the other hand, I [am] afraid it might be imputed to me as a piece of ostentation, if my name should appear in the work." He, however, left it to Young's "prudence" to do what he thought "wisest and best."[54] After Washington's death, Young published the letters.

Encouraged by Young and others, Washington's attachment to the land grew. It was among his greatest pleasures "[t]o see plants rise from the Earth and flourish by the superior skill, and bounty of the laborer." To him, "the life of a husbandman of all others is the most delectable" and, with "judicious management, profitable."[55]

Through "judicious management," Washington did all that he could to improve Mount Vernon's productivity. Thin topsoil, underlaid by hard-packed clay, often bearing a "worn and gullied" look, challenged him. Crop rotation helped. He planted a wide variety of crops, including turnips, oats, corn, beans, wheat, and grass, experimenting altogether with more than sixty plants. He sought constantly to find new ways to "plough—to sow—to mow—to hedge—to Ditch," which enhanced his tillable lands. Fertilizing turned out to be an effective method. He composted, applied gypsum, spread fish guts and marl, and applied mud dug from the river bottom.[56] But the best and most valuable fertilizer came from his own livestock: manure—nourishment that offered "the first transmutation towards gold."[57]

Believing that the "multiplication of useful animals is a common blessing to mankind," in November 1785 Washington spent three days riding around his farms tallying his livestock: 123 horses, 344 cattle (including oxen), and 335 sheep.[58] "Extraordinary in its size and breadth for the period, these animals furnished food for the immediate household, as well as a large population of enslaved Africans, and provided draft labor for farming and transportation, all the while producing valuable manure."[59]

Sheep had always grazed at Mount Vernon. Early in the Washingtons' marriage, Martha's dower had brought a flock of seventy-eight, but they had been of secondary importance to other livestock. Noting, however, that the British, following the precepts of the new husbandry, had made sheep raising "the most profitable branch of husbandry," Washington decided to follow suit. He explained to Sir John Sinclair, the Scottish agricultural writer and statistician, that "after the Peace of Paris in 1783, and my return to the occupations of a farmer, I paid particular attention to my breed of Sheep."[60] For Washington, sheep had become "that part of my Stock in which I most delight."[61]

Curious about American sheep, Young asked Washington to send him a "small lock" of Mount Vernon wool so that he might compare it to other varieties with which he was experimenting.[62] Although willing to send a sample, Washington explained that for the moment he could not, as it was "all wrought into cloth."[63] That from the shearing of such a large flock not a single sample was available seems unlikely. Washington may have been reacting, in a disingenuous fashion, to the policy of Young's government, whose "abominable monopolizing laws" made it difficult for him to obtain superior English stock.[64] Washington, however, persevered, and by the late 1780s he boasted that, in addition to providing mutton, lanolin, and valuable manure, his flock, grown to more than six hundred, was producing twice as much wool as in previous years, five and a quarter pounds compared to two and a half pounds.[65] Enslaved Africans working in the spinning house cleaned, carded, and spun the wool, which was then used to clothe them, saving Washington the considerable expense of buying cloth.[66]

While the number of sheep grew significantly during the years between the Revolution and the presidency, the increase in cattle was modest. Before the war, Washington recorded a herd of nearly 170 head, including oxen. Twenty years later, in the inventory of November 1785, the count stood at 127 cattle and 26 oxen.[67] Visitors commented on the "stunted diminutive size" of cattle in the American South.[68] That American cattle were not as robust and large as those in England and the continent was a problem. Washington attributed the poor size to inadequate grazing land and poor practices: "No more cattle are raised than can be supported by low land meadows, swamps, &ca; and the tops & blades of Indian Corn; as very few persons have attended to sowing grasses & connecting cattle with their Crops."[69] Particularly valuable were his oxen; more powerful and robust than draft horses, they could bear the heavy strain of plowing. Oxen, which Young described "for the labour of a farm have no rivals," had the added benefit that at the end of their working life they might be slaughtered for meat.[70]

Horses were particularly important to Washington. Other than his dogs, used mostly for hunting, Mount Vernon's horses were the only animals to whom he gave names.[71] In March 1777, while in winter camp at Morristown, he wrote to General Thomas Mifflin, the army quartermaster general, about privately purchasing army horses. He had his eye on a "parcel of Mares, to the number of even fifty or an hundred. I have many large Farms and am improving a great deal of Land into Meadow and Pasture, which cannot fail of being profited by a number of Brood Mares." Mifflin was to do this quietly, since even "the most innocent and upright Actions are often misconstrued, & that it would not be surprising, if it should be said, that I was defrauding the public of these Mares by some collusion or other."[72]

In 1781, visiting Mount Vernon, François-Jean de Beauvoir, the marquis de Chastellux, described his host as an "excellent and bold horseman, leaping the highest fences, and going extremely quick, without standing upon his stirrups, bearing on the bridle, or letting his horse run wild."[73] Jefferson agreed. According to him, Washington was "the best horseman of his age, and the most graceful figure that could be seen on horseback."[74] Unlike many of his peers, who simply rode and let others tend to their mounts, Washington took special notice and personal care of his horses. During the Revolution, Blueskin and Nelson were his favorite mounts. Blueskin, a gift from Colonel Benjamin Tasker Dulany in 1773, was half Arabian with a white coat. Although he is the horse most often appearing in portraits of Washington, most likely because of his handsome appearance, he was not Washington's "favourite, on account of his not standing fire so well as the venerable old Nelson," a chestnut with white face and legs.[75]

After the war, both horses accompanied Washington to Mount Vernon. In November 1785, he returned Blueskin to the Dulanys with his "[m]arks of antiquity [which] have supplied the place of those beauties with which this horse abounded—in his better days."[76] Nelson, the battle-hardened veteran, remained at Mount Vernon. Stepgrandson George Washington Parke Custis remembered him as

> a splendid charger, a light sorrel, sixteen hands high, with white face and legs. This famous charger died at Mount Vernon many years after the Revolution, at a very advanced age. After the chief had ceased to mount him, he was never ridden, but grazed in a paddock in summer, and was well cared for in winter; and as often as the retired farmer of Mount Vernon would be making a tour of his grounds, he would

halt at the paddock, when the old war-horse would run, neighing, to the fence, proud to be caressed by the great master's hands.[77]

Although Washington may have had more and better-cared-for animals at Mount Vernon, the collection of livestock in his barns and fields looked much like that of his neighbors, with one exception—mules.

The product of a male donkey (jack) and mare, mules were better draft animals than horses. They ate less, lived longer, required less water, were sure footed, and were easier to manage. The best mules were those bred in Spain. Just as England sought to prevent the export of certain breeds of sheep to protect the domestic industry, so, too, the Spanish refused to allow their jacks to leave the country.[78] Mules were known in America, but the domestic stock was far inferior to the Spanish breed.

Washington was aware of the superiority of Spanish mules. In the spring of 1780, shortly after Spain had joined France (not the United States) in the war against Britain, Washington was entertaining the newly appointed Spanish minister, Juan de Miralles, at his headquarters in Morristown, New Jersey. Having heard a great deal about the superiority of the Spanish jacks (the Andalusian ass), the general took the opportunity to ask Miralles whether he might seek his king's permission to allow him to purchase a jack for Mount Vernon. Miralles agreed, but before he could write to Madrid, the minister took ill and died. It was, Washington lamented regarding his plans for buying a jack, "a disappointment."[79]

Miralles's sudden death delayed but did not end Washington's search for a Spanish jack. Four years later, fully determined to improve the working livestock at Mount Vernon, Washington wrote his friend Robert Townshend Hooe, a merchant in Alexandria, requesting him to contact his partner Richard Harrison, the acting American consul in Cadiz, asking him to use his influence in Spain to persuade the government to allow him to procure a jack. It would be, Washington told Hooe, "a public benefit to this part of the country, as well as private convenience to myself."[80]

Any request from Washington brought attention. Harrison forwarded Washington's inquiry to Madrid, where the American consul, William Carmichael, presented the request to the Spanish foreign minister, José y Redondo, the conde Floridablanca. The count responded that the king (Charles III) was pleased "to permit the extraction of the Jack Ass to General Washington so distinguished a personage."[81]

King Charles sent two jacks. One died on the voyage; the other arrived in Boston. Having lost one at sea, Washington decided not to chance another in the same way. Giving detailed instructions on how to handle the jacks and the precise land route to follow, Washington dispatched the overseer of the mansion farm, John Fairfax (a distant relative of the more affluent Fairfaxes), to bring the jacks overland from Boston to Mount Vernon.[82] On 5 December, Washington noted in his diary, "My Overseer Fairfax returned this Evening with Jack Ass, and his Keeper, a Spaniard from Boston." He named the jack "Royal Gift."[83]

Royal Gift soon had company. During his visit to Mount Vernon in August 1784, Washington had shared with the marquis de Lafayette his interest in breeding mules. On returning to France, Lafayette arranged for two jacks to be sent to Mount Vernon, one from Spain and a second from Malta. The Spanish jack died at sea. The Maltese jack, known as "Knight of Malta," arrived in November 1786.[84]

Washington, hoping "to secure a race of extraordinary goodness, which will stock the Country," shared his enthusiasm over the arrival of the jacks with Young. "Indeed, in a few years," he told Young, "I intend to drive no other in my carriage: having appropriated for the sole purpose of breeding them, upwards of 20 of my best Mares."[85] Young was not convinced, warning Washington about "Spanish asses" who in service "proved so inferior in hardiness & cheapness of Keeping to the little native mule that everybody left them off." Furthermore, Young added, they were "all dead in four years."[86] Fortunately, Washington disregarded Young's concerns, and while he may not have been the father of the American mule, as some have claimed, Royal Gift and Knight of Malta produced numerous progenies.[87] By the time of Washington's death in 1799, donkeys and mules outnumbered horses at Mount Vernon. They were, however, confined to field work and pulling carriages and wagons. There is no portrait of George Washington astride a mule.

Washington's interest in breeding also extended to his favorite pastime: fox hunting. All the rage of the Virginia aristocracy, hunts began in the fall and extended through the winter. Fashionably attired, sporting "knee-length coat, often black or blue with embroidered cuffs, a vest inside, lengthy kid gloves, a tri-cornered hat, leather riding boots, and a requisite whip," riders dashed across the countryside behind baying hounds following the scent of a fox.[88] Not satisfied with his own hounds, Washington asked Lafayette to send him some of the French breed. With a bit of embarrassment, Lafayette responded that "French Hounds are not now very easily got because the King Makes use of english dogs, as Being more swift than those of Normandy."[89] Nonetheless, he found seven and shipped them off to America in the care of young John Quincy Adams, who, after being in France with his parents, was on his way home to attend Harvard.[90] A few days after their arrival, Washington noted in his diary that he "[r]id to the Plantations at the Ferry, Dogue run, and Muddy hole. Took my French Hounds with me for the purpose of Airing them & giving them a knowledge of the grounds round about this place."[91]

While American revolutionaries and English radicals celebrated Washington as their hero for leading a revolution against tyranny, during the years between his return to Mount Vernon on Christmas Eve 1783 and that April morning in 1789 when he "bade adieu to Mount Vernon" and left for New York City to assume the presidency, George Washington preferred to be known as a farmer. In those years, with incredible energy and perseverance, relying on his own experience and the advice of agricultural reformers at home and abroad, he introduced new crops, employed innovative farming implements, and bred superior livestock. Washington's passion for farming made him an important addition to the roster of like-minded trans-Atlantic agricultural reformers. It was a world he entered with "hope and confidence."[92]

8

ANNAPOLIS

Have you heard from Annapolis since Monday? (GW to John
Fitzgerald, 9 September 1786, in *GWP, Conf. Series*, 4:241)

It was the end of August 1785, the harvest season, and, as usual, Washington's much-resorted tavern was busy. On Friday, August 26, "A
Mr. Mar[t]el (or some such name) a Frenchman came in and dined,
and just before dinner Mr. Arthur Lee, and Mr. P. Fendall got here;
all of whom went away after it was over. In the Afternoon—Doctr.
Marshall and his Sister, and Miss Hanson crossed the River, drank Tea,
and returned."[1] On Sunday, Dr. Craik arrived and then left suddenly
the next morning "to see Lund Washington's [daughter] who had been
seized with fits."[2] Martha, concerned for the child, joined him the next
day. She stayed two days helping Elizabeth nurse the patient.[3] During the
same time, Washington kept to his customary daily rounds, riding among
his farms. He was delighted to find "the Corn a good deal improved in
its looks" and the "wheat coming up, very well."[4] On Saturday evening,
3 September, a day that began "[m]uch such a day as yesterday," Washington welcomed an unexpected visitor: "James Madison Esqr."[5]

During their days together in Richmond, advancing legislation
for the Potomac Company, Madison and Washington had developed a
powerful partnership. This, however, was Madison's first visit to Mount
Vernon. He was traveling to New York City intending to press Congress on two issues of deep concern to Virginia: payment for the land
the state had ceded to Congress, and Spain's closure of the Mississippi

River to American navigation. Few people in America knew more about the West, or had deeper commercial interests in that region, than Washington. Madison had decided to make a detour to seek Washington's advice and, ideally, his support for Virginia's cause.

Virginia was one of seven states that, relying on their colonial charters, laid claim to vast areas of territory stretching between the Appalachians and the Mississippi River.[6] Given at a time when little was known of the area, these ill-defined grants often overlapped and conflicted.[7] Virginia's claim was the largest and best founded. The six states without western claims—Delaware, Maryland, New Hampshire, New Jersey, Pennsylvania, and Rhode Island—looked on anxiously as the growing movement westward threatened to tip the scales of political power toward those states with western claims. That vast expanse, they argued, ought not to be viewed as the property of individual states; rather, it should be regarded as a national treasure to be used for the benefit of all. Under pressure from Congress, on 2 January 1781, the Virginia Assembly, after long debate, yielded and enacted a measure granting "to the Congress of the United States, for the benefit of the said United States all right, title and claim that the said Commonwealth hath to the lands northwest of the river Ohio." The cession, however, came with several conditions that the Congress found unacceptable.[8] Negotiations bogged down.

Nearly two years later, 8 December 1783, with the war over and a nation forming, nationalists under Madison's leadership repealed the act of 1781 and passed a revised measure granting to Congress "the right of this Commonwealth to the territory northwest-ward of the river Ohio."[9] Led by Thomas Jefferson, the Virginia delegates presented the revised cession to Congress. On 1 March 1784, with only ten states represented (one more than the required quorum), Congress debated Virginia's offer, including the controversial proviso, "[t]hat the necessary and Reasonable expenses incurred by this state, in subduing any British posts, or maintaining forts and garrisons within, and for the defense, or in acquiring any part of the territory so ceded or relinquished, shall be fully reimbursed by the United States." Despite fears that the "very enormous sum" that Virginia was likely to conjure up might open the floodgates to additional claims, seven states agreed to the terms—sufficient for passage.[10]

Immediately following the vote to accept the cession, a committee, chaired by Jefferson, presented "a plan for the temporary government of the western territory."[11] Sections 4 and 5 drew attention. The first stipulated that, whatever states were created within the cession, "their governments shall be in republican forms and shall admit no person to be a citizen who holds a hereditary title"—a direct slap at the Cincinnati. Section 5 was even more contentious: "That after the year 1800 of the Christian era, there shall be neither slavery nor involuntary servitude in any of the said states" formed in the territory.[12] Six weeks following, on 19 April, the ninth anniversary of Lexington and Concord, the legislation came to the floor. In its final form, both sections were stripped away. According to Jefferson, the slavery proviso "lost by individual vote only. With ten states were present. The 4. Eastern states, N. York, Pennsva. were for the clause. Jersey would have been for it, but there were but two members, one of whom was sick in his chambers. South Carolina, Maryland, and Virginia voted against it. N. Carolina was divided as would have been Virginia had not one of it's delegates been sick in bed."[13] On 23 April, the act passed with the contentious clauses removed.

Two weeks later, 7 May, Jefferson's committee returned to Congress with a second measure, "an ordinance for ascertaining the mode of locating and disposing of lands in the western territories, and for other purposes therein mentioned."[14] It took more than a year (Jefferson left for France on 3 July 1784), but finally, after considerable debate and amendment, on 20 May 1785, Congress enacted the measure. The Land Ordinance of 1785 created a precise system of survey dividing the territory into sections and townships. By establishing a systemic method for settlement, the act brought order to western expansion and much-needed revenue to Congress.[15] Having given over the land, however, Virginia waited for the body to fulfill its pledge to "fully" reimburse the state for its "necessary and reasonable expenses." As was Congress's wont, matters went slowly.[16] Even more concerning to Madison was Spain's closure of the Mississippi.[17]

Although Spain had declared war against Great Britain in 1779, it did not—despite the best efforts of John Jay, the American envoy to Madrid—join the United States in a formal alliance.[18] The French had enticed Spain into the war with promises of regaining Minorca, Gibraltar, and the Floridas. Although Spain aided the American cause, the relationship proved uneasy. The 1783 Treaty of Paris, ending the Revolution, thrust the new republic's western border directly against Spain's Louisiana territory, separated only by the Mississippi River.[19] In Article 8 of the treaty, Great Britain agreed that "[t]he navigation of the river Mississippi, from its source to the ocean, shall forever remain free and open to the subjects of Great Britain and the citizens of the United States."[20] Since Spain was in firm control of the lower Mississippi, including New Orleans, and not a party to the treaty, this provision flew in the face of reality. In June 1784, fretting about the possibility of large numbers of Americans encroaching into their territory and creating unrest, Spain closed the Mississippi to American navigation.[21] Virginians were enraged. In reaction, the House of Delegates resolved "[t]hat it is essential to the prosperity and happiness of the western inhabitants of this Commonwealth to enjoy the right of navigating the river Mississippi to the sea, and that the delegates representing the state in Congress, ought to be instructed to move that honorable body to give directions (unless the same have been already given to the American ministers in Europe) to forward negotiations to obtain that end without loss of time."[22] In a letter dated 19 November 1784 to the president of Congress, delivered by the secretary to the Spanish legation, Francisco Rendon, Spain responded as follows: "Cessation of the navigation to the Mississippi made by the King of Great Britain to the United States, in the treaty of 1783, can have no real force unless the Catholic King, my master, to whom the navigation of that river belongs, shall think proper to ratify it."[23] On 7 December, in the midst of considerable agitation, Congress referred the "note of 19 Nov. and papers enclosed touching the navigation of Mississippi" to a committee that included John Jay of New York, the secretary of foreign affairs. Recently returned from Europe, Jay had represented the United States in Spain and later had been a key player in the Paris peace negotiations.[24]

Reporting back the same day, the committee recommended appointing a minister to Spain to adjust the "interfering claims," with specific instructions to reject Spanish claims to control of the Mississippi.[25] For weeks Congress sat on the report. When news arrived that Spain had appointed a new minister to the United States, Diego de Gardoqui, Jay noted that "it does not seem necessary at present to pursue the idea of treating with his Catholic Majesty on those subjects at Madrid." Congress, lacking a quorum, was easily persuaded to delay. In anticipation of delicate negotiations and fearing that Great Britain, always ready to "blow the flames of discord," might attempt to scuttle any arrangement between the two nations, Jay urged his colleagues to "perfect silence."[26]

Perfect silence was not to be had. Even before Jay delivered his report, Richard Henry Lee wrote Washington, "we have reason soon to expect [Gardoqui's] arrival. Time and wise negotiation will unfold this very important matter, and I hope may secure to the U.S. and those Individual States concerned, the great advantages that will be derived from a free navigation of that river."[27] In another letter to Governor Patrick Henry, Lee was less confident, expressing his suspicion that Gardoqui was likely carrying "some tempting commercial offers, to procure our assent to the loss of this very valuable navigation."[28] Lee suspected that those "tempting offers" involved an offer to reopen Spain's lucrative codfish trade—"fish for gold"—with New England in exchange for abandoning the right to navigate the Mississippi.

Before the Revolution, the Bilbao House of Joseph Gardoqui and Sons was one of Spain's largest importers of New England salt cod, enjoying strong connections with merchants in Boston, Salem, and Marblehead. In the early years of the war, the firm had been among those secretly helping supply arms and gunpowder to Washington's army. When John Jay arrived in Madrid in 1779, the Gardoquis stood as an important link to the Spanish government, especially in the matter of American navigation on the Mississippi River. Jay pressed hard on the issue of free navigation on the Mississippi, telling Diego de Gardoqui, Joseph's second son, that "Americans almost to a Man believed that God Almighty had made that River a highway for the People of the upper Country to go to the Sea by." Gardoqui, the unruffled merchant/

diplomat, brushed aside Jay's hyperbolic rhetoric, suggesting "that the present generation would not want this navigation, and that we should leave future ones to manage their own Affairs."[29] Having accomplished little, Jay left Madrid in June 1782 to join the American commissioners in Paris. By the time Gardoqui presented his credentials to Congress on 2 July 1785, the "future" had arrived. Closure of the Mississippi and the surge of American settlers pressing on Spanish territory resurrected the issue left on the table in Madrid five years earlier.

Amiable, experienced, and shrewd—James Monroe referred to him as "a polite and sensible man"—Gardoqui did his best to smooth the roiling waters.[30] He reminded his American friends that he had helped Washington obtain the prize jack ass (mule) "Royal Gift." He likewise presented Jay with a fine Arabian stallion. To ingratiate himself even further, Gardoqui loaned Virginia delegate Henry Lee $5,000 while lavishing considerable time and money entertaining other members of Congress with fine wines and elegant dinners.[31] Despite his best efforts, however, Gardoqui's charm offensive could not mask the fact that Spain was holding fast—the Mississippi was closed to American navigation.

Even though Congress ordered the negotiations with Gardoqui to be kept secret, leaks sprang everywhere, many flowing from the Virginia delegates.[32] Madison told Gilbert du Motier, the marquis de Lafayette, that the news from New York produced in him an "anxiety concerning the navigation of the Mississippi. If there be any who really looks on the use of that river, as an object not to be sought or desired by the United States I cannot but think they frame their policies on both very narrow and very delusive foundations."[33] Madison warned Monroe, then sitting in Congress, that "the use of the Mississippi is given by nature to our western country, and no power on earth can take it from them." He feared that the "Atlantic States," in return for a commercial treaty with Spain, would push Congress to sacrifice Virginia's western interests and give up its claim for navigation on the Mississippi.[34] Should Spain not relent, the consequences for the new republic would be dire.

Although certain members of Congress leaked information, Jay did not. His silence, however, came at a price, for it gave rise to the suspicion that he, Gardoqui, and the eastern states were "intriguing" to abandon claims to Mississippi navigation in return for a commercial treaty.[35] To preempt the secretary from taking any untoward action, Virginia's delegates moved to rein in his negotiating authority. A committee chaired by James Monroe presented a resolution limiting Jay's authority, instructing him that "in his plan for a treaty particularly to stipulate the right of the United States to their territorial bounds, and the free Navigation of the Mississippi."[36] With warmth and intemperance, Jay replied to the president of Congress, Richard Henry Lee, that "the Instruction which directs me previously to communicate to Congress every Proposition which in the Course of the Negociation I may think expedient to make to Mr. Gardoqui, as well as every Proposition which he may in our Conferences throw out to me, will I apprehend be exceedingly embarrassing." He took the instruction to mean that he could "sign nothing without the previous Approbation of Congress." Under these circumstances, Jay was "at a Loss to conceive how it will be possible for me to comply with this Instruction, and yet do Business in the usual, and in my Opinion, the most natural and proper Way."[37] Over the next few months, he and Gardoqui "had many Conferences and much Reasoning on the Subject."[38] Through it all, however, Jay held to his position and shared little information with Congress.

It was the flood of rumors flowing from New York, none of which favored Virginia, that persuaded Madison to visit Congress, making his stop at Mount Vernon. The visit was brief. He found "the Genl. In perfect health," and having "just returned from a trip up the Potowmac," he was, according to Madison, growing "more and more sanguine [about] the practicability of opening its navigation." On other matters, however, he was more cautious, particularly regarding the recently enacted Land Ordinance. Although he approved the measure, since it would provide for orderly settlement of the West, he was uneasy that offering too much land too soon "would open a more extensive field for land jobbers and speculators." He questioned the wisdom of dispersing sales to the states, putting local loan officers in charge.[39] In this he perceived Congress as "surrendering the little power they have, to the states individually which gave it to them."[40] The plan was, in his opinion, not "a very eligible one."[41] Adding to Washington's concerns was the question of opening navigation on the Mississippi River and its threat to his Potomac plans.

Madison was aware that, in the matter of opening the Mississippi, he and Washington differed. In contrast to his fellow Virginians, Washington confessed to being "singular in my ideas."[42] Two days after Madison left, he wrote to Jean-Baptiste-Donatien de Vimeur, the comte de Rochambeau, that he did "not think the Navigation of the Mississippi is an object of great importance at present." Only "when the Banks of the Ohio are thick settled—and when the fertile plains of that Western Country are covered with people"—would navigation on the river be important.[43] To David Humphreys he confided that, having worked tirelessly to open "the front door" (i.e., the Potomac) to the West so that settlement might "progress regularly and compactly," with strong ties to the East, he feared that opening the Mississippi would ineluctably siphon trade west, down that river into Spanish hands and away from routes leading to tidewater Virginia.[44]

It is unclear how frank Washington was with Madison concerning his views on western settlement and the Mississippi. In controversial matters, he was known to have, as John Adams described it, "the gift of silence." Always cautious about revealing himself, he once advised his nephew Bushrod that he ought "never be agitated by more than decent warmth and offer your sentiments with modest diffidence."[45] On Monday morning, "after breakfast," Madison departed for New York, likely without a clear understanding of the general's position.

When Madison arrived in New York, only two members of the state's delegation were present, Samuel Hardy and William Grayson; the third member, James Monroe, had left to tour the West. In the matter of Virginia's claim for payment, nothing had been done, and the Mississippi question, unresolved, had fallen into a dark hole.[46]

Considerable time elapsed as Gardoqui consulted with Madrid. The answer came. He was authorized to offer a treaty of commerce, but in the matter of American navigation on the Mississippi, "the King will never yield that Point, nor consent to any Compromise about it—for that it always has been and continues to be one of their Maxims of Policy, to exclude all Mankind from their American Shores."[47]

On Saturday, 1 October, having accomplished little, Madison left New York. Pausing for a few days in Philadelphia, he took the opportunity to write a long letter to Jefferson explaining his failed mission.

He spoke plainly, taking direct aim at Congress, which he described as "little redeemed from the confusion which has so long mortified the friends to our national honor and prosperity." He accused the members of harboring a crippling localism so that rather than sitting as "impartial judges," they were in fact "advocates for the respective interest of their constituents." In this, they were acting as servile instruments bowing to their constituents, whose "selfishness or perverseness" prevented them from acting for the benefit of the whole. Concluding his critique, Madison wrote, "The present plan of federal government reverses the first principle of all government. It punishes not the evil doers, but those that do well." In sum, Congress had kept "the vessel from sinking, but it has been by standing constantly at the pump, not by stopping the leaks which have endangered her."[48] Impatient to get home in time to attend the fall session of the Virginia Assembly, Madison hastened on his journey, only allowing time for a return visit to Mount Vernon.

Madison arrived on Wednesday evening, 12 October. Mount Vernon was bustling with activity. Jean-Antoine Houdon and his assistants were putting the finishing touches on Washington's life mask and two plaster of Paris busts. Although Martha was not well and unable to supervise, the household staff were hurriedly preparing for Fanny's wedding only three days distant.[49] On Thursday, the day after Madison arrived, rain caused "a suspension of all outdoors work."[50] Kept to the mansion, Washington and his visitor had ample time to discuss important matters. Through correspondence, conversations with visitors, and newspaper accounts, Washington was well apprised of national affairs. Madison, however, brought him valuable, firsthand information. He listened carefully to Madison, whom, he wrote to Chastellux, he valued as one of "those friends in and out of Congress [who] tells me what is on the carpet."[51] The conversation did little to improve Washington's mood.[52] He remained "sanguine" about the Potomac project, but he despaired over the nation's prospects. Madison's glum report underscored Washington's view that the Confederation was "little more than an empty sound, and Congress a nugatory body."[53] For want of a quorum, which prevented them from conducting business, the members had retreated to their usual state of lethargy, content to "to lie on their oars."[54] Before leaving, Madison likely hinted to Washington the "idea of a convention," a meeting outside of Congress to address issues confounding the Confederation.[55]

By early 1786, Congress, in addition to its chronic financial woes and with attendance "so thin as to render it impracticable for it to undertake any matter of importance," faced a dizzying array of challenges, few of which it was competent to solve.[56] These included a torrent of claims pouring in from soldiers, vendors, and creditors left over from the war, accompanied by persistent pleas from states (Virginia included) seeking to liquidate delinquent accounts. Indian affairs also pressed for attention as the commissioners for Indian affairs continued negotiations seeking ever greater land concessions from the Six Nations and other native peoples. Overall, the question of navigation on the Mississippi loomed ominously.

After many "fruitless arguments," Jay knew that Spain would never yield to the American demands.[57] Quietly, he began to "finesse" the issue, lobbying members of Congress, particularly the president of Congress, Richard Henry Lee, to accept "occlusion" of the Mississippi for a period long enough (twenty-five to thirty years) by which time the United States would be strong enough to force Spain to relent. Jay argued that putting aside this contentious issue would open the way for an immediate commercial treaty.[58] His plan, of course, relied on the utmost secrecy, lest Spain learn of America's long-term intentions. In Congress, however, secrecy was a scarce commodity. Virginia's newly elected delegate, Henry (Harry) "Light Horse" Lee, kept Washington, his old comrade in arms, informed. Lee, as "singular in his opinion as Washington," argued that "no nation in Europe can give us conditions so advantageous to our trade as that kingdom."[59] To bolster "the interest of Virginia," it was critical that "the Potomac & James river companys succeed in their exertions before the navigation of the Mississippi becomes free to the western emigrants."[60] Lee tried to bring Washington to support Jay. Washington was careful. Although concerned about the interests of Virginia, Washington saw an even greater threat—disunion. He responded to Lee that the "navigations of the rivers Potomack & James are pregnant" and were key to "*all* the communications which nature has afforded, between the Atlantic States and the Western territory." Always concerned "that the flanks & rear of the United States were exposed to hostile powers," Washington declared that a premature opening of the Mississippi would bring the West into Spain's orbit and the

> ties of consanguinity which are weakening every day, will soon be no band; and we shall be no more a few years hence to the Inhabitants of that Country than the Spaniards or British are to them at this day; not so much—because commercial connections it is well known introduce others; and united, are difficult to be broken. Whenever the New States become so populous, and so extended to the Westward as really to need it, there is no power that can deprive them of the use of the Mississippi. Why then should we, prematurely, urge a matter which is disagreeable to others, and may be attended with embarrassing consequences, if it is our interest to let it sleep?[61]

Sitting in Congress, Lee saw the reality of the situation. In the face of Spanish intransigence, loud voices in the West, "full of consternation and complaint," were calling for force to compel Spain to open the river.[62] Such demands were pointless and troublesome. "The debilitated condition of the federal government" made any action impossible. From a national perspective, Lee understood

> that in agreeing to the occlusion of the Navigation of the Mississippi, we give in fact nothing, for the moment our western country become populous & capable, they will seize by force what may have been [yielded] by treaty. Till that period, the river cannot be used but by permission of Spain, whose exclusive system of policy, never will grant such permission—Then to be sure, we only give, what we cannot use.

Lee also recognized, however, that the short-term benefits of a treaty carried serious long-term consequences. Surrendering to Spanish pressure would show to all "the inefficiency of the federal government." It would also likely cleave the Congress along sectional lines since Jay's recommendation carried "advantages very great, but not so great to the whole as to a part"—that is, eastern commercial prospects trumping western interests. "Already," he warned, "in every state the amplification of the powers of the Union have too many enemys." This action would provide an even greater "tent for popular declaimers," who feared that a stronger federal government would be controlled by forces hostile to their interests.[63] Lee paid a political price for his opinions. In the fall election for representatives to Congress, Madison reported to Jefferson that "Col. H. Lee of the last delegation was dropt. The causes were different I believe & not very accurately known to me. One of them is said to have been his supposed heterodoxy touching the Mississippi."[64] Washington was wise to keep his distance from Lee.

On 29 May 1786, having kept close about his negotiations with Gardoqui, Jay wrote to the president of the Congress, John Hancock, asking for the appointment of a committee "to direct me on every point and subject relative to the proposed treaty with Spain." The committee, according to Jay, should be "secret to forbear having any conversation on subjects connected with it, except in Congress."[65] The committee consisted of Rufus King (Massachusetts), Charles Pettit (Pennsylvania), and James Monroe (Virginia). After weeks of pointless meetings, the committee deadlocked (Monroe versus King and Pettit). Unable to make a report, they asked to be discharged, leaving matters to Congress. That same day, Tuesday, 1 August, Congress took matters into its own hands, and "[a]fter debate, an order was passed for Secretary for Foreign Affairs to attend Congress on Thursday next, at 12 O'clock on the subject of his letter of 29th May."[66] Jay arrived well prepared. Combining his skills as a diplomat and lawyer, he laid out for the members the tale of his fruitless, though congenial, negotiations with Gardoqui. It took the entire day.

Jay offered Congress a compromise, one that conformed to Washington's "let it sleep" principle.[67] It "would be expedient," he told the body, "to agree that the treaty should be limited to twenty-five or thirty years, and that one of the articles should stipulate that the United States would forbear to use the navigation of that river [Mississippi]." Jay argued that without this concession, a commercial treaty would be impossible. He further suggested that the "navigation is not at present important," and he cautioned that the Confederation, in its weakened state, was "not prepared for a war with any power." In sum, Congress—impoverished, feeble, and fractured—had no choice but to accept Spain's terms.[68] In secret sessions, bitter debate raged for several days.[69] Southern and western interests held firm against concessions. Off and on, the debate lasted nearly a month, longer than it took to declare independence. Little more than a week into the debate, Monroe wrote an ominous report to Virginia's governor, Patrick Henry.

For Monroe, the situation had come to "a crisis." He noted that Jay's original instructions confined him to negotiating boundaries for the Floridas and navigation on the Mississippi. Jay, according to Monroe, had ignored those instructions, abandoned negotiations concerning the Mississippi, and instead focused on a commercial treaty, all the time "intriguing with members" (particularly those from Massachusetts, New York, New Jersey, and Pennsylvania) to achieve his ends. To clear the path to an agreement with Spain, Jay needed Congress to withdraw their original instructions demanding "free navigation of the Mississippi," which, ironically, had been drawn up by a committee chaired by Monroe.[70]

"This," Monroe wrote, was "one of the most extraordinary transactions I have ever known, a minister negotiating expressly for the purpose of defeating the object of his instructions, and by a long train of intrigue and management seducing the representatives of the states to concur in it."[71] To assist Jay in his plan, allies from Massachusetts moved that any change in Jay's instructions needed only seven votes for approval rather than the canonical nine ordinarily required for treaties. Able to muster only five votes out of twelve states present (Delaware was absent), the southern delegates "with some warmth," seeing this development as part of a design "to embarrass the western country to prevent emigration," opposed the change.[72] They succeeded. The nine-vote rule held. When the count was taken on removing the navigation clause, it hewed neatly along sectional lines. With no dissent within any delegation, seven northern states—New Hampshire, Massachusetts, Rhode Island, Connecticut, New York, New Jersey, and Pennsylvania—voted in favor. The five southern states—Maryland, Virginia, North Carolina, South Carolina, and Georgia—stood firmly against. The instructions, by now meaningless, stood.[73] For the moment, Washington's Potomac route remained unchallenged—but at a cost. The vote had revealed deep sectional divisions within the nation, as well as the weakness of a government unable or unwilling to assert its national interests. The treaty fell to the side. Jay continued discussions with Gardoqui, "which produced nothing but Debate and in the Course of which we did not advance one single Step nearer to each other."[74] Some months later, Madison, recalling the sad tale to Jefferson, lamented that "the Spanish project sleeps."[75] It remained tabled until 16 September 1788, when in its waning days the Congress resolved "that the subject be referred to the federal government which is to assemble in March next."[76]

Monroe saw sinister motives afoot. "The object in the occlusion of the Mississippi" was to prevent settlement in the West so that "weight of government and population" would remain in the North. This was the goal "pursued by a set of men so flagitious, unprincipled and determined in their pursuits, as to satisfy me beyond a doubt they have extended their views to the dismemberment of the government."[77] Although the threat of "dismemberment" horrified him, he still held out hope: "I am thoroughly persuaded the government is practicable and with a few alterations, the best that can be devised. To manage our affairs to advantage under it and remedy these defects, in my opinion, nothing is wanting but common sense and common honesty, in both of which necessary qualifications we are, it is to be lamented very defective."[78]

While taking some comfort that his "singular" stand had prevailed, Washington recognized that it might have been a pyrrhic victory. Aware how weak the links were that bound west to east, and how fiercely westerners wanted access to the Mississippi, he forewarned Henry Lee that "[i]t may require some management to quiet the restless & impetuous spirits of Kentucke (of whose conduct I am more apprehensive in this business than I am of all the opposition that will be given by the Spaniards)."[79] Washington was astute and prescient. As he predicted, on Congress's failure to open the Mississippi, a clamor arose in the West. "We can raise twenty thousand troops, this side the Allegheny and Appalachian Mountains," blasted one agitated westerner, "to drive the Spaniards from their settlements." The writer warned that if "we are not countenanced and succored by the United States (if we need it) our allegiance will be thrown off, and some other power applied to."[80] In the face of rising agitation, Monroe hoped that "common sense and common honesty" would steer the nation away from such disasters. Perhaps, he suggested, the "Convention at Annapolis" might offer solutions.[81]

Monroe's mention of "Annapolis" referred to action taken by the Virginia house on the last day of their session, 21 January 1786. Buoyed by the success of the Mount Vernon conference (March 1785), Madison and his allies pushed for a general meeting of the states to address the broad issues confronting the nation. Facing opposition by those "frightened at the idea of a perpetual & irrevocable grant of power" to Congress, the House of Delegates agreed to a modified resolution that confined the agenda to matters of trade and commerce, rather than the more sweeping issues favored by Madison.

> That Edmund Randolph, James Madison, jun. Walter Jones, Saint George Tucker and Meriwether Smith, Esquires, be appointed commissioners, who, or any three of whom, shall meet such commissioners as may be appointed by the other States in the Union, at a time and place to be agreed on, to take into consideration the trade of the United States; to examine the relative situations and trade of the said States; to consider how far a united form system in their commercial regulations may be necessary to their common interest and their permanent harmony and to report to the several States, such an act relative to this great object, as, when unanimously ratified by them, will enable the United States in Congress, effectually to provide for the same.[82]

Three weeks later, meeting at the home of Benjamin Harrison, Speaker of the House, the commissioners agreed to dispatch a circular letter, signed by the chairman of the delegation, Edmund Randolph, inviting the states to attend a convention "to take under their Consideration the Trade of the United States" to be held on the first Monday in September.[83] Apprehensive that powerful commercial and political interests in either New York City (population of thirty-three thousand) or Philadelphia (population of twenty-eight thousand) might influence the proceedings, the commissioners opted to convene at a smaller, southern venue: Annapolis, Maryland (population of two thousand).[84]

The call was not universally welcomed. Northern commercial interests, particularly New Englanders, suspected a plot by "esteemed great [i.e., southern] aristocrats few of them have been in the commercial line, nor is it probable they know or care much about commercial objects."[85]

As time for the convention approached, Madison's feelings "ranged from lukewarm to moderately hot."[86] He confided to Jefferson that he was conflicted: "Gentlemen both within & without Congs. wish to make this Meeting subservient to a Plenipotentiary Convention for amending the Confederation. Tho' my wishes are in favor of such an event, yet I despair so much of its accomplishment at the present crisis that I do not extend my views beyond a Commercial Reform. To speak the truth, I almost despair even of this." Nonetheless, given rising tension over the Spanish question, discontent bubbling up in the West, deepening financial issues (the "epidemic malady" of paper money), and rumors of "dismemberment," Annapolis was "better than nothing."[87] Since "[t]he efforts for bringing about a correction thro' the medium of Congress have miscarried. Let a Convention then be tried."[88]

Although he played no direct role, Washington kept well informed. His role with the Potomac Company, and his other business interests, placed him in close touch with numerous people. At Mount Vernon, the doors continued to swing open. Dozens of visitors came by eager to share the latest news and gossip. Letters from old comrades and politicians in Boston, New York, Philadelphia, and Richmond arrived daily. The nation was in distress. Describing the parlous condition of the Confederation, John Jay suggested that the meeting at Annapolis might be a prelude to a "general convention for revising the Articles of Confederation." Jay was convinced that Washington could not view these events "with the Eye of an unconcerned Spectator." Attempting to draw him in, he wrote that, although "the Plan is not matured—if it should be well concerted and take Effect, I am fervent in my Wishes, that it may comport with the Line of Life you have marked out for yourself, to favor your country with your counsels on such an important & single occasion. I suggest this merely as a Hint for Consideration."[89] Washington took the hint and rejected it:

> We are certainly in a delicate situation, but my fear is that the people are not yet sufficiently misled to retract from error! To be plainer, I think there is more wickedness than ignorance, mixed

with our councils. That it is necessary to revise, and amend the articles of Confederation, I entertain no doubt; but what may be the consequences of such an attempt is doubtful. Yet, something must be done, or the fabrick must fall. It certainly is tottering! Ignorance & design are difficult to combat. Out of these proceed illiberality, improper jealousies, and a train of evils which oftentimes, in republican governments, must be sorely felt before they can be removed. The former, that is ignorance, being a fit soil for the latter to work in, tools are employed which a generous mind would disdain to use; and which nothing but time, and their own puerile or wicked productions, can show the inefficacy and dangerous tendency of. I think often of our situation and view it with concern. From the high ground on which we stood—from the plain path which invited our footsteps, to be so fallen!—so lost! is really mortifying. But virtue, I fear, has, in a great degree, taken its departure from our Land, and the want of disposition to do justice is the sourse of the national embarrassments; for under whatever guise or colourings are given to them, this, I apprehend, is the origin of the evils we now feel, & probably shall labour for some time yet.[90]

As time for the meeting drew closer, nine states (New Hampshire, Massachusetts, Rhode Island, New York, New Jersey, Pennsylvania, Delaware, North Carolina, and Virginia) agreed to attend. Madison grew more optimistic.[91] Always well prepared, the politician/scholar arrived in Annapolis a week early carrying with him a long treatise, "Notes on Ancient and Modern Confederacies," which he had prepared to bolster his argument for a strong national government.[92]

Affairs did not begin well. As Madison waited at Mann's Tavern, only two commissioners arrived, forcing him to conclude that "the prospect of a sufficient no. to make the Meeting respectable is not flattering."[93] By 11 September, only five states were represented. Alexander Hamilton and Egbert Benson sat for New York. New Jersey sent Abraham Clark, William C. Houston, and James Schureman. Tench Coxe represented Pennsylvania. Delaware appointed George Read, John Dickinson, and Richard Bassett. Accompanying Madison were Edmund Randolph and George Tusker. Other than Virginia, no southern states were present, including, paradoxically, Maryland, which refused the invitation, complaining that "the meeting proposed may be misunderstood and misrepresented in Europe, giving umbrage to Congress, and disquiet the citizens of the United States."[94]

Although attendance was "tardy and deficient," those present had experience, talent, and youth.[95] Ten had been (or were) members of the Congress. Seven would attend the Constitutional Convention the following year. The youngest was Alexander Hamilton, age twenty-nine. The oldest was Abraham Clark, sixty, of New Jersey. Madison was thirty-five. The average age was forty. Most important, they all arrived sharing a common goal—strengthening the federal government.

After electing John Dickinson president, the convention "[o]rdered that Mr. Benson, Mr. [Abraham] Clarke, Mr. [Tench] Coxe, Mr. [George] Read, and Mr. [Edmund] Randolph be a Committee to consider of and report the measures proper to be adopted by this Convention."[96]

Quickly reviewing the state resolutions appointing commissioners, the committee found that all except for New Jersey had confined their commissioners' attention to matters of trade and commerce. New Jersey's instructions mentioned trade and commerce but also extended the delegation's remit beyond that narrow scope to include "other important matters." Concluding that "so partial and defective a representation" made it impossible for the convention to act "on the subject immediately committed to the meeting," in a bold move, with uncommon speed, the attendees swerved widely from the original purpose of the convention. Cloaking themselves behind New Jersey's "other important matters," they embraced "radical reform" and voted to prepare an "Address" to Congress, recommending it "call a meeting at Philada. the ensuing year, of Commissrs. with authority to digest & propose a new & effectual system of Govt. for the Union."[97]

Although Hamilton was not a member of the committee, the convention assigned him the task of writing a draft, which he presented two days later. Written in language that some thought unduly harsh toward Congress, the intended recipient, Randolph, suggested modifications; "otherwise, all Virginia will be against you." Madison agreed.[98] By a unanimous vote, the convention approved an amended address.

"With the most respectful deference," the commissioners explained why they "did not conceive it advisable to proceed on their business" as they had been instructed. They asked for "an indulgent construction." That indulgence led them to call "for the appointment of commissioners, to meet at Philadelphia, on the second Monday of May next, to take into consideration the situation of the United States." Casting aside any notion of a limited agenda, they proposed that the meeting should act to "devise provisions as shall appear to them necessary to render the constitution of the federal government adequate to the exigencies of the union."[99] Before adjourning, the convention ordered Dickinson to deliver the address to the Congress then meeting in New York. Other copies were dispatched to the legislatures of the five states represented at Annapolis and to the executives of the absent states.

Events at Annapolis had moved so quickly that the business was done before anyone beyond the twelve, including Washington, knew the details. Desperate for news, he wrote to his friend and business partner, John Fitzgerald, "Have you heard from Annapolis since Monday? Have the Commercial Commissioners met? Have they proceeded to business? How long is it supposed their Session will last? [A]nd is it likely they will do anything effectual?"[100]

9

PHILADELPHIA

> If government shrinks or is unable to enforce its laws anarchy and confusion must prevail. (GW to HK, 3 February 1787, in *GWP, Conf. Series*, 5:7)

Finished with their work, the Annapolis delegates adjourned to Mann's for dinner. The next morning, Friday, 15 September 1786, Madison departed for Philadelphia to collect debts owed to his father from the sale of tobacco, while St. George Tucker went on similar business to New York.[1] Since it was vital that Washington know quickly, and firsthand, that the convention had urged the Congress "to effect a general meeting, of the States," Edmund Randolph agreed to proceed immediately to Mount Vernon. He arrived the next morning, Saturday.

As usual, "Farmer Washington" was making his rounds: "Visited my Mill, Ditchers and the Plantations at the Ferry, Dogue Run, and Muddy hole." Checked on "the fodder (top & blade) of the drilled corn was gathered & the Sowing of the Rye kept up with the plow, and the people [enslaved Africans] had begun to sow Wht. in the drilled Corn by the meadow." Late in the afternoon, arriving home, he welcomed his visitors, "the Attorney General (Randolph) his Lady & two Children and Mr. Charles Lee."[2] Randolph, sharing a copy of the address, recounted events at the meeting. Not ready yet to commit himself but encouraged by the report, after dinner Washington dispatched Lee to Alexandria to "ask Mr. Herbert, Colo. Fitzgerald & others down to dinner tomorrow."[3]

The conversation was lively. Washington and his guests peppered Randolph with questions. In the evening, fresh winds from the east brought heavy rain, which continued "incessantly the whole night." Lest his guests face danger returning to Alexandria in the rain and darkness, Washington invited them to stay the night. In the morning, "as the weather cleared," the visitors from Alexandria returned home, while Randolph, his wife, and his children departed for Richmond. The following Saturday, a week after Randolph's departure, Annapolis again came to the fore when "Mr. Tucker & Lady," returning from New York, joined by "Doctr. Stuart, Mrs. Stuart, Betsy & Patsy Custis, My Nephews George & Lawrence, (whom I had sent Horses) came down before dinner."[4] From the news brought by Randolph and Tucker, Washington concluded that the business at Annapolis gave "indications of a favourable issue" and "may be the spring of animation"; nonetheless, with his usual refrain, he reminded everyone that he "was retired from the world."[5]

Even as Washington learned more about Annapolis and saw its potential, Congress shuffled on the issue. On 20 September, John Dickinson delivered the address to Congress.[6] They received it quietly. Some viewed the Annapolis meeting as an affront to the powers of Congress. Rufus King of Massachusetts dismissed the address as "this project of Virginia" and wrote to John Adams that the meeting "terminated without credit, or prospect of having done much good. Congress can do all that a convention can, and certainly with more safety to original principles."[7] Dickinson spoke cautiously, not wanting to offend those who saw the address as a threat to Congress; others, including James Monroe, were more outspoken. Writing to Madison, he viewed events at Annapolis as a "source of infinite blessings to this country." He assured his friend that he considered "the convention of Annapolis as a most important era in our affairs."[8]

Dickinson's report sat on the table for three weeks. On 11 October, with only ten states present, a bare quorum, and "with difficulty," mostly from the "Eastern states," the members voted to commit the address to a Grand Committee (one member from each state— a device often used to bury proposals), charging them with preparing a report.[9] Two days later, satisfied that Congress would eventually approve the call for a meeting, James Monroe, whose three terms in Congress made him ineligible for reelection, left New York with his wife for Virginia. Since their journey passed through Philadelphia, and aware that Madison was ready to return to Virginia to attend the fall session of the House, he offered his friend "a seat with us in a spacious carriage to Fredricksbg? [Do?] you intend visiting the Genl. before you get to Richmond, in that event we wod. go togeth[er]."[10] Madison readily agreed.

Monday, 23 October, was "calm, clear and pleasant." Washington, in a relaxed mood, spent the day entertaining guests William Drayton and Walter Izard, prominent South Carolinians, passing through on their way home from New York. "In the evening Colo. Monroe, his Lady and Mr. Maddison came in."[11] Late the next morning, "Mr. Drayton and Mr. Izard set out on their rout to South Carolina." Alone with the Monroes and Madison, Washington "remained at home all day."[12] He had now heard accounts from all of Virginia's delegates at Annapolis, as well as Monroe's news from Congress. He was increasingly confident that the call by the Annapolis delegates, asking Congress to convene a meeting of the states on the second Monday in May in Philadelphia, "to devise provisions as shall appear to them necessary to render the constitution of the Federal Government adequate to the exigencies of the Union," would be successful.[13]

Madison and the Monroes left Mount Vernon on Wednesday, 25 October, the latter traveling to Fredericksburg to stay at the home of Joseph Jones, Monroe's uncle and a close friend of Washington's. Madison, late already for the fall session of the House, hurried to Richmond. The visits of Randolph, Tucker, Madison, and Monroe left Washington in a predicament. If not directly, certainly indirectly, they had all hinted that he ought to lead the Virginia delegation to the meeting in Philadelphia. They pointed out to him how convenient attendance would be for him, since he would undoubtedly be in Philadelphia the first Monday in May, the date set for the triennial meeting of the Cincinnati.

On 28 October, Madison was present when "the Speaker laid before the House" the report from Annapolis.[14] The following week, Madison introduced a bill titled "For Appointing Delegates from Their Commonwealth to a Convention to Be Held in the City of Philadelphia in May Next for the Purpose of Revising the Federal Constitution."[15]

Since "no opposition has been yet made and it is ready for the third reading," Madison was certain that the bill would pass, as it did, on 8 November. Although the bill called for delegates, it did not name them. There was, however, no doubt that Washington's name would head the list. On the same day the bill passed, Madison, appealing to Washington as both a Virginian and a national leader, asked him "to give this subject a very solemn dress." It was his intention to place Washington's name at the head of the delegation. "How far this liberty may correspond with the ideas by which you ought to be governed will be best decided where it must ultimately be decided. In every event it will assist powerfully in marking the zeal of our Legislature, and its opinion of the magnitude of the occasion."[16]

Washington took time responding, giving as his excuse that he had not been "to the Post Office with my usual regularity." Rather than chastising him for acting without his consent, Washington began his letter by raising Madison's spirits, telling him that it gave him "most sensible pleasure to hear that the Acts of the present Session, are marked with wisdom, justice & liberality. They are the palladium of good policy, & the only paths that lead to national happiness." Should the other states follow Virginia's example, "those threatening clouds which seem ready to burst on the Confederacy, would soon dispel." He celebrated the "unanimity with which the Bill was received, for appointing Commissioners agreeably to the recommendation of the Convention at Annapolis." These acts might foretell the "spring of reanimation." Having lifted Madison up, Washington then let him down. Despite all "the repeated proofs of confidence" the Virginia Assembly offered him, he could not answer the call. "The cause I will mention."[17]

"The cause" was the triennial meeting of the Cincinnati. Although it had been planned three years in advance, one week after Madison and Monroe left Mount Vernon, in a circular letter to the members of the society, Washington announced that, due to "private concerns, a violent attack of the fever & ague, succeeded by rheumatick pains," and his "desire not to be reelected to the Presidency," he had decided not to attend the meeting.[18] "Under these circumstances," he explained to Madison, "it will readily be perceived that I could not appear at the same time & place on any other occasion, without giving offence to a very respectable & deserving part of the Community—the late officers of the American Army."[19]

Washington's response was unconvincing. While both meetings were in Philadelphia, they were sequential, not conflicting. The Cincinnati was to meet on the first Monday in May, the convention the second Monday. As for Washington's health problems, they seemed not to interfere with his vigorous management of Mount Vernon or his travels on behalf of the Potomac Company.[20] Aware of Washington's strong views on the chronic incapacity of Congress, his advocacy to revise the federal system, and his recognition of the perilous state of the Union, Madison, after consulting with "judicious friends," ignored Washington's wishes and placed his name in nomination. On 4 December, "after members prepared tickets with the names of the persons to be appointed," the House "found a majority of votes in favor of George Washington, Patrick Henry, Edmund Randolph, John Blair, James Madison, George Mason, [and] George Wythe." Henry, sensing a conspiracy to diminish the power of the states and threaten individual liberties, claimed he "smelled a rat" and bluntly refused to attend the convention.[21] The choice turned to Thomas Nelson, who also declined, as did Richard Henry Lee. Finally, George McClurg, a well-known physician who happened, conveniently, to be in Philadelphia at the time, accepted. Although possessed of a "fair and unblemished character," McClurg spoke little and was the person of least consequence in the delegation.[22]

Hoping to woo him with a bit of flattery, Madison appealed to Washington: "Notwithstanding the communications in your favor of the 18th Ult, it was the opinion of every judicious friend whom I consulted that your name could not be spared from the Deputation to the Meeting in May in Philada." Anticipating that he might still decline election, Madison, playing on Washington's sense of duty and the critical importance of his participation, insisted that "having your name in the front of the appointment [would] mark the earnestness of Virginia" and offered "an invitation to the most select characters from every part of the Confederacy" to attend the meeting. These were serious concerns that ought not to give way "to the lesser matter of offending the Cincinnati."[23] Washington agreed "[t]hat the present era is pregnant of great, & strange events; none who will cast their eyes around them, can deny—what may be brought forth between this and the first of May to remove the difficulties which at present labour in my mind." Nonetheless, having already declined to attend the Cincinnati meeting, it would be an "awkward situation to be in Philadelphia on another public occasion during the sitting of this Society." To avoid embarrassment, he would attend neither the society meeting nor the convention.[24]

Madison knew Washington too well to give up easily. Undaunted, he adopted a more strategic approach. He wished "that at least a door could be kept open for your acceptance hereafter, in case the gathering clouds should become so dark and menacing as to supersede every consideration, but that of our national existence or safety." He urged Washington to take his time. "A suspense of your ultimate determination would be no wise inconvenient in a public view."[25] A few days after opening Madison's letter, Washington received a similar message from his friend, the recently elected governor of Virginia, Edmund Randolph, who urged him "not to decide on a refusal immediately." Others from beyond Virginia chimed in, including his former comrade in arms, Congress's secretary at war Henry Knox, who predicted that his attendance would be a tonic to all and "would induce the eastern states to send delegates."[26] That Washington, to whom duty was paramount, would allow the threat of personal embarrassment to override his obligation to a nation in peril was inconceivable. Fear of failure haunted Washington far more deeply than concerns over the Cincinnati. Remembering the meeting at Annapolis, where only five states were represented, he was anxious that the same result might occur in Philadelphia. He shared his concerns with David Humphreys:

> If this second attempt, should also prove abortive it may be considered as an unequivocal proof that the States are not likely to agree in any general measure which is to pervade the Union, & consequently, that there is an end put to Federal Government. The States therefore who make this last dying essay to avoid the misfortune of a dissolution would be mortified at the issue: and their deputies would return home chagrined at their ill success & disappointment. This would be a disagreeable predicament for any of them to be in, but more particularly so for a person in my situation.[27]

As pressure mounted on Washington, disturbing news arrived from Massachusetts. During the summer, tensions had risen in the Commonwealth. Farmers in the central and western parts of the state, weighed down by heavy debt, demanded that the General Court act to relieve their misery by issuing paper money and halting the collection of debts. When the state government ignored their pleas, protesters marched on county courts to halt foreclosures. By early fall, the situation had worsened. Writing to Washington, Henry Lee warned him that "the commotions in Massachusetts had risen to an alarming height." Humphreys, reporting from Connecticut, was equally alarmed and alerted Washington to the "state of Confusion."[28] As he learned more from visitors, letters, and newspaper accounts about the rising crisis in Massachusetts, Washington became increasingly concerned. To Humphreys he wrote, "For God's sake tell me, what is the cause of all these commotions? Do they proceed," he asked, "from licentiousness, British influence disseminated by the Tories, or real grievances which admit of redress? Why are not the powers of government tried at once?" Then, in an ironic twist, the leader of a revolution that had toppled a British regime noted, "Commotions of this sort, like snowballs, gather strength as they roll, if there is no opposition in the way to divide & crumble them."[29]

As the situation deteriorated, Daniel Shays, a former captain in the Continental army, emerged as the leader of the "rebellion." Responding to the threat, while ignoring the farmers' plight, the Supreme Judicial Court of the Commonwealth indicted Shays and others as "disorderly, riotous, and seditious persons." An equally unsympathetic legislature suspended habeas corpus and granted Governor James Bowdoin extraordinary powers to suppress the revolt.[30]

Unwilling to rely on the "vague & contradictory reports which are handed to us in Newspapers," Washington called on Knox to keep him informed about the tumult in Massachusetts.[31] Knox obliged willingly. Between 23 October 1786 and 29 February 1787, Knox dispatched eighteen letters to Washington describing the disorders in Massachusetts.[32] He set the tone for his reports in his first letter declaring that the "government of Massachusetts has given way, and its laws arrested and trampled underfoot."[33] By December, Knox was predicting that "during the Winter, it is possible that 12, or 15000, men may be embodied next spring or summer, whose views may be directed to any object whatever even the establishment of a tyranny, or a return to great Britain."[34] "Extremely anxious," Washington warned Knox that "[i]f government shrinks or is unable to enforce its laws anarchy and confusion must prevail."[35] Force prevailed. On 25 January, state militia repulsed a Shaysite attack on the Springfield Armory, and the following month state militia, commanded by Benjamin Lincoln, surprised the rebels at Petersham; "without time to call in their out parties or even their guards," the insurgents scattered. Shays's rebellion was over.[36]

Washington described Knox as a "fountain of intelligence," and his reliance on Knox went beyond reporting on affairs in Massachusetts. He queried him about the "General Convention to revise and amend the federal Constitution. What are the prevailing sentiments, how will it be attended?"[37] Not fully aware of his former commander's sentiments on the matter, Knox was careful in his response. On 14 January, he wrote, "how various are the opinions of men." Yet, he added, despite "the contrary opinions respecting the proposed convention were I to presume to give my own judgement, it would be in favor of the convention, and I sincerely hope that it may be generally attended." Turnout would be assured "if you were determined to attend the convention."[38] Replying quickly (3 February) to Knox's suggestion, Washington continued to hedge: "It is not, at this time, my purpose to attend it."[39] While Washington played Hamlet—to go or not to go—others moved quickly.

Ignoring the question as to whether a "convention" could take place without the consent of Congress, several states acted on their own. By early February, New Jersey, Virginia, Pennsylvania, North Carolina, Delaware, and Georgia had elected delegates.[40] Congress remained inert. The Grand Committee elected the previous October to take into consideration the report from the "commissioners assembled at the city of Annapolis" had yet to make a report. On 12 February, the same day that Knox reported to Congress "that the rebellion in Massachusetts is in a fair train of being speedily and effectually suppressed," Congress renewed the committee.[41] Nine days later, five months after Congress had received the address from Annapolis, in an attempt to recoup their own authority, they resolved that

it is expedient that on the second Monday in May next a convention of delegates who shall have been appointed by the several states
be held at Philadelphia for the sole and express purpose of revising
the Articles of Confederation and reporting to Congress and the
several legislatures such alterations and provisions therein as shall
when agreed to in Congress and confirmed by the states render the
federal constitution adequate to the exigencies of government and
the preservation of the Union.[42]

Congress's action solved the question posed by Madison to Monroe,
"whether it will be better to correct the vices of the Confederation by
recommendation gradually as it moves along, or by a Convention."[43] By
their call, Congress gave the meeting legitimacy.

The echoes of Shays's rebellion, the uncertain state of the union,
and a rising chorus of entreaties from his friends urging him to attend the convention were having an impact on Washington.[44] From
Richmond, Edmund Randolph, calling on their "friendship," asked
to be excused "for again mentioning the convention at Philadelphia.
But every day brings forth some new crisis, and the confederation is,
I fear, the last anchor of our hope."[45] Washington's wall of resistance,
never very robust, was crumbling. Knowing that he could depend on
his "friendship and candor," he wrote to Knox: "A thought has lately
run through my mind, which is attended with embarrassment. It is,
whether my non-attendance in this Convention will not be considered
as a dereliction to republicanism—nay more—whether other motives
may not (however injuriously) be ascribed to me for not exerting myself on this occasion in support of it." He asked Knox to share with
him "what the public expectation is on this head—that is, whether I
will, or ought to be there?"[46]

Knox's reply was quick and firm: "Your name has had already
great influence to induce the States to come into the measure—your
attendance will be grateful, and your absence chagrining." His "presence would confer on the assembly a national complexion, and more
than any other circumstance induce a compliance to the propositions
of the convention." Knox argued that the present Confederation was
too "defective" to be remedied by amendments. A new, "energetic and
judicious system" must come into being. Such a new order, "with Your

signature, would be a circumstance highly honorable to your fame, in the judgement of the present and future ages; and doubly entitle you to the glorious republican epithet—The Father of Your Country." As to the matter of the Cincinnati, the issue could be solved easily if Washington came to Philadelphia a week earlier to attend the triennial meeting, at which, Knox hoped, he might accept reelection as president.[47] The matter was settled. Shortly after reading Knox's letter, Washington wrote to Randolph that unless the Virginia Assembly had "turned its thoughts to some other character," and despite "a rheumatic complaint in my shoulder," he was willing to join the Virginia delegation. He asked Randolph for his "earliest advice," noting that in a similar reversal, he had decided to attend the Society of the Cincinnati meeting called for the first Monday of May, one week before the convention.[48]

Excitement and tension were rising as the nation prepared for the Philadelphia convention. All the while, Washington, the farmer, kept to his usual routine, including riding "to all the plantations," "sowing, harrowing and rolling the clover," "spreading dung," "planting corn," "raising a trunnel fence," and taking "a good many herring."[49] Back at the mansion house, his "well resorted tavern," he continued to entertain a steady stream of visitors. Dr. Craik, Arthur Lee, Henry Lee, Benjamin Franklin's nephew Jonathan Williams, and George Mason, as well as numerous relatives and neighbors, came and stayed.

The pressure worked. On 4 April, after receiving Washington's letter of 28 March, Randolph wrote to Madison, "Genl. Washington is prevailed upon to agree to go to Phila."[50] Madison was elated. "The attendance of Genl Washington is a proof of the light" in which he regarded the convention.[51]

As news of Washington's decision to go to Philadelphia spread, the business of the convention began to press on him, including pleas from job seekers. On 24 April, William Jackson, an officer who had served on Washington's staff, wrote to offer himself as a "candidate for the office of Secretary to the Federal Convention." Although Jackson had few qualifications, he enjoyed the strong backing of Robert Morris and Alexander Hamilton. However, his competitors, Temple Franklin and John Beckley, were equally well connected. Temple Franklin was Benjamin Franklin's grandson, who had acted as secretary to the American commissioners in Paris during the peace negotiations. John Beckley, supported by Edmund Randolph, was clerk of the Virginia House.[52]

Washington's preparations for Philadelphia were interrupted on 26 April when an "Express [arrived] between 4 & 5 O'clock this afternoon informing me of the extreme illness of my Mother and Sister Lewis, I resolved to set out for Fredericksburg by daylight in the Morning."[53] Leaving at sunrise, he arrived Friday afternoon to find "both my Mother & Sister better than I expected—the latter out of danger as is supposed, but the extreme low State in wch. the former was left little hope of her recovery as she was exceedingly reduced and much debilitated by age and the disorder."[54] For three days Washington remained with his mother and sister. His presence drew considerable local attention. Numerous people came by, and several offered their views on the upcoming convention. None of the visitors, however, was more interesting to Washington, a farmer always curious about agricultural experimentation, than Charles Yates, "a Gentleman," he noted in his diary, "on whose veracity entire confidence may be placed." Yates was "raising Irish Potatoes by laying them on unbroken, hard, or grassy ground & covering them with straw and found them to succeed admirably." He also shared with Washington a method for growing potatoes in cornfields.[55]

The summons to Fredericksburg had cost Washington several days that he had intended to use to prepare Mount Vernon for his absence. Although the convention was not scheduled to convene until 14 May, he planned to be in the city the week before so that he might attend the Society of Cincinnati meeting, in order "that he may apologize to the Cincinnati for his refusal of their presidency."[56] Not willing to delay his departure any longer, and despite his "fatigue," to make up for the time lost visiting his mother, Washington pursued a grueling pace, riding to all of his farms "with my Nephew G. W. to explain to him the Nature, and the ordr. of the business at each as I would have it carried on during my absence at the Convention in Philadelphia."[57] He also spent many hours surveying his growing fishing enterprise, negotiating western land sales, and managing the nonstop flow of visitors.

Madison, too, was at work preparing for Philadelphia. His plans centered on Washington. On 16 April, writing from New York, in a long letter to Washington, he laid out his thoughts: "Having been lately led to revolve the subject, which is to undergo the discussion of the Convention, and formed in my mind some outlines of a new system, I take the liberty of submitting them without apology, to your eye."[58] He continued with a detailed prescription based on the bold assumption "that an individual independence of the States is utterly irreconcilable with their aggregate sovereignty."[59] Washington, in his usual careful manner, reflected on Madison's letter, as well as ones he had received from Jay and Knox. Weighing them all, shortly before he left for Philadelphia, he wrote a private memo titled "Notes on the Sentiments of Government: John Jay, Henry Knox and James Madison."[60] He concluded that Jay was skeptical of giving "any further powers to Congress," while Knox and Madison saw no other course.

On Wednesday, 9 May 1787, "[a] little after sunrise," leaving Martha, who had become "too Domestick, and too attentive to two little Grand Children to leave home," Washington departed for Philadelphia accompanied by three enslaved Africans: his longtime companion Billy Lee, who had been with him throughout the Revolution; coachman Giles; and Paris, the postilion rider.[61]

Hampered by "turbulent and squally" weather, Washington took four days to reach Chester, Pennsylvania, on the Delaware River, where "he was met by the Genls. Mifflin (now Speaker of the Pennsylvania Assembly) Knox and Varnum—The Colonels Humphreys and Minges and Majors Jackson and Nicholas—With whom I proceeded to Philada."[62] The *Pennsylvania Packet* recorded his entrance into the city: "His Excellency General Washington, a member of the grand convention, arrived here. He was met at some distance and escorted into the city by the troop of horse and saluted at his entrance by the artillery. The joy of the people on the coming of this great and good man was shewn by their acclamations and the ringing of bells."[63]

Enthusiastic throngs followed him through the city to the corner of Fifth and Market Streets, where he stepped from his carriage at Mary House's boardinghouse, an "upscale" establishment that enjoyed a reputation for quality food and comfortable rooms. Madison, who had stayed there before, thought so well of Mrs. House's hospitality that he had reserved accommodations for the entire Virginia delegation. Having the delegation room together, reckoned Madison, would allow them the opportunity to caucus privately and lay out their plans for the convention. However, with the influx of delegates, servants, and others into the city, good accommodations had grown scarce. At Mrs. House's, rooms were crowded, overbooked, and renting at a premium. Initially, Washington had agreed to lodge with the Virginia delegation. Indeed, before leaving for Philadelphia, he had politely declined an invitation from Robert Morris to stay with his family, explaining that since it was unlikely the convention would "be brought to a speedy conclusion," a long stay would "give so much trouble to a private family" that he was forced to "decline the polite and obliging offer."[64] By the time he arrived in Philadelphia, however, the prospect of being lodged in Mrs. House's cramped quarters was quite unappealing, particularly given that, living with his fellow delegates, he would enjoy little privacy and no respite from politics. Mrs. House's boardinghouse would not do. Fortunately, at this moment, "being again warmly and kindly pressed by Mr. & Mrs. Rob. Morris to lodge with them I did so and had my baggage removed thither." Leaving his carriage, Washington made his way through the crowd, walking a few doors down Market Street to Morris's impressive three-story brick mansion, which, during the British occupation, had served as General Sir William Howe's headquarters. Washington's decision to live apart from his colleagues threw a twist into Madison's plans to keep the delegation in the same quarters so that they might caucus more easily. Barely settled at Morris's, that afternoon Washington made his first visit: "Waited on the President, Doctr. Franklin."[65]

The next morning "being the day appointed for the Convention to meet, such Members as were in town assembled at the State Ho[use]; but only two States being represented—viz.—Virginia & Pennsylvania—agreed to attend at the same place at 11 'Oclock tomorrow."[66] That night Washington "[d]ined in a family way at Mr. Morris's."[67] For the next ten days, each morning Washington and a scattering of delegates gathered at the State House to hear the same announcement—those present were "not sufficient to form a quorum."

As arranged, on Tuesday evening, 15 May, Washington "[d]ined with the Members, to the Genl. Meeting of the Society of the Cincinnati."[68] Disappointed that the state societies had ignored recommendations he made at the 1784 meeting, Washington had indicated that he would not seek reelection as president. His decision, distressing to many, raised concerns about the future of the society. Before leaving for Philadelphia, several members had written to him, urging him as a matter of duty to remain. Although the society met until 19 May, Washington's only appearance was at a dinner on 15 May. Among those present were Knox, Humphreys, and Mifflin. Two days later, Hamilton arrived. Under pressure from these men and others, with little enthusiasm, Washington, to whom duty was always true north, relented and accepted reelection as president general.[69]

As irksome as it was, the failure of delegates to arrive on time gave Washington, who was besieged with invitations, ample time to keep a full social calendar. On the evening of 18 May, Benjamin Franklin invited him, and the other delegates, to "une assemble des notables"—a dinner party in his newly enlarged dining room. "When the cask was broached," the host wrote to his sister, "its contents [were] met with the most cordial reception and universal approbation. In short, the company agreed unanimously, that it was the best porter they had ever tasted."[70]

Others among Philadelphia's elite were equally keen to invite Washington, including his close friends Elizabeth Willing Powel and her husband, Samuel. He ate with the prominent lawyer Jared Ingersoll, one of Pennsylvania's delegates to the convention, and on another evening, in "great splendor," he dined with Elizabeth Powel's nephew William Bingham, one of Philadelphia's richest merchants. Twice he dined at the Hills, Robert Morris's country estate overlooking the Schuylkill River. On another evening, after dining at Grey's Ferry, a natural garden on the west bank of the Schuylkill River, he "accompanied Mrs. [Morris] and some other Ladies to hear a Mrs. O'Connell read (a charity affair). The lady being reduced in circumstances had had recourse to this expedient to obtain a little money. Her performance was tolerable—at the College-Hall." Wednesday, 23 May, was an especially full day. After presenting himself at the State House, "[n]o more States being represented," Washington went "to Genl. Mifflin's to breakfast—after which in Company with him Mr. Madison, Mr. Rutledge and others I crossed the Schuylkill above the Falls. Visited Mr. Peters—Mr. Penn's Seat, and Mr. Wm. Hamilton's." He then "[d]ined at Mr. Chews—with the Wedding guests (Colo. Howard of Baltimore having married his daughter Peggy). Drank Tea there in a very large Circle of Ladies."[71]

While Washington swept through Philadelphia's high society, family and Mount Vernon remained present in his mind. On Thursday evening, after returning from the Powels', he wrote to George Augustine. He was in a good mood. The trip to Philadelphia had been "easy," and a recent rain had made "all nature alive." Since many delegates had yet to arrive, it was impossible to predict at this point when the business would begin, let alone "when it will end." He reminded his nephew how "anxious" he was for "the weekly remarks" that they had agreed he would send. "These you will have time to transcribe between Saturday and Monday Night; by which time your letter should be in the Post Office, in order that it may come off with the Mail on Tuesday Morning & be here on Friday."[72]

George Mason's arrival on 17 May "completed the whole number" of Virginia's delegation.[73] Still, other states remained absent. "These delays," Washington complained to Arthur Lee, "greatly impede public measures, and serve to sour the temper of the punctual members, who do not like to idle away their time."[74] That time, however, was well spent by the Virginia delegates, who, George Mason reported to his son, "meet and confer together two or three hours every day in order to form a proper correspondence of sentiments; and for form's sake, to see what new deputies are arrived, and to grow into some acquaintance with each other, we regularly meet every day at three o'clock."[75]

Finally, on Friday, 25 May, David Brearly, a delegate from New Jersey, took his seat, making a quorum.[76] Almost immediately, Robert Morris rose to nominate Washington to be president of the convention. Morris's nomination came, Madison noted, "with particular grace as Docr Franklin alone could have been thought of as a competitor. The Docr was himself to have made the nomination of General Washington, but the state of the weather and of his health confined him to his house."[77]

Seconded quickly by John Rutledge of South Carolina, "I was," recorded Washington, "by a unanimous vote called to be President of the body." As the delegates sat in solemn silence, Washington, "like Gustavus Vasa, the deliverer of his country, like Peter the Great, the politician and States-man and like Cincinnatus returned to his farm perfectly contented with being only a plain citizen," addressed the convention. He "thanked the Convention for the honor they had conferred on him, reminded them of the novelty of the scene of business in which he was to act, lamented his want of better qualifications, and claimed the indulgence of the House towards the involuntary errors which his inexperience might occasion."[78] The *Pennsylvania Gazette* went into raptures over Washington's election: "Who can read or hear, that the immortal Washington has again quitted his beloved retirement, and obeyed the voice of God and his country, by accepting the chair of this illustrious body of patriots and heroes, and doubt of the safety and blessings of the government we are to receive from their hands?"[79]

That same day, pushing aside Temple Franklin and John Beckley, the convention elected William Jackson, five states to two, as secretary.[80] Temple's grandfather, according to William Shippen, a prominent Philadelphia merchant, was "much mortified that he had no interest enough to procure the place for his grandson."[81]

With Washington presiding and Jackson recording, the members elected a committee, chaired by George Wythe of Virginia, joined by Alexander Hamilton of New York and South Carolina's Charles Pinckney, "to prepare rules & regulations for conducting the business and after [ap]pointing door keepers the Convention adjourned till Monday [28 May], to give time to the Comee. to report the matters referred to them."[82] The business of the day completed, Washington "[d]ined at Mr. Thos. Willing's and sp[en]t the evening at my lodgings."[83]

Washington had the weekend at leisure. On Saturday "returned all my visits this forenoon." Later, he "dined with a club at the City Tavern," an establishment John Adams described as "the most genteel one in America," where the setting for suppers was "as elegant as ever was laid on a table." He left the club and spent the rest of "the evening at my quarters writing letters." Always savvy when it came to his public image, on Sunday he "went to the Romish Church [St. Mary's]—to high mass."[84]

On Monday, 28 May, the committee "to prepare rules and regulations" made their report. Discussion lasted through Tuesday, with the members finally agreeing to procedures similar to those of the Confederation Congress. The quorum was set at seven states, with "all questions decided by the greater number of those which shall be fully represented." Each state had one vote, which was determined by a vote within the delegation.[85] A state with only one delegate present could not vote, and if a state's delegation was divided, its vote did not count. Each day "after the President shall have taken the Chair, and the members their seats, the minutes of the preceding day shall be read by the Secretary." Over and above the awe he inspired, Washington, as the presiding officer, held considerable authority—most important, the power to decide "all questions of order without appeal or debate." The next day the delegates approved additional rules. In contrast to the usual legislative procedures in the states and the Congress, they agreed "[t]hat no copy be taken of any entry on the Journal, during the sitting of the House, without leave of the House. That members only be permitted to inspect the Journal. That nothing spoken in the House be printed, or otherwise published, or communicated, without leave." While all the delegates agreed to secrecy, not all obeyed. In a more open gesture, they adopted a rule allowing members at almost any time "to reconsider a matter which had been determined by a majority."[86] Such latitude gave wide opportunity for endless backtracking. However, it also permitted delegates to reflect and revise their opinions.

Given the place in which they were meeting—the Pennsylvania State House—members might well have been reminded of the words of William Penn: "Governments, like clocks, go from the motion men give them."[87] The same could be said about the convention, where much of the "motion" was directed by Washington, in whom they had invested considerable power. Washington felt the weight of the moment. If the convention failed, he confided to Jefferson, "anarchy and confusion will inevitably ensue."[88] Seated on a raised platform in an elegant chair positioned behind a simple table, he moderated debate, issued rulings on procedure (not subject to appeal), announced the results of votes, and recognized speakers (or did not), and when he left the chamber, "all members stood while he passed."[89] Although no one doubted that he favored a strong federal government, Washington knew that there was a "diversity of sentiments on this important subject; and to inform the judgment, it is necessary to hear all arguments that can be advanced."[90] Stern, distant, and laconic, Washington rarely spoke in the convention. His magisterial presence was enough to keep order in what might otherwise have been an unruly body. No one questioned his rulings. Gouverneur Morris learned the power of his silent authority when, to win a bet with Alexander Hamilton that he could break Washington's reserve, he approached Washington at an evening reception. He "bowed, shook hands, laid his left hand on Washington's shoulder, 'My dear General I am very happy to see you so well!' Washington withdrew his hand, stepped suddenly back, fixed his eye on Morris for several minutes with an angry frown, until the latter retreated abashed, and sought refuge in the crowd."[91] Later, at dinner, Morris confided to Hamilton, "I have won the bet, but paid dearly for it, and nothing could induce me to repeat it."[92]

Except for Sundays and the time taken for the Committee of Detail to perform its work (26 July–6 August), the convention met six days a week, several hours each day, until adjournment on 17 September. Twelve states—Rhode Island did not attend—elected seventy delegates. Fifty-five attended at various times. Washington and Madison were among only fourteen delegates present at every session. Seven of the delegates had sat in this chamber and voted for independence. Most had served in their state legislatures or Congress. Eighteen were in their twenties or thirties. The average age was forty-two. At eighty-two, Benjamin Franklin was by far the oldest.

While lines of political division were drawn boldly, debates heated, and threats of withdrawal occasionally bandied about, the delegates were tethered by a deference to Washington and a general agreement on two fundamental points: the Articles of Confederation were an inadequate governing tool and ought to be revised or scrapped, and the new government should have three separate branches—executive, a two-house legislature, and a judiciary. Could they fashion, within this framework, a government competent to grapple with issues of national concern, but not so powerful as to overwhelm the authority of the states? How to divide sovereignty? How to account for representation between big states and small states? Not since the heady days of 1775–1776 had the nation seen such a distinguished gathering, including the nation's most eminent citizens, Washington and Franklin. John Dickinson, author of the *Farmers Letters* and former president of Pennsylvania, expressed the sentiments of many, writing to his wife, "My hopes of something good for our Country are strong. Virtue and Wisdom must be employed. May Heaven bless our Endeavours."[93] Having adopted the final set of rules, on Tuesday, 29 May, the convention was ready to begin its "main" work.[94]

Shortly after ten o'clock, having called the meeting to order, Washington, using his power to recognize speakers, gave the floor to Edmund Randolph. Washington's recognition of Randolph was likely part of a strategy that the Virginians had crafted during those hours they had spent together at Mrs. House's. From years of legislative experience, Randolph and his fellow Virginians, skilled parliamentarians, understood that by being the first to put a plan on the floor, they could guide the debate. They decided that Randolph, "being the governor of the State, of distinguished talents, and in the habit of public speaking," would present their plan for the union. James McHenry recalled that Randolph stood before the convention and "decanted with energy on our respective situations from New Hampshire to Georgia, on the situation of our joint national affairs at home and abroad and drew the conclusion that all were on the brink of ruin and dissolution."[95] He laid before the convention a series of fifteen resolutions.[96] W. R. Davie of North Carolina sensed the moment, "the great business of the meeting was brought forward by Virginia with whom the proposition for a convention had originated."[97]

The precise authorship of the fifteen Virginia Resolutions is difficult to discern. Madison later claimed that they were the work of the entire delegation; however, his influence is clear.[98] These resolutions, the essence of which he had shared previously with Jefferson, Randolph, and Washington, called for the creation of a strong central government that could provide "common defense, security of liberty and general welfare." Although they described a separation of powers—legislative, executive, and judicial—the preponderance of authority rested in a "National Legislature to be proportioned to the Quotas of contribution, or to the number of free inhabitants, as the one or the other rule may seem best in different cases." In his speech introducing the resolutions, Randolph was blunt, warning that the nation's "chief danger arises from the democratic parts of our [state] constitutions. It is a maxim which I hold incontrovertible, that the powers of government exercised by the people swallows up the other branches. None of the constitutions have provided sufficient checks against the democracy." The Virginians favored "a strong consolidated union, in which the idea of states would be nearly annihilated," and a system of government established that clearly favored the large states.[99] Randolph's "long and elaborate speech," and the grand sweep of his plan, shook the convention. Needing time to digest what they had heard, the members adjourned the meeting, agreeing that in the morning they would meet as "a Committee of the Whole House to consider of the state of the American Union," and ordered "that the propositions moved by Mr. Randolph be referred to the said Committee."[100]

10

PRESIDENT

Heaven alone can foretell. Integrity and firmness is all that
I can promise—these, be the voyage long or short; never
shall forsake me although I may be deserted by all men.
(GW to HK, 1 April 1789, in *GWP, Pres. Series*, 2:3)

As agreed, on Wednesday morning, 30 May 1787, after "the order
of the day being approved," the convention resolved itself into a
Committee of the Whole House.[1] A convenient parliamentary maneuver, the committee, made up of all the members but meeting outside
the regular session, was less encumbered by rigid rules. Like all commit-
tees, it could not take any final action itself and was empowered only to
report its findings to the full body for action. The committee elected its
own presiding officer, Nathaniel Gorham of Massachusetts, a firm supporter of strong government. As Gorham took the chair, Washington
temporarily relinquished his position to sit with the Virginia delegation.
Calling the committee to order, Gorham recognized Edmund Randolph, who, with a "harmonious voice and striking manners, in a long
and elaborate speech," laid out "the defects in the system of the present
federal government as totally inadequate to the peace, safety and security of the confederation, and the absolute necessity of a more energetic
government." The "confederation," he declared, "is incompetent."[2]

For two weeks the committee, making "progress in the matter to
them referred," debated the resolutions. On 13 June, the committee
reported on "Mr. Randolph's propositions," which during debate had
grown from fifteen to nineteen. In broad terms, Randolph's plan called

for a tripartite "National Government" consisting "of a supreme Legislative, Executive and Judiciary." The "Supreme Legislative," consisting of two chambers, held sweeping powers. It could elect a "National Executive" (which enjoyed veto power over "any legislative act") and appoint all judges in both the "supreme tribunal" and "Inferior tribunals," and, to ensure its national supremacy, it could "negative all laws passed by the several states contravening in the opinion of the National Legislature the articles of union." Firm in support of states' rights, several members bridled at the words "national" and "supreme." Particularly discomforting was the provision that both chambers of the legislature would be chosen on the basis of population determined by "the whole number of white and other free citizens and inhabitants, of every age, sex and condition, including those bound to servitude for term of years, and three fifths of all other persons, not comprehended in the forgoing description, except Indians not paying taxes in each state." By this calculation, Virginia, in combination with two or three other large states, might easily control the nation. Alarmed at such a dire prospect, New York delegate Robert Yates warned that Virginia's plan of national government would "annihilate" state governments.[3]

As debate continued, William Paterson, a delegate from New Jersey, speaking for those who opposed the Virginia Plan, rose and asked for time "to contemplate the plan reported from the Committee of the Whole." Agreeing to Paterson's request, the convention adjourned until the next day (16 June), when Paterson "laid before the Convention the plan which he said several of the deputations wished to be substituted in place of that proposed by Mr. Randolph."[4]

Paterson proposed nine amendments to the articles, representing the views of the less populous states that feared a strong central government with a powerful legislature apportioned by population would run roughshod over their interests. To preserve state sovereignty, the "New Jersey Plan," by simply amending the articles, held to a more federal system in which states, standing equal in the legislature, one state one vote, held the ultimate authority.[5] To give the resolutions "a fair deliberation," the convention agreed to return to a Committee of the Whole "in order to place the two plans in due comparison."[6] On Saturday, 16 June, debate began, with James Wilson of Pennsylvania comparing the two plans point by point, arguing in favor of Virginia's position. Washington sat silent.

On Sunday, 17 June, Washington joined the Morrises at Christ Church to hear Robert Morris's brother-in-law, the recently consecrated bishop William White, "preach and ordain two gentlemen into the order of deacons." After the ceremony, he rode "8 Miles into the Country, dined with Mr. Jno. Ross and returned to Town agn. about dusk."[7]

Debate resumed Monday, 18 June, and continued into Tuesday, when, late in the afternoon, Rufus King of New York moved "that the Committee should rise, and Mr. Randolph's propositions be re-reported without alteration, which was in fact a question whether Mr. Randolph's should be adhered to as preferable to those of Mr. Pater-son." By a vote of 7 (Massachusetts, Connecticut, Pennsylvania, Virginia, North Carolina, South Carolina, and Georgia) to 3 (New York divided, Delaware, New Jersey), King's motion passed.[8] While the large states had scuppered Paterson's resolutions to amend the articles, alone they could not form a new government. They might have won the battle, but they could never win the war. Unless the disaffected states joined, there would be no "government of the United States." A powerful "National" and "Supreme" legislature apportioned by population was unacceptable. Hoping to allay fears, James Wilson, who had argued forcefully against the New Jersey Plan, assured his colleagues that "by National Government, he did not mean one that would swallow up the state governments." He was, he said, "tenacious" to preserve them.[9]

Deadlock loomed. The large states held to their position—a strong legislature apportioned by population. Unwilling to bend, the smaller states threatened to abandon the convention. In the midst of crisis, Washington wrote to Nelly's stepfather, David Stuart:

> Our disorders lie in the different State Governments, and in the tenacity of that power which pervades the whole of their systems. Whilst independent sovereignty is so ardently contended for, whilst the local views of each State and seperate interests by which they are too much govern'd will not yield to a more enlarged scale of politicks; incompatibility in the laws of different States, and disrespect to those of the general government must render the situation of this great Country weak, inefficient, and disgraceful. It has

already done so, almost to the final dissolution of it—weak at home and disregarded abroad is our present condition, and contemptible enough it is.[10]

On 2 July, Roger Sherman of Connecticut, speaking for the small states, declared the convention "at a full stop." Hugh Williamson of North Carolina, a man described by William Pierce as a "Gentleman of education and talents," rose to warn that "[i]f we do not concede on both sides, our business must soon be at an end." Although he opposed "equality of votes in the 2nd branch," to calm the waters, Charles Cotesworth Pinckney of South Carolina, known to speak warmly but not well, proposed a Grand Committee composed of members from each state to consider the issue.[11] Randolph, sensing calamity, acknowledged that "the large states could not subsist of themselves any more than the small." He continued that "although he did not expect much benefit from the expedient," like a majority of the delegates, he supported the appointment of the committee. So "that time might be given to the committee, and to such as choose to attend to the celebration on the anniversary of Independence, the convention adjourned till Thursday."[12]

Taking advantage of a welcome break in the proceedings, on 3 July Washington "attended the Agricultural Society at Carpenters Hall." The Fourth of July was particularly busy. He visited Dr. Abraham Chovet's "Anatomical Museum," an exhibition of wax human figures located on Vidal's Alley. From there he went "to hear an Oration on the anniversary of Independence delivered by a Mr. Mitchell, a student of Law." He dined later that day, "agreeable to invitation" with the Pennsylvania Society of the Cincinnati at the Sign of the Rainbow, a tavern owned by Henry Epple. He ended the day, as was often his custom, enjoying "[t]ea at Mr. Powells."[13] In the midst of this flurry of social activities, Washington also sat, once again, for his portrait painters, Robert Edge Pine and Charles Willson Peale. Pine, anxious "to correct his portrait of me" that he had begun during his whirlwind visit to Mount Vernon nearly two years before, invited Washington to pose for him in his Philadelphia studio. Washington agreed. The next day he took the painter's chair again, this time for Charles Willson Peale, "who wanted my picture to make a print or Metzotinto."[14] To "make the business as convenient as possible," Peale offered to bring his "Pallette and Pensils to Mr. Morris's that [you] might sett at your leisure."[15]

While Washington and other members were at their "leisure," with Elbridge Gerry of Massachusetts in the chair, moving at unwonted speed, the committee, meeting over the holiday, went to work. Oliver Ellsworth of Connecticut, who had been a member of the committee, took ill and was replaced by his colleague Roger Sherman. Together, two men—Sherman, an experienced politician representing a small state, and Benjamin Franklin, the consummate political sage, standing for Pennsylvania—steered the committee toward compromise. On Thursday, 5 July, Gerry reported the committee's recommendation: "That in the first branch of the Legislature each of the States now in the union be allowed one Member for every forty thousand inhabitants," and "that in the second Branch of the Legislature each State shall have an equal Vote."[16] Debate lasted eleven days. Hugh Williamson explained to his fellow North Carolinian James Iredell that "the diverse and almost opposite interests that are to be reconciled, occasion us to progress very slowly."[17] Washington listened and worried. To Alexander Hamilton, who had returned to New York, he wrote that the convention was "in a worse train than ever; you will find but little ground on which the hope of a good establishment, can be formed. In a word, I almost despair of seeing a favourable issue to the proceedings of the Convention and do therefore repent having had any agency in the business."[18] Having exhausted the issues, James Madison noted that Luther Martin of Maryland summed up the feelings of many delegates, arguing to his colleagues that he "did not like having two branches, nor the inequality of votes in the 1st branch. He was willing however to make trial of the plan, rather than do nothing."[19] On 16 July, as the first order of business, by a narrow vote (five in favor, four opposed, one abstention) the convention approved the scheme of representation presented by the committee.[20]

"The Great Compromise" opened the path allowing the convention to move forward. Buoyed by what he saw, Williamson reported to Iredell that "after much labor the Convention have nearly agreed on the principles and outlines of a system, which we hope may fairly be called an amendment of the Federal Government."[21] Following ten days of debate, the convention, by a unanimous vote, ordered that the proceedings be referred to a Committee of Detail "to prepare and report a constitution." They then "adjourned till Monday August 6, that the Committee might have time to prepare and report the Constitution."[22]

During the break, several delegates returned home; Washington, however, remained in Philadelphia. On Monday, 30 July, Washington, "[i]n company with Mr. Govr. Morris, and in his Phaeton with my horses, went up to one Jane Moores to get Trout."[23] The day carried longer than expected, forcing him to cancel a planned evening with Elizabeth Powel, to whom he wrote a hasty note of apology:

> Genl. Washington presents his respectful compliments to Mrs. Powell, and would, with great pleasure, have made one of a party for the School for Scandal this evening; had not everything been arranged, & Mr. Govr. Morris and himself on the point of stepping into the Carriage for a fishing expedition at Jenny Moores; at Which place Mr. & Mrs. Robt. Morris is to be tomorrow, to partake of the successes, of Mr. Govr. Morris & himself this day. The Genl. can but regret that matters have turned out so unluckily, after waiting so long to receive a lesson in the School for Scandal.[24]

Morris's fishing spot was close by Valley Forge. Leaving the trout to Morris, the next day, Tuesday, 31 July, Washington "rid over the old Cantonment of the American [army] of the Winter 1777, & 8. Visited all the Works, wch. were in Ruins; and the Encampments in woods where the ground had not been cultivated." On his return he stopped to chat with "some farmers at work" to inquire about growing buckwheat.[25] After a few days back in Philadelphia, he went fishing again with the Morrises, "not very successfully."[26]

Washington returned to Philadelphia late on 5 August. The next morning, the convention reconvened with Washington in the chair. John Rutledge presented the committee's report, which was "read once throughout and copies thereof given to the members."[27] Although several changes were still to come, the printed document—a preamble and twenty-three articles—carried the essence of the final constitution: a bicameral legislature, with equal representation in the Senate and apportionment by population in the House; an executive titled president; an independent judiciary; a list of powers granted to the legislature, including authority "to make all laws that shall be necessary and proper for carrying into execution the foregoing powers."[28] Given a day to review the report, debate got underway on Tuesday morning, at which point Charles Pinckney moved to refer the report to a Committee of the Whole. Several members "strongly opposed" the motion "as likely to produce unnecessary delay." The motion failed. Debate proceeded.[29] For the next six weeks, the convention met (Sundays excepted) without interruption from 10:00 a.m. to 4:00 p.m., pausing only for lunch or refreshments.[30]

Debate was often boring, as members repeated arguments. Washington, silent as always except when procedural matters required his attention, kept to his routine, often dining "in a family way at Mr. Morris's" and then spending the rest of the evening "in my own room" writing letters.[31] During his stay in Philadelphia, Washington wrote and received more than 130 letters. His most frequent correspondent was George Augustine. Abiding by the rules, none of Washington's letters contained any specific information about the convention.[32]

It had been twelve weeks since he had arrived in Philadelphia. Washington was frustrated. Writing to his faraway friend, Gilbert du Motier, the marquis de Lafayette, with whom he often shared opinions he withheld from those closer to home, he lamented the weakness of America:

> Vain is it to look for respect from abroad, or tranquility at home—vain is it to murmur at the detention of our Western Posts—or complain of the restriction of our commerce—vain are the attempts to remedy the evil complained of by Mr Dumas to discharge the interest due on foreign loans, vain is it to talk of chastising the Algerines, or doing ourselves Justice in any other respect, till the wisdom and force of the Union can be more concentrated and better applied.[33]

Others were equally concerned. John Dickinson, fearing his colleagues were veering wildly from practical concerns, warned the convention that "[e]xperience must be our only guide. Reason may mislead us."[34]

On Sunday, 19 August, after listening patiently to testy debates over requirements for election to the House, congressional pay, executive veto, issuing paper money, the war powers of Congress, and the role of a standing army, Washington yearned for compromise. He hoped, he wrote to Henry Knox, that "a disposition may be found in Congress— the several State Legislatures—and the community at large to adopt the Government which may be agreed on in Convention; because I am fully persuaded it is the best that can be obtained at the present moment, under such diversity of ideas as prevail."[35] While Washington hoped for resolution and compromise, other delegates grew increasingly impatient. The convention debated the articles line by line.[36] In an irascible mood, Elbridge Gerry, "a man of sense but a Grumbletonian," wrote home to his wife, Ann, "I never was sicker of anything than I am of conventionering: had I known what would have happened, nothing would have introduced me to come here. I am and must be patient a little longer."[37] Hope, patience, and exhaustion were propelling the convention to finish its work.

As August passed, debate focused on what vote in the convention was necessary for approval of the document. Daniel Carroll of Maryland called for "unanimity." He stood alone. Sherman came partway to Carroll's position, noting that since "the states now confederated by articles require unanimity in changes, he thought the ratification in this case of ten states at least ought to be made necessary." Edmund Randolph held that nine was the proper number. James Wilson argued eight was "preferable." Dickinson wondered about the "refusing states, could they be deserted?" To that, Madison responded strongly "that if the blank should be filled with seven eight or nine, the Constitution as it stands might be put in force over the whole body of the people tho' less than a majority of them should ratify it." On that harsh note, the meeting adjourned.[38] With the issue unresolved, two days later, Friday, 31 August, "a private conference" according to James McHenry was held "before the meeting of this convention."[39] Likely, it was at this "private" meeting that Washington let it be known that he favored seven.[40] When the convention reconvened, in rapid succession the members turned away motions calling for the approval of thirteen, ten, or seven states, settling on nine; a neat compromise, it passed 10–1. Next came the issue of state ratification. After opponents failed to postpone consideration, by a vote of 10–1 the convention agreed "[t]hat the Constitution shall be laid before the U.S. in Congress assembled; and it is the opinion of this Convention that it should afterwards be submitted to a convention chosen in each State in order to receive the ratification of such convention: to which end the several Legislatures ought to provide for the calling Conventions within their respective States as speedily as circumstances will permit."[41]

The convention continued its work until Saturday, 8 September, when, having approved the amended articles, they elected "a Committee of five (Gouverneur Morris, Alexander Hamilton, James Madison, Samuel Johnson, and Rufus King) to revise the style of and arrange the articles agreed to by the House."[42] That same day, an expectant Washington wrote George Augustine, "The probability is, that the Convention will have completed the business which brought the delegates together in the course of this week. God grant I may not be disappointed in this expectation, as I am quite homesick."[43] Leaving a good deal of the work to Morris, from Saturday afternoon, 8 September, until Tuesday evening, 11 September, the committee reworked the preamble while consolidating and reorganizing the twenty-three articles into a succinct seven. On Wednesday morning, the committee report was "read by paragraph." George Mason, noting its absence, stood to argue for a bill of rights that "*would* give great quiet to the people; and with aid of the State declarations, a bill might be prepared in a few hours." Gerry supported him. All ten states present rejected the proposal.[44] Members presented other changes. Finally, late Saturday (15 September), after a lengthy session that lasted until six o'clock in the evening, the members, approving the final text, adjourned the convention. That evening, Washington, alone in his room at the Morrises', confided to his diary, "Concluded the business of Convention, all to signing the proceedings; and adjourned till Monday that the Constitution which it was proposed to offer to the People might be engrossed and a number of printed copies struck off."[45]

Secretary William Jackson carried the final document to Jacob Shallus, the assistant clerk of the Pennsylvania Assembly, for engrossing. Following the English tradition of copying important documents on parchment (a specially treated animal skin far more durable than paper), Shallus began the painstaking work. He first drew faint guidelines, and then, using quill pens dipped in iron gall ink, he spent Sunday carefully copying the document onto four pages each measuring twenty-eight by twenty-three inches.[46]

On Monday, 17 September, the delegates gathered for the signing, but not before an important change was made. On the previous Wednesday, Hugh Williamson of North Carolina, wishing to reduce the number of constituents per House member—then set at forty thousand—to a lesser figure, had moved "to increase the number of representatives." His effort failed. Sensing this idea might be popular at home, while nodding to the interest of his southern colleagues, Nathaniel Gorham asked Washington, "if it was not too late, he could wish, for the purpose of lessening objections to the Constitution, that" the number forty thousand be reduced to thirty thousand. In a rare moment, "when rising for the purpose of putting the question," Washington noted, "late as the present moment was for admitting amendments," he offered his own opinion, thinking "this of so much consequence that it would give much satisfaction to see it adopted." With Washington's blessing, Gorham's motion passed unanimously.[47] The convention then returned to the main question, Washington asking whether the body "agree to the Constitution enrolled to be signed. It was agreed to by all the States."[48]

As the members approached to sign, Franklin, according to Madison,

> [l]ooking towards the President's chair from which Washington had presided, on the back of which a rising sun happened to be painted, observed to a few members near him, that Painters had found it difficult to distinguish it in their art a rising from a setting sun. I have, said he, often in the course of the session, and the vicissitudes of my hopes and fears as to its issue, looked at that behind the President without being able to tell whether it was rising or setting: But now at length I have the happiness to know that it is a rising and not a setting Sun.[49]

All the members signed, "except Mr. Randolph, Mr. Mason and Mr. Gerry who declined giving it the sanction of their names."[50] Randolph would later support ratification; Mason and Gerry did not. Having approved the document, the convention instructed Secretary Jackson to carry the Constitution to Congress. Members were given printed copies, and the "injunction of secrecy [was] taken off."[51] They adjourned at four o'clock, "sine die."[52] That evening the New Hampshire delegate, Nicholas Gilman, a late arrival to the convention, summed up the feelings of many, including Washington, when he wrote to his brother that the constitution was "the best that could meet the unanimous concurrence of the states in Convention; it was done by bargain and compromise, yet notwithstanding its imperfections on the adoption of it depends whether we shall become a respectable nation, or a people torn to pieces by intestine commotions, and rendered contemptible for ages."[53]

In his last official act as president of the convention, Washington wrote to Congress that it was his "honor to submit that Constitution which has appeared to us the most advisable." For their guidance, he enclosed the convention's "opinion" that the Constitution "should be submitted to a Convention of Delegates, chosen in each State by the People thereof, under the Recommendation of its Legislature, for their Assent and Ratification." As soon as nine states had ratified it, Congress "should fix a Day on which Electors should be appointed by the States which shall have ratified the same, and a Day on which the Electors should assemble to vote for the President, and the Time and Place for commencing Proceedings under this Constitution."[54]

That evening, as was his wont, Washington recorded the day: "The business being thus closed, the Members adjourned to the City Tavern, dined together, and took a cordial leave of each other—after which I returned to my lodgings." Shortly after he retired, Secretary Jackson arrived. "Having," at the instructions of the convention, "burned all the loose scraps of paper," he delivered to "the General the journal and other papers" of the convention, which he was to retain, "subject to the order of Congress, if ever formed under the Constitution."[55] Alone, Washington took the moment "to meditate on the momentous wk. which had been executed, after not less than five, for a large part of the time Six, and sometimes 7 hours sitting every day, sundays & the ten days adjournment to give a Comee. opportunity & time to arrange the business for more than four Months."[56]

In the morning, Washington sent copies of the Constitution to Thomas Jefferson and Lafayette. His accompanying note to the former was brief and without comment, but to Lafayette he confided that the Constitution "is now a Child of fortune, to be fostered by some and buffeted by others. [W]hat will be the General opinion on, or the reception of it, is not for me to decide, nor shall I say anything for or against it—if it be good I suppose it will work its way good—if bad it will recoil on the Framers."[57] Washington's letter to Lafayette, distancing himself from events in Philadelphia, is surprising only in that he did not, yet again, repeat his claim of retiring in "the shadow of my own Vine and my own fig tree."[58] Even as far away as Paris, it was clear, as his friend Lafayette noted, that Washington "Cannot Refuse Being Elected president."[59]

After finishing his "private business," Washington dined with the Morrises, and then, bidding farewell to his hosts, in his newly refurbished chariot, "in Company with Mr. Blair," he set off for home. Staying the night in Chester, the next morning, "[p]revented by Rain much of wch. fell in the Night," Washington and Blair, hoping for better weather, delayed their departure until later in the day. Not all went well. Washington recorded a near disaster trying to cross Christiana Creek:

> The rain which had fallen the preceding evening having swelled the Water considerably there was no fording it safely. I was reduced to the necessity therefore of remaining on the other side or of attempting to cross on an old, rotten & long disused bridge. Being anxious to get on I preferred the latter and in the attempt one of my horses fell 15 feet at least the other very near following which (had it happened) would have taken the Carriage with baggage along with him and destroyed the whole effectually. However, by prompt assistance of some people at a Mill just by and great exertion, the first horse was disengaged from his harness, the 2d. prevented from going quite through and drawn off and the Carriage rescued from hurt.[60]

The remainder of the trip proved uneventful. Finally, on Saturday, 22 September, Washington "[b]reakfasted at Bladensburg—passed thro George Town—dined at Alexandria and reached home by Sun set after being absent 4 Months & 14 days."[61] The next day, to welcome him, more than a dozen friends and relatives gathered, including "Cols. Fitzgerald, Simms, Ramsay & Lyles, Mr. Hunter, Mr. Murray Mr. Taylor Doctr. & Mrs. Stuart & the Girls."[62] Released from the pledge of secrecy, the conversation was lively.

At the time Washington and Blair were heading south, Secretary Jackson was riding hard for New York, arriving in the city on 19 September. The next day the papers from Philadelphia were "received and read," and although, according to William Bingham, "every State on the Floor of Congress is disposed to adopt it," action was postponed until "Wednesday next."[63] On Wednesday, 26 September, Congress opened debate on the Constitution. After two days of deliberation, in language deliberately neutral, they "[r]esolved unanimously, That the said report with the resolutions and letter accompanying the same be transmitted to the several legislatures in order to be submitted to a convention of delegates chosen in each state by the people thereof in conformity to the resolves of the Convention made and provided in that case."[64] That afternoon, Charles Thomson, repeating the language of Congress, dispatched a "Circular Letter to the Executives of the States," ordering them to submit "the report of the convention lately assembled in Philadelphia, to a convention of delegates chosen by the people thereof, in conformity to the resolves of the Convention made and provided in that case."[65]

Thanks to the dispersal of the members back to their homes, and the printing press, news spread rapidly. In Philadelphia, only a few hours after the convention adjourned, John Dunlap and David Claypoole, publishers of the *Pennsylvania Packet*, printed five hundred copies of a six-page broadside that included a copy of the Constitution, Washington's letter to Congress, and the resolutions of the convention concerning ratification.[66] As they left, each delegate received several copies, which they carried home to state executives, families, and friends. By late October, nearly every newspaper in America had printed the Constitution.

Washington was pleased with the results of the convention. While he wished for a stronger central government (i.e., the Virginia Plan), he was willing to accept compromise.[67] Reflecting on the weeks spent in Philadelphia and the "diversity of interests" at play, he told David Humphreys, who had initially been skeptical, that the Constitution "is not free from imperfections; but there are as few radical defects in it as could well be expected." Having lived through more than two decades of revolutionary change, Washington grasped the evolving nature of politics. He confided to Humphreys, "I think it would be wise in the People to adopt what is offered to them," but then, with an eye to posterity, he went on to emphasize that the convention had opened "a constitutional door for future alterations and amendments."[68] To his friend and admirer, Catharine Sawbridge Macaulay Graham, he wrote that after the "various & opposite interests" were accounted for, it was "much to be wondered at, that anything could have been produced with such unanimity as the Constitution proposed."[69]

With his customary reserve—always useful in political matters—Washington again stood as the great leader, shunning fame and glory. Nonetheless, it is likely that nothing would have come forth from the convention without his participation. James Monroe, who had not been at the convention but was well informed, had no doubt about Washington's role. Washington, he told Jefferson, "carried this government."[70] "His largest contribution," according to his preeminent biographer, Douglas Southall Freeman, "was not that of his counsel but that of his presence."[71] There was little doubt that Washington, silent except in his role as chair but never absent from a session, supported the Virginia Plan—a strong central government dominated by a legislature apportioned by population.[72] Eight years of experience in a war during which he answered to a weak Congress, riven by rancorous states, convinced him that the "monster—sovereignty which have taken such fast hold on the states" must be lodged in a central government competent to rein in the states and govern a nation.[73] Washington and his fellow Virginians watched with dismay as the convention gradually dismantled important parts of their plan. In the end, Mason, lamenting the absence of a Declaration of Rights, declared that he would rather "bury his bones" in Philadelphia than leave without the bill of rights.[74] Randolph, casting a second (albeit less dramatic) *no*, thought a second convention ought to be called to remedy certain defects. Whatever sympathy he might have had with Mason and Randolph, Washington, satisfied with the document and having wagered his reputation on a successful outcome, stood steady in support.

Having spent four months closeted in a stuffy chamber listening to long, often repetitive speeches, Washington was pleased to be home. On Monday morning, 24 September, he returned happily to his usual schedule. "After breakfast I rid to the Plantatns. at the Ferry—Frenchs—Dogue run & Muddy hole." It was harvest time, and the "hands were getting out Wheat & Rye."[75] That evening he forwarded a copy of the Constitution to Virginia's governor, Benjamin Harrison, offering "no observations."[76]

While citizens digested the "Constitution," Washington resumed offering his standard hospitality. Visitors continued to arrive. Early in November, "Mr. & Mrs. Powell of Philadelphia came in." They stayed a week, during which Washington took them "to view the Ruins of Belvoir." It was here as a young man that he had made, in company with his brother Lawrence and the Fairfaxes, lifelong friendships. Those were, he said, "the happiest moments of my life."[77] Alexander Donald, a Richmond tobacco merchant, visited Washington shortly after his return from Philadelphia and reported to Jefferson that the general "is in perfect good health, and looks almost as well as he did Twenty years ago. I never saw him so keen for anything in my life, as he is for the adoption of the new Form of Government." Donald went on to note, "As the eyes of all America are turned towards this genuinely Great and Good Man, for the First President, I took the liberty of sounding him upon it." Washington gave his usual response that he was "greatly against going into Publick Life again, Pleads in Excuse for himself, His Love of Retirement, and his advanced Age, but Notwithstanding of these," Donald concluded, "I am fully of opinion he may be induced to appear once more on the Publick Stage of Life."[78]

Early news boded well. By the end of the year, ten states had called conventions.[79] From Boston, Knox reported, "The new constitution is received with boundless joy by all the commercial part of the community. The people of Boston are in raptures with it. The people of Jersey and Connecticut who are not commercial embrace it with ardor."[80] In Virginia, meetings in Alexandria, Williamsburg, and Fredericksburg called for a ratifying convention. Nonetheless, Washington worried. He told Knox affairs did not auger well in Virginia. Opposition was rising.[81] "The refusal of our Govr and Colo. Mason to subscribe to the proceedings of the Convention will have a bad effect in this State."[82] Sensing adverse political winds, Madison warned Washington that, while momentum was moving in their favor, opponents were lying in wait and "will naturally be latest in shewing."[83] Madison was prescient. A few days later, Washington received a letter from Patrick Henry, portending problems. Long an opponent of a stronger federal government, and a key figure in Virginia politics, Henry wrote, "I have to lament, that I cannot bring my Mind to accord with the proposed Constitution. The Concern I feel on this Account, is really greater than I am able to express."[84] Mason, too, shared his opinions with Washington, announcing that the Constitution "shall have every Opposition in my Power to give it."[85] Randolph, however, although he had not signed the Constitution, was more equivocal. His faithful correspondent, Madison, sitting with Congress in New York, kept Washington well informed— eleven letters from 30 September to 31 December.[86] Nearer to home Washington had another trusted correspondent—David Stuart. Sitting in the Virginia House as a delegate from Fairfax County, he informed Washington that they had voted that "the proceedings of the Federal Convention transmitted to the General Assembly through the medium of Congress, be submitted to a Convention of the people for their full and free investigation, discussion, and decision." The convention was called for "Monday in June next."[87] Elected to the convention, Stuart wrote frequently to Washington, often providing detailed personal information.[88] "Pope and Chichester have been very active in alarming the people. The later had his pockets full of Mason's objections, which he leaves wherever he calls."[89]

From New York, Madison reported to Washington that Congress, unable to assemble a quorum, had fallen into an "interregnum" that might "continue throughout the winter." That interregnum might well have been a blessing, since it permitted Madison time to help write *The Federalist Papers*, the first seven of which he sent to Washington on 18 November.[90] Although he was "one of the pens concerned in the task," to hide his involvement, he asked Washington whether he might put the essays, without revealing authorship, "into the hand of some of your confidential correspondents at Richmond who would have them reprinted there."[91] Washington, recalling the heady days of the polemical writings of the 1760s and 1770s, and understanding that ratification "will depend on literary abilities, & the recommendation of it by good pens," readily complied, and, a few days after receiving the essays, he forwarded them to Stuart in Richmond.[92] The essays were, he said, an "antidote" to those "who wish to see these states divided into several confederacies." He told Stuart, "If there is a Printer in Richmond who is really well disposed to support the New Constitution, he would do well to give them a place in his Paper. They are written by able men; and before they are finished, will, if I mistake not, place matters in a true point of light." He was "not at liberty to disclose their names," and, concurrently, he asked that his name not appear as well.[93]

Washington's request to Stuart was typical of his posture during the ratification process. While Federalists touted his support, pointing out that he had signed the Constitution, in public, aside from his transmittal letter to Congress, he was cautious. Privately, he was less restrained. In one instance, his openness cost him dearly. Penning a long letter to Charles Carter, dealing almost entirely with potatoes, carrots, and turnips, he went astray. In a final paragraph, he gave his candid opinion, telling Carter that "there is no alternative between the adoption of the [Constitution] and anarchy."[94] To his dismay, two weeks later portions of the letter appeared in the *Virginia Herald*. From there it was widely reprinted. Deeply annoyed, Washington, who loathed seeing his private views bandied about in public, chastised Carter, writing that it gave him great "pain to see the hasty, and indigested production of a private letter, handed to the public, to be animadverted upon by the adversaries of the new Government."[95]

Momentum was on the side of ratification. By the end of 1787, three states—Delaware, Pennsylvania, and New Jersey—had ratified. The day after New Year's, Georgia did the same. As the "high probability of a general adoption of the Federal Constitution" grew, so, too, did the call for Washington to be president.[96] Even Humphreys came around. Writing from New Haven, he urged Washington to listen to his "good Angel. What will tend, perhaps, more than anything to the adoption of the new System, will be a universal opinion of your being elected President of the United States, and an expectation that you will accept it for a while."[97] A month later, Gouverneur Morris was even more blunt: "As it is, should the Idea prevail that you would not accept of the Presidency it would prove fatal in many Parts. Truth is, that your great and decided Superiority leads Men willingly to put you in a Place which will not add to your personal Dignity, nor raise you higher than you already stand." Three weeks later, the brace of Morrises—Robert and Gouverneur—arrived at Mount Vernon to lobby in person.[98] Other friends and public figures chimed in as well, including John Armstrong; Lafayette; Jean-Baptiste-Donatien de Vimeur, the comte de Rochambeau; and Hamilton, all urging him to accept the presidency.[99]

No one in America possessed greater stature. Washington was the only living person in the nation whose birthday was celebrated.[100] Newspapers, including the widely read *Pennsylvania Packet*, repeatedly mentioned him. At Fourth of July festivities, the paper reported, a toast was drunk to "Farmer Washington—may he be like a second Cincinnatus, be called from the plow to rule a great people." Echoes reverberated in Frederick, Maryland: "May the Saviour of America gratify the ardent wishes of his countrymen by accepting the position which the voice of mankind has assigned him." In York, Pennsylvania, "Great Washington shall rule the land," and from New England Benjamin Lincoln urged him to "the acceptance of the presidency."[101] As ratification advanced, more letters, praising and pressuring, arrived. Sensitive to the impropriety of being seen as ambitious, or self-serving, Washington sought to deflect the attention.[102] It was a losing battle.

On 23 May 1788, South Carolina became the eighth state to ratify. Since Article 7 provided that "nine States, shall be sufficient for the Establishment of this Constitution," the news from the South meant that only one more state needed to act. Since conventions in New Hampshire and Virginia were well advanced, Washington was optimistic, writing to Lafayette, "The plot thickens fast. A few short weeks will determine the political fate of America."[103] From Madison he continued to receive almost daily accounts of the convention's proceedings in Richmond. Although there were those who would "leap into the dark consequences of rejection," Washington had "no doubt but that the good sense of this Country will prevail." Late on Wednesday, 25 June, following long debate, the vote was taken. Madison, in a hurried note, reported the good news to Washington: "ratification passed 89 ayes—79 noes."[104] Reveling in the victory, on Friday, 27 June, the citizens of Alexandria, "federal to a man," hosted Washington and his family at a celebration where "the Cannon roared, and the Town was illuminated." In his tavern at the corner of Fairfax and Cameron Streets, John Wise provided a "magnificent" dinner. "Ears were saluted at every quaff with the melody of federal Guns."[105] Guests offered toasts celebrating that Virginia, the ninth state to ratify, made the union possible. Before dawn, as the guests recovered from their celebratory evening, an express rider from New York, Colonel David Henley, arrived with news that tempered local enthusiasm.[106] Virginia was not the ninth state to ratify. Four days before Virginia had acted, the New Hampshire convention, voting 57–47, had ratified. Putting the best face on it, Washington noted that Henley's dispatches were simply part of a "flood of good news that gave abundant cause for rejoicing in a place, the Inhabitants of which are all federal."[107]

On 2 July, receiving news of New Hampshire's ratification, the president of Congress, Cyrus Griffin, ordered a committee to "report an act to Congress for putting the said constitution into operation."[108] Following more than two months of debate, much of it swirling around where the new government ought to meet, on 13 September, Congress set

> the first Wednesday in January next [1789] to be the day for appointing electors in the several states, which before the said day shall have ratified the said constitution; that the first Wednesday in February next be the day for the electors to assemble in their respective states and vote for a president; and that the first Wednesday in March next be the time and the present seat [i.e., New York City] of Congress the place for commencing proceedings under the said constitution.[109]

In accordance with Article 2 of the Constitution, votes of the electors were to be counted "in the presence of the Senate and the House of Representatives, where the person with the greatest number of votes shall be the president [and] after the Choice of the President, the Person having the greatest Number of Votes of the Electors shall be the Vice

President."[110] While Congress debated, on 26 July New York, by a narrow vote, 30–27, ratified, becoming the "eleventh pillar."[111]

Although Washington trotted out the usual disclaimers shunning public office (how many times had he offered them?), it was clear that he was "the unanimous voice of this rising empire" to be the first president.[112] Less certain was the vice president. As usual, sectionalism was key.

In a situation reminiscent of June 1775 when Congress, seeking to unite the colonies in rebellion, selected a Virginian to command a predominantly Yankee army, this instance again called for geographical balance. Two candidates emerged, both from Massachusetts—John Hancock and John Adams. Ironically, in 1775 it was Hancock, then president of the Congress with "an ambition to be appointed commander-in-chief," who lost out to Washington, whose strongest supporter was John Adams.[113]

Vexed by chronic gout, an ailment he often used to avoid difficult political situations, Hancock—whose own personality would hardly allow him to ever play a secondary role, particularly under his former rival, Washington—was, despite rumors to the contrary, an unlikely candidate. Adams, although stubborn and outspoken, had impeccable credentials. Only recently returned from England (June 1788), he enjoyed the advantage of having been abroad for most of the Revolution, earning an impressive reputation as a successful diplomat while avoiding direct involvement in domestic politics. Like Washington, when his name was mentioned for higher office, Adams rejected such notions, arguing that his only desire was to return to "Braintree and embrace it with both arms and all my might. There to live. There to die, there to lay my bones."[114] Abigail ("Nabby"), his young daughter, who knew her father well, had a more sensible view: "Shall he retire from the world and bury himself amongst his books, and live only for himself? No—I wish it not. . . . He would not, I am well convinced, be happy in private life."[115] Whatever public pronouncements they uttered in the name of public virtue, neither Washington nor Adams were ready for retirement.

On 6 April 1789, Richard Henry Lee's arrival gave the Senate a quorum. The president of the Senate, New Hampshire's John Langdon, ordered that "Mr. Ellsworth inform the House of Representatives that the Senate is now ready in the Senate Chamber, to proceed, in the presence of the House, to discharge its duty." Members of the House attended. The clerk opened and counted the ballots "for President and Vice President of the United States." Out of the 138 ballots cast, Washington received 69, a unanimous vote; John Adams, second with 34 votes, was chosen vice president.[116] The next morning Langdon dispatched the ever-reliable Charles Thomson with a letter informing Washington that he had "the honor to transmit to your Excellency the information of your unanimous election to the office of President of the United States of America." Langdon added, "Suffer me, Sir to indulge the hope, that so auspicious a mark of public confidence will meet your approbation and be considered as a sure pledge of the affection and support you are to expect from a free and enlightened people."[117]

As he awaited the news, Washington told Knox that he had "feelings not unlike those of a culprit who is going to the place of his execution: so unwilling am I, in the evening of a life nearly consumed in public cares, to quit a peaceful abode for an Ocean of difficulties, without that competency of political skill—abilities & inclination which is necessary to manage the helm. I am sensible, that I am embarking the voice of my Countrymen."[118]

Although "much impeded by tempestuous weather, bad roads, and the many large rivers I had to cross, on Tuesday, the 14th about 12 o'clock," Thomson arrived at Mount Vernon.[119] Washington was ready. On Thursday morning "[a]bout ten o'clock I bade adieu to Mount Vernon, to private life, and to domestic felicity; and with a mind oppressed with more anxious and painful sensations than I have words to express, set out for New York in company with Mr. Thomson, and colonel Humphries, with the best dispositions to render service to my country in obedience to its call, but with less hope of answering its expectations."[120] The "vine and fig tree" would have to wait.

ABBREVIATIONS

BF	Benjamin Franklin
DEGW	*Digital Encyclopedia of George Washington*
DHRC	*The Documentary History of the Ratification of the Constitution*
Farrand	Max Farrand, ed., *The Records of the Federal Convention of 1787*, 3 vols.
FOL	Founders Online
GAW	George Augustine Washington
GW	George Washington
GWP, Col. Series	*George Washington Papers, Colonial Series*
GWP, Conf. Series	*George Washington Papers, Confederation Series*
GWP, Diaries	*George Washington Papers, Diaries*
GWP, Pres. Series	*George Washington Papers, Presidential Series*
GWP, Ret. Series	*George Washington Papers, Retirement Series*
GWP, Rev. Series	*George Washington Papers, Revolutionary War Series*
HK	Henry Knox
Idzerda	Stanley J. Idzerda, ed., *Lafayette in the Age of the American Revolution: Selected Letters and Papers, 1776–1790*, 5 vols.
JAW	John Augustine Washington
JCC	*Journals of the Continental Congress*
JJ	John Jay
JJP	*Papers of John Jay*
JM	James Madison
JMP, Cong. Series	*Papers of James Madison, Congressional Series*
JMP, Ret. Series	*Papers of James Madison, Retirement Series*

JMP, Sec. State Series	*Papers of James Madison, Secretary of State Series*
JVHD	*Journal of the Virginia House of Delegates (Journal of the House of Delegates of the Commonwealth of Virginia)*
LC	Library of Congress
LD	*Letters of Delegates to Congress*
LW	Lund Washington
ML	Gilbert du Motier, Marquis de Lafayette
MW	Martha Washington
ODNB	*Oxford Dictionary of National Biography*
OED	*Oxford English Dictionary*
PMH and B	*Pennsylvania Magazine of History and Biography*
RHL	Richard Henry Lee
TJ	Thomas Jefferson
TJP, Main Series	*Papers of Thomas Jefferson, Main Series*
TJP, Ret. Series	*Papers of Thomas Jefferson, Retirement Series*
VMH and B	*Virginia Magazine of History and Biography*
WMQ	*William and Mary Quarterly*

NOTES

INTRODUCTION

1. Founders Online, "Editorial Note: George Washington's Resignation as Commander-in-Chief," National Archives, https://founders.archives.gov /documents/Jefferson/01-06-02-0319-0001.

2. Joseph Hillman, "Resignation of Military Commission," in *Digital Encyclopedia of George Washington*, https://www.mountvernon.org/library/digital history/digital-encyclopedia/article/resignation-of-military-commission.

3. Mary V. Thompson, "Eleanor 'Nelly' Parke Custis," in *Digital Encyclopedia of George Washington*, https://www.mountvernon.org/library/digitalhis tory/digital-encyclopedia/article/eleanor-nelly-parke-custis.

CHAPTER 1. HOME

1. JM to TJ, 10 December 1783, in *JMP, Cong. Series*, 7:401. Irma Jaffe, *John Trumbull: Patriot Artist of the American Revolution* (New York: Graphic Society, 1975), 234–63. Also depicted but not present was James Madison.

2. GW to Patrick Henry, 28 March 1778, in *GWP, Rev. Series*, 7:401.

3. "Report of a Committee on Arrangements for the Public Audience," 22 December 1783, in *TJP, Main Series*, 6:142; *JCC*, 25:837–38.

4. "Washington's Address to Congress 23 December 1783," in *JCC*, 25:837–38. One month later, Washington had second thoughts about returning his commission. He wrote to Charles Thomson, "If my Commission is not necessary for the files of Congress, I should be glad to have it deposited amongst my own Papers. It may serve some fifty or a hundd. years hence for

a theme to ruminate upon, contemplatively disposed" (*GWP, Conf. Series*, 2 January 1784, 1:71). The commission was never returned and resides today among the Washington Papers at the Library of Congress.

5. James McHenry to Margaret Caldwell, 23 December 1783, in *LD*, 21:221.

6. "An Account of a Visit Made to Washington at Mount Vernon by an English Gentleman [John Hunter] in 1785," *PMH and B* 17 (1893):7; GW to James McHenry, 29 May 1797, *GWP, Rev. Series*, 1:159.

7. Quoted in "George Washington's Study," in *DEGW*, https://www.mountvernon.org/library/digitalhistory/digital-encyclopedia/article/george-washingtons-study.

8. GW to David Humphreys, 25 July 1785, in *GWP, Conf. Series*, 3:148; Stanley Cushing, *The George Washington Library Collection* (Boston: Boston Athenaeum, 1997), 9; Paul K. Longmore, *The Invention of George Washington* (Berkeley: University of California Press, 1989), 214.

9. GW to William Stephens Smith, 21 May 1783, FOL.

10. Kevin J. Hayes, *George Washington: A Life in Books* (New York: Oxford University Press, 2017), 94.

11. "Library on the Potomac," George Washington's Mount Vernon, https://www.mountvernon.org/george-washington/take-note/library-on-the-potomac/; Cushing, *George Washington Library Collection*, 28–36.

12. Mary V. Thompson, "Christmas at Mount Vernon," in *Mount Vernon Ladies Association Annual Report* (Mount Vernon, VA: Mount Vernon Ladies Association, 1990), 24–30.

13. The marriage date was 6 January 1759.

14. David Ludlum, *Early American Winters, 1604–1820* (Boston: American Meteorological Society, 1966), 151; Anne-Cesar de La Luzerne de Beuzeville, Chevalier to GW, 18 February 1784, in *GWP, Conf. Series*, 1:128.

15. GW to Burwell Bassett, 20 June 1773, in *GWP, Col. Series*, 9:243.

16. GW to Jonathan Boucher, 16 December 1770, in *GWP, Col. Series*, 8:411.

17. Helen Bryan, *Martha Washington: First Lady of Liberty* (New York: Wiley, 2002), 255.

18. Eleanor Parke Custis to Elizabeth Bordley, 19 October 1795, in *George Washington's Beautiful Nelly: The Letters of Eleanor Parke Custis to Elizabeth Bordley Gibson, 1794–1851*, ed. Patricia Brady (Columbia: University of South Carolina Press, 1991), 21–23.

19. Lund's and George Washington's great-grandfathers were brothers.

20. Gerald Edward Kahler, "Gentlemen of the Family: General George Washington's Aides-de-Camp and Military Secretaries" (MA thesis, University of Richmond, 1997), https://scholarship.richmond.edu/cgi/viewcontent.cgi?article=1623&context=masters-theses.

21. Frank Landon Humphreys, *Life and Times of David Humphreys* (New York: Putnam, 1917), 148; David Humphreys, *Life of General Washington*, ed. with an introduction by Rosemary Zagarri (Athens: University of Georgia Press, 1991), xvi; David Humphreys, "An Address to the Armies of the United States of America" (New Haven, CT: T. and S. Green, 1780).

22. Emily Stone Whiteley, *Washington and His Aides-de-Camp* (New York: Macmillan, 1936), 65.

23. For a discussion of the role of fame among leaders of the Revolution, see *The Spur of Fame: Dialogues of John Adams and Benjamin Rush, 1805–1813*, ed. John A. Schutz and Douglass Adair (San Marino, CA: Huntington Library, 1966). This discussion of Washington's papers relies on William M. Fowler Jr., *American Crisis: George Washington and the Dangerous Two Years after Yorktown, 1781–1783* (New York: Walker, 2011), 225–26.

24. GW to John Hancock, 13 August 1776, in *GWP, Rev. Series*, 6:4.

25. GW to Colonel Richard Varick, 25 May 1781, FOL.

26. GW to Bezaleel Howe, 9 November 1783, FOL.

27. GW to Richard Varick, 1 January 1784, in *GWP, Conf. Series*, 1:2.

28. For a discussion of the papers, see GW to Richard Varick, 1 January 1784, note, in *GWP, Conf. Series*, 1:2.

29. Quoted in Bryan, *Martha Washington*, 264.

30. GW to David Humphrey, 26 December 1786, in *GWP, Conf. Series*, 4:477; Nancy Carter Crump, "Yorkshire Christmas Pie," in *Dining with the Washingtons*, ed. Stephen A. McLeod (Mount Vernon, VA: Mount Vernon Ladies Association, 2011), 152–53.

31. "An Account of a Visit Made to Washington," 76–80.

32. GW to ML, 1 February 1784, in *GWP, Conf. Series*, 1:87. The quote is a paraphrase of 1 Kings 4:25.

33. MW to Hannah Stockton Boudinot, 15 January 1784, in *"Worthy Partner": The Papers of Martha Washington*, comp. Joseph E. Fields (Westport, CT: Greenwood, 1994), 193.

34. Washington was hardly forgotten. The *United States Chronicle*, 26 February 1784, noted his birthday.

35. GW to Robert Morris, 4 January 1784, in *GWP, Conf. Series*, 1:9; Whiteley, *Washington and His Aides-de-Camp*, 188.

36. David Humphreys to GW, 6 January 1784, in *GWP, Conf. Series*, 1:13. Humphreys offered a shopping list of posts for which he felt qualified. Secretary of foreign affairs was first.

37. GW to David Humphreys, 14 January 1784, in *GWP, Conf. Series*, 1:40.

38. GW to Thomas Mifflin, 14 January 1784, in *GWP, Conf. Series*, 1:41.

39. *JCC*, 27:375.

40. GW to LW, 26 November 1775, in *GWP, Rev. Series*, 2:431.

41. GW to LW, 20 August 1775, in *GWP, Rev. Series*, 1:334.

42. LW to GW, 29 February 1776, in *GWP, Rev. Series*, 3:393.

43. LW to GW, 17 January 1776, in *GWP, Rev. Series*, 3:126.

44. GW to LW, 19 August 1776, in *GWP, Rev. Series*, 6:82.

45. GW to LW, 10–17 December 1776, in *GWP, Rev. Series*, 7:289.

46. Robert E. Dalzell and Lee Baldwin Dalzell, *George Washington's Mount Vernon: At Home in Revolutionary America* (New York: Oxford University Press, 1998), 109.

47. GW to LW, 14 September 1779, in *GWP, Rev. Series*, 22:427; Dalzell and Dalzell, *George Washington's Mount Vernon*, 182–87.

48. "HMS *Savage*," in *DEGW*, https://www.mountvernon.org/library/digitalhistory/digital-encyclopedia/article/h-m-s-savage.

49. Marquis de Chastellux, *Travels in North America in the Years 1780, 1781, and 1782 by the Marquis de Chastellux*, 2 vols., ed. Howard C. Rice Jr. (Chapel Hill: University of North Carolina Press, 1963), 2:597n; Mary V. Thompson, *"The Only Unavoidable Subject of Regret": George Washington, Slavery, and the Enslaved Community at Mount Vernon* (Charlottesville: University of Virginia Press, 2019), 279–80.

50. Chastellux, *Travels in North America*, 2:597n.

51. "Waters of Despair." On 6 September 1781, the *Savage* was captured by the privateer *Congress*. Gardner W. Allen, *A Naval History of the American Revolution*, 2 vols. (Williamstown, MA: Corner House, 1970), 2:565.

52. Commissioners of Embarkation to GW, 18 January 1784, in *GWP, Conf. Series*, 1:5; Fowler, *American Crisis*, 198–210.

53. ML to GW, 23 April 1781, in *Lafayette in the Age of the American Revolution: Selected Letters and Papers, 1776–1790*, 5 vols., ed. Stanley J. Idzerda (Ithaca, NY: Cornell University Press, 1977–), 4:60–61.

54. GW to LW, 30 April 1781, FOL.

55. GW to LW, 12 February 1783, FOL.

56. GW to Robert Morris, 4 January 1784, in *GWP, Conf. Series*, 1:9.

57. GW to Fielding Lewis, 27 February 27, 1784, in *GWP, Conf. Series*, 1:161.

58. GW to Tankerville, 20 January 1784, in *GWP, Conf. Series*, 1:64. Charles Bennett, Fourth Earl of Tankerville, had asked Washington to help him settle estate matters in Virginia. Washington declined.

59. GW to LW, 11 June 1783, FOL.

60. GW to LW, 11 June 1783, FOL.

61. Battaile Muse to GW, 28 November 1785, in *GWP, Conf. Series*, 3:413.

62. GW to LW, 11 June 1783, FOL.

63. For a summary of GW's western landholdings, see GW to Samuel Lewis, 1 February 1784, unnumbered note, in *GWP, Conf. Series*, 1:91; Colin Calloway, *The Indian World of George Washington* (New York: Oxford University Press, 2018), 283–318.

64. GW to Samuel Lewis, 1 February 1784, in *GWP, Conf. Series*, 1:91; GW to Thomas Lewis, 1 February 1784, in *GWP, Conf. Series*, 1:95; GW to John Harvie, 10 February 1784, in *GWP, Conf. Series*, 1:107; GW to Gilbert Simpson, 13 February 1784, in *GWP, Conf. Series*, 1:117; GW to John Witherspoon, 10 March 1784, in *GWP, Conf. Series*, 1:197.

65. GW to Gilbert Simpson, 13 February 1784, in *GWP, Conf. Series*, 1:117.

66. Gilbert Simpson to GW, 5 October 1772, in *GWP, Col. Series*, 9:113.

67. GW to LW, 20 August 1775, in *GWP, Rev. Series*, 1:334.

68. GW to HK, 20 February 1784, in *GWP, Conf. Series*, 1:136.

69. GW to John Lewis, 14 February 1784, in *GWP, Conf. Series*, 1:123.

70. GW to Gilbert Simpson, 13 February 1784, in *GWP, Conf. Series*, 1:117.

71. Gilbert Simpson to GW, 27 April 1784, in *GWP, Conf. Series*, 1:315. Included in the property were "6 young Negroes and one more expected."

72. David Bradford to John Lewis, 28 March 1784, in *GWP, Conf. Series*, 1:314; John Lewis to GW, 27 April 1784, *GWP, Conf. Series*, 1:312.

73. GW to Gilbert Simpson, 10 July 1784, in *GWP, Conf. Series*, 1:496.

74. "To the Officers of the Army," in *JCC*, 24:295–97.

75. George Washington, *Newburgh Address* (Boston: Massachusetts Historical Society, 1966).

76. Philip Schuyler to Stephen Van Rensselaer, 17 March 1783, in Benson John Lossing, *Life and Times of Philip Schuyler* (New York: Sheldon, 1873), 48.

77. *General Orders of George Washington Issued at Newburgh on the Hudson, 1782–1783*, comp. Major Edward C. Boynton (Harrison, NY: Harbor Hill Books, 1973), 78–81.

78. Knox prepared the Institution by April 15. Minor Myers, *Liberty without Anarchy: A History of the Society of the Cincinnati* (Charlottesville: University of Virginia Press, 1983), 23.

79. Pierre Charles L'Enfant to General von Steuben, 10 June 1783, Society of the Cincinnati Archives, Washington, DC.

80. Arthur St. Clair to GW, 20 April 1784, in *GWP, Conf Series*, 1:295.

81. Elnathan Haskell to JM, 12 September 1783, FOL.

82. Edmund Randolph to JM,13 September 1783, in *JMP, Cong. Series*, 7:311.

83. GW to HK, 23 September 1783, FOL.

84. Aenanus Burke, *Consideration on the Society or Order of Cincinnati; Lately Instituted by the Major-Generals, Brigadier-Generals, and Officers of the American Army Proving That It Creates a Race of Hereditary Patricians, or Nobility* (Philadelphia: Bell, 1783).

85. "Circular Letter to the State Societies of the Cincinnati," 1 January 1784, in *GWP, Conf. Series*, 1:1.

86. Benjamin Lincoln to GW, 2 March 1784, in *GWP Conf. Series*, 1:167; HK to GW, 21 February 1784, in *GWP, Conf. Series*, 1:142.

87. South Carolina *Gazette*, 19 February 1784; BF to Sarah Bache, 26 January 1784, FOL.

88. GW to Jonathan Trumbull, 4 April 1784, in *GWP, Conf Series*, 1:260.

89. GW to TJ, 8 April 1784, in *GWP, Conf. Series*, 1:275.

90. TJ to GW, 16 April 1784, in *GWP, Conf. Series*, 1:287.

91. Jonathan Blanchard to Nathaniel Peabody, 2 May 1784, in *LD*, 21:571.

92. TJ to GW, 16 April 1784, in *GWP, Conf. Series*, 1:287; *JCC*, 26:250.

93. "Account of Expenditures in Attending General Meeting of the Society of the Cincinnati," 24 May 1784, in *GWP, Conf. Series*, 1:402.

94. TJ to Martin Van Buren, 29 June 1824, FOL.

95. Winthrop Sargent Journal, "General Meeting of the Society of the Cincinnati," 4 May 1784, in *GWP, Conf. Series*, 1:332–49; Winthrop Sargent Journal, 4 May 1784, note 16, in *GWP, Conf. Series*, 1:351.

96. Winthrop Sargent Journal, 4 May 1784, in *GWP, Conf. Series*, 1:333.

97. Winthrop Sargent Journal, note 20, in *GWP, Conf. Series*, 1:351.

98. "Thomas Jefferson's Notes on the Fifth Volume of John Marshall's *Life of George Washington* [circa 4 February 1818]," FOL.

99. Myers, *Liberty without Anarchy*, 61.

100. Winthrop Sargent Journal, "Institution," in *GWP, Conf Series*, 1:342.

101. GW to Philip Schuyler, 15 May 1784, in *GWP, Conf. Series*, 1:384.

102. GW to Elizabeth Powel, 18 May 1784, in *GWP, Conf Series*, 1:398; *Pennsylvania Packet*, 8 June 1784.

103. Charles Thomson to TJ, 19 May 1784, in *TJP, Main Series*, 7:272.

104. TJ to Martin Van Buren, 29 June 1824, FOL.

CHAPTER 2. THE WEST

1. Arthur St. Clair to GW, 20 April 1784, in *GWP, Conf. Series*, 1:295; GW to Arthur St. Clair, 31 August 1785, in *GWP, Conf. Series*, 3:212.

2. GW to Jonathan Trumbull, 5 January 1784, in *GWP, Conf. Series*, 1:12.

3. "Circular Letter to States on the Distress of the Army Headquarters, Newburgh, New York," 18 June 1783, FOL.

4. HK to GW, 4 June 1784, in *GWP, Conf. Series*, 1:424.

5. *JCC*, 26:314.

6. Jacob Read to GW, 6 August 1784, in *GWP, Conf. Series*, 2:25.

7. ML to Adrienne de Noailles de Lafayette, 20 August 1784, in *Lafayette in the Age of the American Revolution: Selected Letters and Papers, 1776–1790*, 5 vols., ed. Stanley J. Idzerda (Ithaca, NY: Cornell University Press, 1983), 5:237–38.

8. Quoted in James Gaines, *Liberty and Glory: Washington, Lafayette and Their Revolutions* (New York: Norton, 2007), 37.

9. *JCC*, 5:592.

10. ML to Adrienne de Noailles de Lafayette, in Idzerda, 1:91.

11. Lafayette, "Memoirs," in Idzerda, 5:146.

12. Idzerda, 5:xxi.

13. Louis Gottschalk, *Lafayette between the American and the French Revolution (1783–1789)* (Chicago: University of Chicago Press, 1950), 68–82.

14. Dana Goodman, *The Republic of Letters* (Ithaca, NY: Cornell University Press, 1994), 15, quoting Paul Dibon, "L'Universite de Leyde et la Republique des Lettres au 17e siècle," *Quaerendo* 5c (1975): 25.

15. ML to GW, 10 January 1784, in *GWP, Conf. Series*, 1:26.

16. The period is December 23, 1783–December 20, 1784.

17. ML to GW, 12 April 1782, in Idzerda, 5:27; ML to GW, 9 March 1784, in Idzerda, 5:207.

18. GW to ML, 1 February 1784, in *GWP, Conf. Series*, 1:87.

19. ML to GW, 9 March 1784, in Idzerda, 5:207.

20. ML to Samuel Adams, 7 August 1784, in Idzerda, 5:233.

21. APS Members Bibliography, "Motier Theodore Lafayette (402)," https://membib.amphilsoc.org/member/pub/402.

22. Charles Gillispie, *The Montgolfier Brothers and the Invention of Aviation* (Princeton, NJ: Princeton University Press, 1983), 34–44.

23. Duportail to GW, 3 March 1784, in *GWP, Conf. Series*, 1:168; GW to Duportail, 4 April 1784, in *GWP, Conf. Series*, 1:255.

24. John Morgan, "Air Balloons" (June 19, 1784), *Early Proceedings of the American Philosophical Society for the Promotion of Useful Knowledge Compiled by*

One of the Secretaries Manuscript Minutes of Its Meetings from 1744 to 1838 (Philadelphia, 1884): 126.

25. *Maryland Gazette*, 19 August 1784.

26. J. Bennett Nolan, "Lafayette and the American Philosophical Society," *Proceedings of the American Philosophical Society* 73, no. 2 (1934): 120.

27. ML to GW, 14 May 1784, in *GWP, Conf. Series*, 1:380; Robert Darnton, *Mesmerism and the End of the Enlightenment in France* (Cambridge, MA: Harvard University Press, 1968), 88–90.

28. Friedrich Anton Mesmer to GW, 16 June 1784, in *GWP, Conf. Series*, 1:454.

29. GW to Mesmer, 25 November 1784, in *GWP, Conf. Series*, 2:151.

30. *Virginia Journal and Alexandria Advertiser*, 19 August 1784.

31. GW to Marquis de Chastellux, 20 August 1784, in *GWP, Conf. Series*, 2:44; GW to Stephen Sayre, 1 September 1784, in *GWP, Conf. Series*, 2:65.

32. ML to Adrienne de Noailles de Lafayette, 20 August 1784, in Idzerda, 5:237.

33. ML to Adrienne de Noailles de Lafayette, 20 August 1784, in Idzerda, 5:237.

34. Nathanael Greene to GW, 29 August 1784, in *GWP, Conf. Series*, 2:59.

35. Helen Bryan, *Martha Washington: First Lady of Liberty* (New York: Wiley, 2002), 275.

36. "Dogs," in *DEGW*, https://www.mountvernon.org/library/digitalhistory/digital-encyclopedia/article/dogs.

37. *GWP, Diaries*, 24 August 1785, 4:185; GW to ML, 25 July 1785, note 5, *GWP, Conf. Series*, 3:151.

38. Elkanah Watson, *Men and Times of the Revolution; or, Memoirs of Elkanah Watson, Including Journals of Travel in Europe and America from 1777 to 1842*, ed. Winslow Watson (New York: Dana, 1856), 243–44.

39. ML to Adrienne de Noailles de Lafayette, 20 August 1784, in Idzerda, 5:237.

40. JM to TJ, 17 October 1784, in *JMP, Cong. Series*, 8:118.

41. *Maryland Gazette*, 8 July 1784; *JCC*, 26:332–33.

42. ML to Adrienne de Noailles de Lafayette, 13 August 1784, in Idzerda, 5:233–34.

43. ML to Comte de Vergennes, 15 September 1784, in Idzerda, 5:244.

44. Condorcet shared this sentiment with Lafayette shortly after he returned from America. Marquis de Condorcet to ML, 24 February 1785, in Idzerda, 5:299.

45. ML to GW, 5 February 1783, in Idzerda, 5:91–92.

46. GW to ML, 5 April 1783, in Idzerda, 5:121. Washington also found himself under pressure from William Gordon. Gordon to GW, 30 August 1784, in *GWP, Conf. Series*, 2:63.

47. John Adams to Benjamin Rush, 11 November 1807, in *The Spur of Fame: Dialogues of John Adams and Benjamin Rush, 1805–1813*, ed. John A. Schutz and Douglass Adair (San Marino, CA: Huntington Library, 1966), 98; GW to Bushrod Washington, 9 November 1787, in *GWP, Conf. Series*, 5:420.

48. Virginians' Petition to Prevent the Emancipation of Slaves, Citizens of Mecklenburg, Amelia, and Pittsylvania Counties (Virginia), *To the Honourable the General Assembly of Virginia, the Remonstrance and Petition of the Free Inhabitants of Amelia County, 8–10 November 1785* (Richmond, VA: Legislative Petitions, 1784–1785, Virginia State Library).

49. GW to ML, 10 May 1786, in *GWP, Conf. Series*, 4:41.

50. ML to GW, 5 February 1783, FOL; ML to John Adams, 8 March 1784, in Idzerda, 5:202.

51. GW to James Craik, 10 July 1784, in *GWP, Conf. Series*, 1:492. Preparing for the trip, Washington conducted an extensive inquiry into the status of his lands. See GW to Laurence Muse, 11 March 1784, in *GWP, Conf. Series*, 1:204; GW to Edmund Randolph, 18 March 1784, in *GWP, Conf. Series*, 1:224; GW to John Harvie, 18 March 1784, in *GWP, Conf. Series*, 1:223.

52. Quoted in Robert C. Alberts, *A Charming Field for an Encounter* (Washington, DC: National Park Service, 1975), 20.

53. *GWP, Diaries*, 5 October 1770, unnumbered note, 2:227.

54. Otho Holland Williams to GW, 12 July 1784, in *GWP, Conf. Series*, 1:502. In partnership with George Clinton, Washington attempted to purchase land at the springs. The plan fell through. GW to George Clinton, 25 November 1784, in *GWP, Conf. Series*, 2:145.

55. GW to Marquis de Chastellux, 12 October 1783, FOL; GW to George Clinton, 25 November 1784, in *GWP, Conf. Series*, 2:145.

56. He also had considerable property in Alexandria, Virginia. Lawrence Martin, preface to *The George Washington Atlas* (Washington, DC: George Washington Bicentennial Commission, 1932).

57. *GWP, Diaries*, 1 September 1784, 4:1; GW to Jacob Read, 3 November 1784, in *GWP, Conf. Series*, 2:118.

58. GW to JAW, 29 July 1784, unpublished letter, Washington Papers. My thanks to Katie Blizzard for supplying a copy.

59. GW to Thomas Richardson, 5 July 1784, note 3, in *GWP, Conf. Series*, 1:485.

60. GW to David Luckett, 10 July 1784, in *GWP, Conf. Series*, 1:493.

61. ML to Adrienne de Noailles de Lafayette, 20 August 1784, in Idzerda, 5:238.

62. Gottschalk, *Lafayette between the American and the French Revolution*, 97; Colin Calloway, *The Indian World of George Washington* (New York: Oxford University Press, 2018), 301–2.

63. ML to GW, 8 October 1784, in Idzerda, 5:264–65.

64. JM to TJ, 7 September 1784, in *JMP, Cong. Series*, 8:113.

65. JM to James Madison Sr., 6 September 1784, in *JMP, Cong. Series*, 8:112.

66. JM to TJ, 7 September 1784, in *JMP, Cong. Series*, 8:113.

67. Barbe de Marbois, "Journal," 23 September 1784, in Idzerda, 5:245–53.

68. JM to TJ, 17 October 1784, in *JMP, Cong. Series*, 8:118.

69. "Account of Lafayette's Meeting with the Six Nations," in Idzerda, 5:256; "Journal of Griffith Evans, 1784–1785," Notes and Documents, *PMH and B* 65 (1941): 207–8.

70. JM to TJ, 17 October 1784, in *JMP, Cong. Series*, 8:118.

71. In a letter to Alexander Hamilton, only a few days after the meeting at Fort Stanwix, Lafayette indicated his dislike of Lee. ML to Hamilton, 8 October 1784, in Idzerda, 5:264. The final treaty was signed on 22 October 1784. The treaty was the first of several that opened native land to American settlers.

72. Barbe Marbois, "Journal," in Idzerda, 5:252.

73. ML to Alexander Hamilton, 22 October 1784, in Idzerda, 5:275.

74. GW to JAW, 30 June 1784, in *GWP, Conf. Series*, 1:477.

75. GW to James Craik, 10 July 1784, in *GWP, Conf. Series*, 1:492.

76. GW to James Craik, 26 April 1777, unnumbered note, in *GWP, Rev. Series*, 9:272; James Thacher, *American Medical Biography; or, Memoirs of Eminent Physicians Who Have Flourished in America*, 2 vols. (Boston: Richardson and Lord, 1828), 1:238–39; Wyndham B. Blanton, *Medicine in Virginia in the Eighteenth Century* (Richmond, VA: Byrd, 1930), passim.

77. GW to James Craik, 26 April 1777, in *GWP, Rev. Series*, 9:272.

78. Craik to GW, 13 May 1777, in *GWP, Rev. Series*, 9:409.

79. *Diaries*, 1 September 1784, 4:1.

CHAPTER 3. SETTLERS

1. *GWP, Diaries*, 15 March 1748 and 20 March 1748, 1:9, 1:12.

2. *GWP, Diaries*, 13 and 14 March 1748, 1:7.

3. GW to François-Jean de Beauvoir, Marquis de Chastellux, 12 October 1783, FOL.

4. *GWP, Diaries*, 22 September 1784, 4:31.

5. Dennis J. Pogue, "Drink and Be Merry: Liquor and Wine at Mount Vernon," in *Dining with the Washingtons*, ed. Stephen A. McLeod (Mount Vernon, VA: Mount Vernon Ladies Association, 2011), 204.

6. *GWP, Diaries*, 22 September 1784, 4:31.

7. During the Revolution, Washington had several marquee tents. They came in a variety of sizes and configurations. The one he took on this journey was rectangular in shape, measuring fourteen feet in length with a protected entrance.

8. *GWP, Diaries*, 1 September 1784, 4:403.

9. Samuel had nine children with five wives. At the time of Washington's visit, only four were still living: Thornton, George Steptoe, Lawrence Augustine, and Harriot. Justin Glenn, *The Washingtons: A Family History*, vol. 1, *Seven Generations of a Presidential Branch* (Hagerstown, MD: Savas, 2014), 78. Charles Washington to GW, 16 November 1784, notes 1 and 2, in *GWP, Conf. Series*, 2:137. For Harriot Washington's movements, see Harriot Washington to GW, 2 April 1790; GW to Betty Washington Lewis, 7 October 1782, in *GWP, Pres. Series*, 5:310.

10. *GWP, Diaries*, 3 September 1784, 4:3.

11. *GWP, Diaries*, 4 September 1784, 4:5.

12. *GWP, Diaries*, 3 September 1784, 4:3.

13. Morgan lived near Winchester in a home he named Saratoga after the battle in which he had played a conspicuous part. Don Higginbotham, *Daniel Morgan: Revolutionary Rifleman* (Chapel Hill: University of North Carolina Press, 1961).

14. GW to Daniel Morgan, 4 September 1784, in *GWP, Conf. Series*, 2:67.

15. Ralph Wormeley to GW, 16 July 1784, in *GWP, Conf. Series*, 1:530; GW to Edmund Randolph, 12 April 1780, in *GWP, Rev. Series*, 25:389; GW to Francis Lightfoot Lee and Ralph Wormeley, 20 June 1784, in *GWP, Conf. Series*, 1:458. "Rosegill," National Register of Historic Places, www.rosegill.com/Library/HistoricPlaces/HistoricPlaces.html.

16. Edward Snickers to GW, 17 May 1784, unnumbered note, in *GWP, Conf. Series*, 1:392.

17. *GWP, Diaries*, 3 September 1784, 4:3.

18. "Address to the Army," 2 November 1783, FOL.

19. GW to James Craik, 10 July 1784, in *GWP, Conf. Series*, 1:492.

20. *GWP, Diaries*, 4 October 1784, 4:57.

21. Johann Schoepf, *Travels in the Confederation, 1783–1784*, ed. and trans. Alfred Morrison (Philadelphia: Campbell, 1911), 312.

22. Currently located in West Virginia, the name was changed to Bath in 1776; however, it continued to be called, conventionally, Berkeley Springs. Since that is the name most often mentioned by Washington, it is the name used in the text.

23. *GWP, Diaries*, 18 March 1748, 1:12; GW to Andrew Burnaby, 27 July 1761, in *GWP, Col. Series*, 7:58; GW to Charles Green, 26–30 August 1761, in *GWP, Col. Series*, 7:68. Washington was so impressed that over the next few years he bought land in the area.

24. "Cash Accounts," 31 July–17 September 1767, in *GWP, Col. Series*, 8:20.

25. Schoepf, *Travels in the Confederation*, 310.

26. Carl Bridenbaugh, "Baths and Watering Places of Colonial America," *WMQ* 3, no. 2 (1946): 161.

27. *Maryland Gazette*, quoted in James Thomas Flexner, *Steamboats Come True: American Inventors in Action* (New York: Viking, 1944), 67.

28. GW to Charles Green, 26–30 August 1761, in *GWP, Col. Series*, 7:68; Schoepf, *Travels in the Confederation*, 311.

29. Thomas Jefferson, *Notes on the State of Virginia* (Richmond, VA: Randolph, 1853), 36. The temperature of the springs averaged 72 degrees. Schoepf, *Travels in the Confederation*, 309.

30. GW to Dr. James Craik, 10 July 1784, in *GWP, Conf. Series*, 1:492.

31. Francis Asbury, *The Journal and Letters of the Rev. Francis Asbury, Bishop*, 3 vols., ed. Elmer T. Clark (London: Epworth, 1958), 2:53.

32. *Maryland Gazette*, 13 June 1784; Flexner, *Steamboats Come True*, 67.

33. JM to TJ, 9 January 1785, in *JMP, Cong. Series*, 8:222.

34. Flexner, *Steamboats Come True*, 67.

35. *GWP, Diaries*, 6 September 1784, 4:9.

36. GW to James Rumsey, 7 September 1784, in *GWP, Conf. Series*, 2:69.

37. *GWP, Diaries*, 6 September 1784, note 2, 4:9; George Lewis to GW, 25 August 1786, in *GWP, Conf. Series*, 4:228.

38. *GWP, Diaries*, 8 September 1784, 4:14.

39. Charles Calvert, Fifth Lord Baltimore (1699–1751); Frederick Calvert, Lord Baltimore (1731–1771).

40. GW to JAW, 26 October 1778, in *GWP, Rev. Series*, 17:595.

41. *GWP, Diaries*, 8 September 1784, 4:14; Catherine Van Cortlandt Mathews, *Andrew Ellicott: His Life and Letters* (New York: Grafton, 1908), 34.

42. *GWP, Diaries*, 10 September 1784, note 3, 4:16.

43. *GWP, Diaries*, 12 September 1784, 4:18.

44. Philip C. F. Smith, *The Empress of China* (Philadelphia: Philadelphia Maritime Museum, 1984), 31–42, 75–76.

45. *GWP, Diaries*, 13 September 1784, 4:20.

46. *GWP, Diaries*, 13 September 1784, 4:20.

47. *GWP, Diaries*, 14 September 1784, 4:21; GW to David Luckett, 10 July 1784, in *GWP, Conf. Series*, 1:493.

48. *GWP, Diaries*, 14 September 1784, 4:21.

49. *GWP, Diaries*, 15 September 1784, 4:23.

50. *GWP, Diaries*, 19 September 1784, note 1, 4:26; Solon J. Buck and Elizabeth Buck, *The Planting of Civilization in Western Pennsylvania* (Pittsburgh: University of Pittsburgh Press, 1939), 120, 408.

51. *GWP, Diaries*, 18 September 1784, 4:25.

52. *GWP, Diaries*, 19 September 1784, 4:26.

53. *GWP, Diaries*, 20 September 1784, 4:27.

54. *Diary*, 20 September 1784, in *GWP, Diaries*, 4:27.

55. Boyd Crumine, *History of Washington County* (Philadelphia: Everts, 1882), 859.

56. Crumine, *History of Washington County*, 859.

57. *GWP, Diaries*, 20 September 1784, 4:27.

58. In advertising his lands, Washington always spoke of renting/leasing. See GW to Dolphin Drew, 25 February 1784, in *GWP, Conf. Series*, 1:157; GW to Thomas Richardson, 5 July 1784, in *GWP, Conf. Series*, 1:485; GW to Thomas Freeman, 23 September 1784, in *GWP, Conf. Series*, 2:78.

59. *GWP, Diaries*, 20 September 1784, 4:27.

60. Crumine, *History of Washington County*, 859.

61. *GWP, Diaries*, 21 September 1784, 4:31.

62. *GWP, Diaries*, 22 September 1784, 4:32.

63. Thomas Smith to GW, 9 February 1785, editorial note, in *GWP, Conf. Series*, 2:356; Thomas Smith to GW, 17–26 November 1785, in *GWP, Conf. Series*, 2:356.

64. GW to Thomas Smith, 7 December 1785, in *GWP, Conf. Series*, 3:438.

65. Thomas Smith to GW, 17–26 November 1785, in *GWP, Conf. Series*, 2:356.

66. John Seelye, *Beautiful Machine: Rivers and the Republican Plan, 1755–1825* (New York: Oxford University Press, 1991), 63. Only a few weeks before, Brackenridge, a classmate of James Madison and Philip Freneau at Princeton, had written a blubbery masque in honor of the commander in chief. Later, as

one of the founders of the *Pittsburgh Gazette*, the first newspaper west of the Alleghenies, Brackenridge became a fervent Federalist. Claude Milton Newlin, *The Life and Writings of Hugh Henry Brackenridge* (Princeton, NJ: Princeton University Press, 1932), 65–67.

67. Thomas Smith to GW, 9 February 1785, editorial note, in *GWP, Conf. Series*, 2:356.

68. Brice McGeehan to GW, 18 October 1788, in *GWP, Pres. Series*, 1:51.

69. Thomas Smith to GW, 7 November 1786, in *GWP, Conf. Series*, 4:339.

70. Thomas Smith to GW, 7 November 1786, in *GWP, Conf. Series*, 4:339.

71. GW to George McCarmick, 27 November 1786, in *GWP, Conf. Series*, 4:401; Hugh Henry Brackenridge, *Law Miscellanies* (Philadelphia: Byrne, 1814), 258.

72. Brice McGeehan to GW, 18 October 1788, in *GWP, Pres. Series*, 1:51.

73. *GWP, Diaries*, 22 September 1784, 4:31.

74. *GWP, Diaries*, 4 October 1784, 4:57.

75. *GWP, Diaries*, 4 October 1784, 4:57. For an overview of some of Washington's holdings and his tenants, see "List of Tenants," 18 September 1785, in *GWP, Conf. Series*, 3:256.

76. *GWP, Diaries*, 4 October 1784, 4:57; GW shared these concerns. GW to Benjamin Harrison, 10 October 1784, in *GWP, Conf. Series*, 2:86; GW to George Plater, 25 October 1784, in *GWP, Conf. Series*, 2:106.

77. GW to Francis Halkett, 2 August 1758, in *GWP, Col. Series*, 5:360.

78. GW to Benjamin Harrison, 10 October 1784, in *GWP, Conf. Series*, 2:90.

79. Lawrence Martin, *The George Washington Atlas* (Washington, DC: George Washington Bicentennial Commission, 1932), plate 24.

80. *GWP, Diaries*, 26 September 1784, 4:45; Washington reflects on some of these difficulties and the problem of questionable information.

81. GW to Benjamin Harrison, 10 October 1784, in *GWP, Conf. Series*, 2:90.

82. *GWP, Diaries*, 4 October 1784, 4:57.

83. GW to Benjamin Harrison, 10 October 1784, in *GWP, Conf. Series*, 2:90.

84. GW to Benjamin Harrison, 10 October 1784, in *GWP, Conf. Series*, 2:91.

85. GW to George Plater, 25 October 1784, in *GWP, Conf. Series*, 2:106.

86. John Hunter, "An Account of a Visit Made to Washington at Mount Vernon by an English Gentleman [John Hunter] in 1785," *PMH and B* 17 (1893): 7.

87. GW to HK, 5 December 1784, in *GWP, Conf. Series*, 2:170.

88. ML to GW, 8 October 1784, in *GWP, Conf. Series*, 2:84.

CHAPTER 4. POTOMAC COMPANY

1. *Virginia Journal and Alexandria Advertiser*, 2 December 1784.
2. GW to Virginia House of Delegates, 15 November 1784, in *GWP, Conf. Series*, 2:136.
3. JM to TJ, 9 January 1785, *JMP, Cong. Series*, 8:222; GW to JM, 28 November 1784, in *GWP, Conf. Series*, 2:155.
4. *JVHD*, 1 November 1784.
5. JM to James Monroe, 27 November 1784, in *JMP, Cong. Series*, 8:156.
6. Stuart Leibiger, *Founding Friendship: George Washington, James Madison and the Creation of the American Republic* (Charlottesville: University of Virginia Press, 1999), 23.
7. GW to JM, 12 June 1784, in *GWP, Conf. Series*, 1:445; Leibiger, *Founding Friendship*, 53.
8. GW to Officials of the City of Richmond, 15 November 1784, note 1, in *GWP, Conf. Series*, 2:135; *Virginia Journal and Alexandria Advertiser*, 2 December 1784.
9. GW to Officials of the City of Richmond, 15 November 1784, note 1, in *GWP, Conf. Series*, 2:135.
10. JM to TJ, 9 January 1785, in *JMP, Cong. Series*, 8:222.
11. JM to TJ, 9 January 1785, in *JMP, Cong. Series*, 8:222; *JVHD*, 15 November 1784.
12. Edmund Randolph to TJ, 15 May 1784, in *TJP, Main Series*, 7:259.
13. Johann David Schoepf, *Travels in the Confederation, 1783–1784*, ed. and trans. Alfred J. Morrison (Philadelphia: Campbell, 1911), 55.
14. *JVHD*, 7 December 1784.
15. Henry Lee to GW, 18 November 1784, in *GWP, Conf. Series*, 2:139.
16. GW to JM, 28 November 1784, in *GWP, Conf. Series*, 2:155.
17. GW to JM, 28 November 1784, in *GWP, Conf. Series*, 2:155.
18. ML to GW, 8 October 1784, note 2, in *GWP, Conf. Series*, 2:84.
19. GW to JM, 3 December 1784, in *GWP, Conf. Series*, 2:165.
20. GW to JM, 3 December 1784, in *GWP, Conf. Series*, 2:165.
21. *JVHD*, 13 December 1784.
22. GW and Horatio Gates to Virginia Legislature, 28 December 1784, in *GWP, Conf. Series*, 2:235. The house did not meet again until October 1785. In the following October, Blackburne's daughter, Julia Ann, married Bushrod Washington.
23. Jonathan Gregory Rossie, *The Politics of Command in the American Revolution* (Syracuse, NY: Syracuse University Press, 1975), 188–203.

24. John Rutledge to Horatio Gates, 14 August 1782, note 1, in *LD*, 19:66n.

25. GW to Alexander Hamilton, 4 March 1783, FOL; William M. Fowler Jr., *American Crisis: George Washington and the Dangerous Two Years after Yorktown, 1781–1783* (New York: Walker, 2011), 180.

26. Fowler, *American Crisis*, 173–88.

27. GW to HK, 5 January 1785, in *GWP, Conf. Series*, 2:253.

28. Horatio Gates to GW, 24 December 1784, in *GWP, Conf. Series*, 2:229.

29. GW to JM, 28 December 1784, in *GWP, Conf. Series*, 2:231; Maryland House of Delegates, *Votes and Proceedings*, 22 December 1784; Maryland House of Delegates, *Votes and Proceedings*, 27 December 1784.

30. GW to JM, 28 December 1784, in *GWP, Conf. Series*, 2:231.

31. GW to HK, 5 January 1785, in *GWP, Conf. Series*, 2:253; GW and Horatio Gates to Virginia Legislature, including enclosures, 28 December 1784, in *GWP, Conf. Series*, 2:235.

32. GW to Aloys Graf Bruhl, 3 January 1784, in *GWP, Conf. Series*, 1:4. Bruhl, a privy councilor to the elector of Savoy, was the elector's envoy in London.

33. GW to HK, 5 January 1785, in *GWP, Conf. Series*, 2:253.

34. *GWP, Diaries*, 26 July 1785, 4:168. Shaw proved unreliable and lasted only thirteen months.

35. In July, James Madison had provided strong support for the promotion of Alexandria as a port. JM to TJ, 3 July 1784, in *TJP, Main Series*, 7:359. The legislation was typical "logrolling." The measure also included the ports of York, Tappahannock, and Bermuda Hundred. JM to GW, 9 January 1785, in *GWP, Conf. Series*, 2:260.

36. "Bill for Providing Funds for a James River Canal," in *JVHD*, 18 December 1784.

37. JM to GW, 1 January 1785, in *GWP, Conf. Series*, 2:248.

38. JM to TJ, 9 January 1785, enclosures 1, 2, 3, in *JMP, Cong. Series*, 7:588.

39. JM to GW, 9 January 1785, in *GWP, Conf. Series*, 2:260.

40. JM to GW, 1 January 1785, note 4, in *GWP, Conf. Series*, 2:248.

41. JM to TJ, 9 January 1785, in *TJP, Main Series*, 7:588.

42. JM to TJ, 16 March 1784, in *JMP, Cong. Series*, 7:32.

43. Corra Bacon-Foster, *Early Chapters in the Development of the Potomac Route to the West* (Washington, DC: Columbia Historical Society, 1912), 41.

44. "Resolutions Authorizing an Interstate Compact on Navigation and Jurisdiction of the Potomac," in *JVHD*, 28 December 1784; JM to TJ, 9 January 1785, in *JMP, Cong. Series*, 7:588.

45. GW to Samuel Chase, 17 January 1785, in *GWP, Conf. Series*, 2:272.

46. GW to ML, 15 February 1785, in *GWP, Conf. Series*, 2:363.

47. Benjamin Harrison to GW, 8 February 1785, in *GWP, Conf. Series*, 2:328.

48. GW to ML, 15 February 1785, in *GWP, Conf. Series*, 2:263.

49. GW to ML, 15 February 1785, in *GWP, Conf. Series*, 2:363.

50. William Waller Hening, *Statutes at Large, 1619–1792* (Richmond, VA: printed for the editor by George Cochran, 1819–1823), 11:525–26; *JVHD*, 5 January 1785; Benjamin Harrison to GW, 6 January 1785, in *GWP, Conf. Series*, 2:256; JM to TJ, 9 January 1785, in *TJP, Main Series*, 7:588.

51. GW to TJ, 29 March 1784, in *GWP, Conf. Series*, 1:231.

52. GW to ML, 15 February 1785, in *GWP, Conf. Series*, 2:363. Washington sought advice from others as well, including Patrick Henry, who, in an unusual response, told Washington that his grandson was ill, and he was "under a state of uneasiness and perturbation" and could not reply. Patrick Henry to GW, 12 March 1785, in *GWP, Conf. Series*, 2:430. Henry later told Washington that he should take the stock. Patrick Henry to GW, 19 March 1785, in *GWP, Conf. Series*, 2:447.

53. ML to GW, 13 May 1785, in *GWP, Conf. Series*, 2:556.

54. Hening, *Statutes at Large*, 12:42–44.

55. "George Washington's Last Will and Testament," 9 July 1799, FOL. Liberty Hall Academy is present-day Washington and Lee University.

56. *Maryland Gazette*, 17 February 1785; GW to Thomas Richardson, 5 July 1784, in *GWP, Conf. Series*, 1:485.

57. GW to ML, 15 February 1785, in *GWP, Conf. Series*, 2:363.

58. Bacon-Foster, *Early Chapters*, 52; GW to HK, 5 January 1785, in *GWP, Conf. Series*, 2:253; GW to RHL, 8 February 1785, in *GWP, Conf. Series*, 2:330; GW to William Paca, 31 January 1785, in *GWP, Cong. Series*, 2:306; GW to Robert Morris, 1 February 1785, in *GWP, Conf. Series*, 2:309.

59. Elkanah Watson, *Men and Times of the Revolution; or, Memoirs of Elkanah Watson, Including Journals of Travel in Europe and America from 1777 to 1842*, ed. Winslow Warren (New York: Dana, 1856), 243–46.

60. Joel Achebach, *The Grand Idea: George Washington's Potomac and the Race to the West* (New York: Simon & Schuster, 2014), 129.

61. "Resolutions Authorizing an Interstate Compact on Navigation and Jurisdiction of the Potomac," in *JVHD*, 28 December 1784.

62. As early as January, Washington knew of the meeting. He did not know that Henry had made no arrangements for attendance. Thomas Stone to GW, 28 January 1785, in *GWP, Conf. Series*, 2:297.

63. Pennsylvania was also invited to attend. Given Henry's mishandling, it is likely that the invitation never reached the state. Edmund Randolph to JM, 17 July 1785, note 2, in *JMP, Cong. Series*, 8:324; *GWP, Diaries*, 20–28 March 1785, 4:104–9; George Mason to JM, 9 August 1785, in *JMP, Cong. Series*, 8:337.

64. Edmund Randolph to JM, 17 July 1785, in *JMP, Cong. Series*, 8:324.

65. Maryland-Virginia Compact 1785. This meeting is often referred to as the Mount Vernon Conference. *Papers of George Mason*, ed. Robert Rutland (Chapel Hill: University of North Carolina Press, 2011), 2:816–22.

66. "Act Ratifying the Chesapeake Compact with Maryland," in *JVHD*, 24–26 December 1785; Kate Mason Rowland, "The Mount Vernon Convention," *PMH and B* 11, no. 4 (January 1888): 410–25.

67. "Resolution Authorizing a Commission to Examine Trade Regulations," in *JVHD*, 21 January 1786.

68. JM to James Monroe, 22 January 1786, in *JMP, Cong. Series*, 8:482.

69. JM to TJ, 18 March 1786, in *JMP, Cong. Series*, 8:500. Congress had moved to New York City in January 1785.

70. Bacon-Foster, *Early Chapters*, 59.

71. GW to Thomas Johnson and Thomas Sim Lee, 18 May 1785, in *GWP, Conf. Series*, 2:562. Nearly all the remaining enslaved Africans were eventually purchased by investors in Amsterdam. Bacon-Foster, *Early Chapters*, 62. Although Virginians held a majority of the shares, sales in Richmond did not go well. Jacquelin Ambler to GW, 12 May 1785, in *GWP, Conf. Series*, 2:552.

72. *GWP, Diaries*, 17 May 1785, 4:140. Both Gilpin and Fitzgerald were merchants in Alexandria and had served as aides to Washington during the Revolution. Washington was also offered the presidency of the James River Company. He declined, explaining that he could not give the "punctuality and attention which the trust desires." GW to Edmund Randolph, 16 September 1785, in *GWP, Conf. Series*, 3:250.

73. Bacon-Foster, *Early Chapters*, 60.

74. Hening, *Statutes at Large*, 11:510–42.

75. GW to TJ and Thomas Sim Lee, 18 May 1785, in *GWP, Conf. Series*, 2:562.

76. Hartshorne was a prominent merchant in Alexandria. Potts was from Pennsylvania. Bacon-Foster, *Early Chapters*, 61, 62.

77. Bacon-Foster, *Early Chapters*, 62.

78. Bacon-Foster, *Early Chapters*, 62 63.

79. GW to ML, 15 February 1785, in *GWP, Conf. Series*, 2:363.

80. GW to James Rumsey, 5 June 1785, in *GWP, Conf. Series*, 3:40.

81. GW to James Rumsey, 2 July 1785, in *GWP, Conf. Series,* 3:99.

82. Also spelled "Suters." Oliver W. Holmes, "Suter's Tavern: Birthplace of the Federal City," *Records of the Columbia Historical Society* 49 (1973–1974): 1–34.

83. *GWP, Diaries,* 1 August 1785, 4:169.

84. *GWP, Diaries,* 2 and 3 August 1785, 4:170–71.

85. *GWP, Diaries,* 7 August 1785, 4:177.

86. Thomas Johnson to GW, 4 November 1785, in *GWP, Conf. Series,* 3:339.

87. Douglas R. Littlefield, "Eighteenth-Century Plans to Clear the Potomac River: Technology, Expertise, and Labor in a Developing Nation," *VMH and B* 93, no. 3 (1985): 307.

88. GW to William Grayson, 22 August 1785, in *GWP, Conf. Series,* 3:193.

89. Bacon-Foster, *Early Chapters,* 72–73; GW to Thomas Johnson, 20 December 1785, in *GWP, Conf. Series,* 3:475.

90. GW to James Rumsey, 31 January 1786, in *GWP, Conf. Series,* 3:527.

91. *GWP, Diaries,* 4 July 1786, 5:2.

92. Littlefield, "Eighteenth-Century Plans," 314.

93. *GWP, Diaries,* 2–3 October 1786, 5:47.

94. Despite these setbacks, Rumsey continued to be part of Washington's life. See James Rumsey to GW, 24 March 1788, in *GWP, Conf. Series,* 6:175; James Rumsey to GW, 15 May 1788, in *GWP, Conf. Series,* 6:276; Joseph Barnes to GW, 17 September 1796, in *GWP, Pres. Series,* 20:693.

95. GW to George Gilpin and Thomas Fitzgerald, 2 August 1788, in *GWP, Conf. Series,* 6:418.

96. George Washington made his last annual report in September 1788. *GWP, Diaries,* 4 August 1788, 5:373.

97. "George Washington's Last Will and Testament," 9 July 1799, FOL.

98. Bacon-Foster, *Early Chapters,* 151.

99. W. P. Smith, *A History and Description of the Baltimore and Ohio Railroad* (Baltimore: Murphy, 1853), 9–10.

CHAPTER 5. FAMILY

1. GW to William Gordon, 3 November 1784, in *GWP, Conf. Series,* 1:116; GW to William Gordon, 3 November 1784, in *GWP, Conf. Series,* 2:116. "Tub," George Washington Parke Custis, was Martha's grandson.

2. *GWP, Diaries,* 1 January 1785, 4:72.

3. MW to Maria Dandridge Bassett, 18 November 1777, in *"Worthy Partner": The Papers of Martha Washington*, comp. Joseph E. Fields (Westport, CT: Greenwood, 1994), 174–75.

4. MW to Burwell Bassett, 22 December 1777, in Fields, *"Worthy Partner,"* 175.

5. Benjamin Harrison to GW, 3 April 1784, note 4, in *GWP, Conf. Series*, 1:250.

6. GW to GAW, 26 November 1784, FOL.

7. MW to Elizabeth Powel, 18 January 1788, in Fields, *"Worthy Partner,"* 201.

8. GW to GAW, 26 November 1784, in *GWP, Conf. Series*, 2:154.

9. *GWP, Diaries*, 13 May 1785, 4:137.

10. GAW to GW, 25 February 1785, in *GWP, Conf. Series*, 2:382.

11. GW to William Washington, 25 November 1784, in *GWP, Conf. Series*, 2:153.

12. William Washington to GW, 21 April 1785, in *GWP, Conf. Series*, 2:513.

13. GW to Burwell Bassett, 23 May 1785, in *GWP, Conf. Series*, 3:9.

14. GW to Burwell Bassett, 23 May 1785, in *GWP, Conf. Series*, 3:9; Burwell Bassett to GW, 1 June 1785, note 3, in *GWP, Conf. Series*, 3:30.

15. GW to Burwell Bassett, 23 May 1785, in *GWP, Conf. Series*, 3:30.

16. Burwell Bassett to GW, 1 June 1784, in *GWP, Conf. Series*, 3:30.

17. *GWP, Diaries*, 14 October 1785, unnumbered note, 4:205.

18. *GWP, Diaries*, 15 October 1785, 4:206.

19. Although the record is not clear, it appears that Lund and his wife had three daughters. All died young.

20. GW to LW, 20 November 1785, in *GWP, Conf. Series*, 3:373.

21. "Notes and Observations," 1785–1786, Henry Lee to GW, 16 April 1785, FOL.

22. Most of the letters passing between George and Lund Washington between June 1776 and December 1783 have been lost, but, from those that have survived, the impression is that Lund took Washington's criticism with remarkable patience. GW to LW, 20 November 1785, note 3, in *GWP, Conf. Series*, 3:373.

23. After a long, lingering illness, George Augustine Washington died on 5 February 1793. Subsequently, Fanny married Washington's secretary, Tobias Lear, in 1795. She died the next year of tuberculosis.

24. George Steptoe (1771–1809) was named for his mother, Ann Steptoe. Lawrence Augustine's (1774–1824) name honored his late uncle. A third,

Thornton (1760–1787), son of Samuel's second wife, Mildred Thornton, remained near his father's house, Harewood.

Family of Samuel Washington

- Jane Champe (1724–1755)
- Mildred Thornton (ca. 1741–1763)
  - Thornton Washington (1760–1787)
  - Tristram Washington (b. 1763)
- Lucy Chapman (1743–1762)—died during childbirth
  - Infant Washington (1762)
- Anne Steptoe (1737–1777)
  - Ferdinand Washington (1767–1788)
  - George Steptoe Washington (1773–1809)
  - Lawrence Augustine Washington (1775–1824)
  - Harriot Washington (1776–1822)
- Susannah Perrin (1740–1783)
  - John Perrin Washington (1781–1784)

Source: "Samuel Washington—Marriages and Children," Liquisearch, www.liqui search.com/samuel_washington/marriages_and_children.

25. GW to JAW, 16 January 1783, FOL.

26. Nourse, a prominent local politician, lived a few miles east of Berkeley on his plantation, Piedmont. "James Nourse of Virginia," *VMH and B* 8, no. 2 (1900): 199–202.

27. GW to Bushrod Washington, 17 November 1788, in *GWP, Pres. Series*, 1:116.

28. *GWP, Diaries*, 18 February 1788, 5:277–78; Jean Gibo to GW, 22 May 1788, in *GWP, Conf. Series*, 6:286; GW to Robert Chambers, 28 January 1789, in *GWP, Pres. Series*, 1:259.

29. GW to Betty Washington Lewis, 7 October 1792, in *GWP, Pres. Series*, 11:201.

30. GW to Bushrod Washington, 17 November 1788, in *GWP, Pres Series*, 1:116; GW to James Nourse, 22 January 1784, in *GWP, Conf. Series*, 1:69; GW to Charles Washington, 12 April 1785, in *GWP, Conf. Series*, 2:494.

31. David Griffith to GW, 12 July 1784, FOL.

32. GW to James Nourse, 22 January 1784, unnumbered note, in *GWP, Conf. Series*, 1:69.

33. GW to David Griffith, 29 August 1784, in *GWP, Conf. Series*, 1:499.

34. "A Brief History," Georgetown Presbyterian Church, https://www.gtownpres.org/history.

35. At the time, it was simply referred to as "The Academy." A. C. Clark, "Rev. Stephen Bloomer Balch: A Pioneer Preacher of Georgetown," *Records of the Columbia Historical Society* 15 (1912): 78–80.

36. GW to Stephen Bloomer Balch, 26 June 1785, in *GWP, Conf. Series*, 3:84.

37. Benjamin Stoddert to GW, 21 June 1785, in *GWP, Conf. Series*, 3:68; GW to Stephen Bloomer Balch, 22 November 1785, in *GWP, Conf. Series*, 3:378; GW to William Bailey, 2 August 1785, in *GWP, Conf. Series*, 3:169.

38. *GWP, Diaries*, 2 July 1785, 4:158; GW to Stephen Bloomer Balch, 22 November 1785, in *GWP, Conf. Series*, 3:378.

39. *GWP, Diaries*, 25 November 1785, 4:240.

40. William Brown to GW, 7 October 1785, in *GWP Conf. Series*, 3:296. Brown's letter has not been found, but Wshington's reply of 24 November 1785 makes the contents plain. *GWP, Conf. Series*, 3:382.

41. GW to William Brown, 24 November 1785, in *GWP, Conf. Series*, 3:382; GW to William Brown, 30 June 1786, in *GWP, Conf. Series*, 4:135.

42. "Alexandria Academy," in *DEGW*, https://www.mountvernon.org/library/digitalhistory/digital-encyclopedia/article/alexandria-academy. Pleading that he did not at the time have sufficient cash, he pledged £50 per year and agreed that at his death £1,000 would come to the Academy. GW to Trustees Alexandria Academy, 17 December 1785, in *GWP, Conf. Series*, 3:463.

43. Samuel Hanson to GW, 27 January 1787, in *GWP, Conf. Series*, 4:544.

44. William McWhir to GW, 24 December 1787, note 1, in *GWP, Conf. Series*, 5:504.

45. *GWP, Diaries*, 1 November 1787, 5:256.

46. GW to GAW, 2 September 1787, in *GWP, Conf. Series*, 5:309; Samuel Hanson to GW, 23 September 1787, note 1, in *GWP, Conf. Series*, 5:337. Tobias Lear succeeded William Shaw as Washington's secretary in May 1786. Tobias Lear to GW, 7 May 1786, in *GWP, Conf. Series*, 4:34.

47. GW to GAW, 2 September 1787, in *GWP, Conf. Series*, 5:309.

48. Samuel Hanson to GW, 23 September 1787, in *GWP, Conf. Series*, 5:337.

49. GW to Samuel Hanson, 27 September 1787, in *GWP, Conf. Series*, 5:341.

50. Samuel Hanson to GW, 18 November 1787, in *GWP, Conf. Series*, 5:442; Samuel Hanson to GW, 16 March 1788, in *GWP, Conf. Series*, 6:157.

51. Samuel Hanson to GW, 18 November 1787, note 2, in *GWP, Conf. Series*, 5:442.

52. William McWhir to GW, 8 March 1788, in *GWP, Conf. Series*, 6:148.

53. Samuel Hanson to GW, 16 March 1788, in *GWP, Conf. Series*, 6:157.

54. Samuel Hanson to GW, 16 March 1788, in *GWP, Conf. Series*, 6:157.

55. GW to Samuel Hanson, 18 March 1788, in *GWP, Conf. Series*, 6:160; Samuel Hanson to GW, 23 March 1788, in *GWP, Conf. Series*, 6:171.

56. Samuel Hanson to GW, 4 May 1788, in *GWP, Conf. Series*, 6:260.

57. GW to Samuel Hanson, 4 June 1788, in *GWP, Conf. Series*, 6:311.

58. Samuel Hanson to GW, 7 August 1788, in *GWP, Conf. Series*, 6:431; GW to George Steptoe Washington, 6 August 1788, in *GWP, Conf. Series*, 6:430.

59. George Steptoe Washington to GW, 8 August 1788, in *GWP, Conf. Series*, 6:433.

60. GW to George Steptoe Washington, 6 August 1788, in *GWP, Conf. Series*, 6:430.

61. George Steptoe Washington to GW, 8 August 1788, in *GWP, Conf. Series*, 6:433.

62. GW to George Steptoe Washington, 23 March 1789, in *GWP, Pres. Series*, 1:438; James Craik to GW, 24 August 1789, in *GWP, Conf. Series*, 3:529; Samuel Hanson to GW, 23 March 1788, in *GWP, Conf. Series*, 6:171.

63. Washington may have felt that Craik owed him this favor. He had previously agreed to "contribute One hundred Dollars pr Ann., as long as it is necessary, towards the education of His Son Geo. Washington either in this Country or Scotland." GW to James Craik, 4 August 1788, note 1, in *GWP, Conf. Series*, 6:423.

64. GW to Tobias Lear, 10 October 1790, in *GWP, Pres. Series*, 6:549.

65. There is a slight discrepancy. University of Pennsylvania, *Biographical Catalogue of the Matriculates of the College, 1749–1893* (Philadelphia: Society of the Alumni, 1894), 35. Compare to GW to James Craik, 19 December 1790, in *GWP, Pres. Series*, 7:99.

66. "George Washington's Last Will and Testament," 9 July 1799, FOL.

67. GW to HK, 27 April 1787, in *GWP, Conf. Series*, 5:157; GW to Bushrod Washington, 10 January 1787, in *GWP, Conf. Series*, 4:509.

68. Frank E. Grizzard Jr., "Mary Ball Washington," in *George! A Guide to All Things Washington* (Buena Vista, VA: Mariner, 2005), 335–37. Augustine Washington had four children with his first wife, Jane Butler. A son, Butler, died in infancy. Lawrence, Augustine, and Jane were alive at the time of the second marriage in 1732, although Jane died in 1735. With Augustine, Mary Ball had six children. Five survived into adulthood: George, Betty, Samuel, John, and Charles. Mildred died in infancy.

69. Craig Shirley, *Mary Ball Washington: The Untold Story of George Washington's Mother* (New York: HarperCollins, 2019), 1–10.

70. Moncure Daniel Conway, *Barons of the Potomack and the Rappahannock* (New York: Grolier Club, 1892), 238.

71. GW to Hugh Mercer, 28 March 1774, in *GWP, Col. Series*, 10:9.

72. Benjamin Harrison to GW, 25 February 1781, FOL.

73. GW to Benjamin Harrison, 21 March 1781, FOL.

74. Mary Ball Washington to GAW, January 1787, and GW to Mary Ball Washington, 15 February 1787, note 1, in *GWP, Conf. Series*, 5:33.

75. Martha's reaction is uncertain. She destroyed a good deal of her correspondence. In what remains of her letters, she does not mention her mother-in-law.

76. GW to Mary Ball Washington, 15 February 1787, in *GWP, Conf. Series*, 5:33.

77. For an example of her literacy, see Mary Ball Washington to GW, 13 March 1782, FOL.

78. Quoted in Shirley, *Mary Ball Washington*, 265.

79. Burgess Ball to GW, 25 August 1789, in *GWP, Pres. Series*, 3:536.

80. GW to Betty Lewis, 13 September 1789, note 3, in *GWP, Pres. Series*, 4:32.

81. Betty and John Augustine were the exception.

82. GW to Bushrod Washington, 10 January 1787, in *GWP, Conf. Series*, 4:509.

83. GW to BF, 26 September 1785, in *GWP, Conf. Series*, 3:275.

84. *GWP, Diaries*, 30 June 1785, 4:157.

85. RHL to GW, 3 May 1785, in *GWP, Conf. Series*, 2:532; Catharine Sawbridge Macaulay to GW, 13 July 1785, in *GWP, Conf. Series*, 3:115. Catharine Sawbridge Macaulay was born Catharine Sawbridge and was married twice (to George Macaulay and William Graham); I shall refer to her as Macaulay. The breakdown of visitors is taken from Mary V. Thompson, "Visitors to Mount Vernon, 1784–1789: A Study Undertaken for the Bill of Rights Institute and the Mount Vernon Education Department" (unpublished paper, Mount Vernon Ladies' Association, July 2003).

CHAPTER 6. VISITORS

1. "Resolution House of Burgesses," 26 February 1759, note 1, in *GWP, Col. Series*, 6:192.

2. *GWP, Diaries*, 13 October 1773, unnumbered note, 3:209.

3. GW to John Baker, 29 May 1781, FOL.

4. GW to William Stephens Smith, 15 May 1783, FOL. Smith later became secretary to the American legation in London. In 1786, he married Abigail "Nabby" Adams, daughter of John and Abigail.

5. GW to William Stephens Smith, 15 May 1783, FOL.

6. William Stephens Smith to GW, 20 May 1783, FOL.

7. Washington wrote to thank Le Mayeur for three items he had sent. One of them may have been a set of false teeth. GW to Le Mayeur, 16 July 1783, FOL.

8. Jean Pierre Le Mayeur to GW, 20 January 1784, in *GWP, Conf. Series*, 1:63.

9. Jean Pierre Le Mayeur to GW, 20 January 1784, note 2, in *GWP, Conf. Series*, 1:63.

10. *GWP, Diaries*, 15 September 1785, unnumbered note, 4:193.

11. Jean Pierre Le Mayeur to GW, 2 November 1785, in *GWP, Conf. Series*, 3:337.

12. Jean Pierre Le Mayeur, "From the City of New York, Dentist, Notes and Queries," *VMH and B* 10 (1902–1903): 325.

13. *GWP, Diaries*, 15 June 1786, 4:347; Jean Pierre Le Mayeur to GW, 10 April 1786, in *GWP, Conf. Series*, 4:11. Le Mayeur had left a mare to be serviced by Washington's Magnolio.

14. TJ to Rev. William Smith, 19 February 1791, FOL.

15. For an overview of portraits of Washington done during his lifetime, see David Meschutt, "Life Portraits of George Washington," in *George Washington: American Symbol*, ed. Barbara J. Mitnick (New York: Hudson Hills, 1990), 25–37.

16. "Pine, Robert Edge," in *ODNB*, https://www.oxforddnb.com/view/10.1093/ref:odnb/9780198614128.001.0001/odnb-9780198614128-e-22294.

17. Robert Edge Pine, *America Lamenting*, LC, https://www.loc.gov/pictures/item/2003690788/. Fairfax's sister Hannah was married to Washington's cousin Warner. George William Fairfax to GW, 23 August 1783, note 4, FOL.

18. George William Fairfax to GW, 23 August 1784, in *GWP, Conf. Series*, 2:51. A copy of Fairfax's subscription is at Mount Vernon.

19. George William Fairfax to GW, 23 August 1784, in *GWP, Conf. Series*, 2:51.

20. Stuart returned to America in 1793.

21. Francis Hopkinson to GW, 19 April 1785; Thomas McKean to GW, 23 April 1785; and Thomas Mifflin to GW, 24 April 1785, note 1, in *GWP, Conf. Series*, 2:507.

22. GW to Francis Hopkinson and Thomas McKean, 16 May 1784, note 1, in *GWP, Conf. Series*, 2:561.

23. Robert Edge Pine to John Vaughan, 29 April 1784, in *Robert Edge Pine: A British Portrait Painter in America, 1784–1788*, by Robert G. Stewart (Washington, DC: Smithsonian Institution Press, 1979), 20. Quoted in "Robert Edge Pine," National Gallery of Art, https://www.nga.gov/collection/artist-info.1788.html.

24. GW to Francis Hopkinson, 16 May 1785, in *GWP, Conf. Series*, 2:561. Washington may have been particularly interested in what Pine could tell him about the Countess of Huntington, Selena Hastings, who was living in Bath. She had written him with her plans for "the conversion and civilization of the Indians." "Lady Huntington's Scheme for Aiding the American Indians," 8 April 1784, FOL.

25. *GWP, Diaries*, 28 April 1785, 4:129.

26. John Hopkinson to ?, 6 May 1833, in William Dunlap, *A History of the Rise and Progress of the Arts of Design in the United States*, new ed., 3 vols., ed. Frank William Bayley and Charles Eliot Goodspeed (New York: Bloom, 1965), 1:377.

27. Washington was going to Richmond to attend a meeting of the Dismal Swamp Company. Thomas Walker to GW, 24 January 1784, note 1, in *GWP, Conf. Series*, 1:76; GW to Thomas Walker, 10 April 1785, in *GWP, Conf. Series*, 2:488; Michael A. Blaakman, "Dismal Swamp Company," in *DEGW*, https://www.mountvernon.org/library/digitalhistory/digital-encyclopedia/article/dismal-swamp-company.

28. "Robert Edge Pine," National Gallery of Art, https://www.nga.gov/collection/artist-info.1788.html.

29. RHL to GW, 3 May 1785, in *GWP, Conf. Series*, 2:532; *GWP, Diaries*, 4 June 1785, 4:148. Born Catharine Sawbridge, she first married Dr. George Macaulay (1716–1766). Her second husband was William Graham (m. 1778). She was most often referred to as Mrs. Macaulay. "Macaulay [nee Sawbridge; Other Married Name Graham], Catharine," in *ODNB*, https://www.oxforddnb.com/display/10.1093/ref:odnb/9780198614128.001.0001/odnb-9780198614128-e-17344?rskey=m6osvx&result=2.

30. "Catharine Macaulay (née Sawbridge)," National Portrait Gallery, https://www.npg.org.uk/collections/search/portrait/mw07627/Catharine-Macaulay-ne-Sawbridge.

31. Bridget Hill, *The Republican Virago: The Life and Times of Catharine Macaulay, Historian* (Oxford: Clarendon, 1992), 10.

32. Hill, *Republican Virago*, 11.

33. Edmund Rack, quoted in Richard Polwhelve, *Traditions and Recollections*, 2 vols. (London: Nichols, 1826), 1:122–23; Hill, *Republican Virago*, 118.

34. Mercy Otis Warren to John Adams, 27 April 1785, in *Warren Adams Letters: Being Chiefly a Correspondence among John Adams, Samuel Adams, and James Warren*, 2 vols. (Boston: Massachusetts Historical Society, 1917–1925), 2:254; Lucy Martin Donnelly, "The Celebrated Mrs. Macaulay," *WMQ* 6 (1949): 189.

35. Paul M. Smith, comp., *English Defenders of American Freedoms, 1774–1778* (Washington, DC: Library of Congress, 1972), 107.

36. Hill, *Republican Virago*, 173; Catharine Macaulay, *Loose Remarks on Certain Propositions to Be Found in Mr. Hobbes's Philosophical Rudiments of Government and Society with a Short Sketch of a Democratical Form of Government in a Letter to Signor Paoli* (London: printed for T. Davies, 1767); Carla H. Hay, "Catharine Macaulay and the American Revolution," *Historian* 56, no. 2 (Winter 1994): 303–4. The *Oxford English Dictionary* defines the word *virago* as "[a] man-like, vigorous and heroic woman" (*OED*, https://www.oed.com/search/dictionary/?scope=Entries&q=virago).

37. The following is a list of works by Catharine Macaulay:

The History of England from the Accession of James I to that of the Brunswick Line, vol. 1, 1763; vol. 2, 1765; vol. 3, 1767; vol. 4, 1768; vol. 5, 1771; vol. 6, 1781; vol. 7, 1781; vol. 8, 1783 (various printers)

Loose Remarks on Certain Positions to Be Found in Mr. Hobbes's Philosophical Rudiments of Government and Society with a Short Sketch of a Democratical Form of Government in a Letter to Signor Paoli (1767)

Observations on a Pamphlet Entitled "Thoughts on the Cause of the Present Discontents" (1770)

A Modest Plea for the Property of Copyright (1774)

An Address to the People of England, Scotland, and Ireland on the Present Important Crisis of Affairs (1775)

The History of England from the Revolution to the Present Time in a Series of Letters to a Friend, vol. 1 (1778)

Treatise on the Immutability of Moral Truth (1783)

Letters on Education with Observations on Religions and Metaphysical Subjects (1790)

38. John Adams to Catharine Macaulay, 9 August 1770, FOL.

39. Smith, *English Defenders*, 108.

40. Catharine Macaulay, *Address to the People of England, Ireland, and Scotland* (New York: Holt, 1775), 7–8.

41. Mercy Otis Warren to Winslow Warren, 11 November 1784, in *Mercy Otis Warren: Selected Letters*, ed. Jeffrey H. Richards and Sharon M. Harris (Athens: University of Georgia Press, 2009), 192.

42. Ezra Stiles, *Literary Diary of Ezra Stiles*, 3 vols., ed. Franklin Bowditch (New York: Scribner, 1901), 3:172; Richards and Harris, *Mercy Otis Warren*, 198–99; Martha Washington to Mercy Otis Warren, 9 June 1785, in *"Worthy Partner": The Papers of Martha Washington*, comp. Joseph E. Fields (Westport, CT: Greenwood, 1994), 196; Kate Davies, *Catharine Macaulay and Mercy Otis Warren: The Revolutionary Atlantic and the Politics of Gender* (Oxford: Oxford University Press, 2005), 228–47.

43. RHL to GW, 3 May 1785, in *GWP, Conf. Series*, 2:532.

44. *GWP, Diaries*, 4 June 1785, 4:148.

45. GW to RHL, 22 June 1785, in *GWP, Conf. Series*, 3:70; GW to David Stuart, 5 June 1785, in *GWP, Conf. Series*, 3:43.

46. Gordon visited Washington in June 1784. William Gordon to GW, 8 March 1784, in *GWP, Conf. Series*, 1:177; GW to William Gordon, 8 May 1784, in *GWP, Conf. Series*, 1:370. For Washington's view on biographers, see GW to James Craik, 25 March 1784, in *GWP, Conf. Series*, 1:234.

47. *GWP, Diaries*, 8 June 1785, 4:149. Macaulay was giving thought to writing either a history of the Revolution or a biography of Washington.

48. Quoted in Hay, "Catharine Macaulay," 303; Trevor Colbourn, *The Lamp of Experience: Whig History and the Origins of the American Revolution* (Chapel Hill: University of North Carolina Press, 1965), 153–54.

49. Hay, "Catharine Macaulay," 313.

50. Thomas Paine, *Common Sense* (Philadelphia: Bell, 1776).

51. GW to RHL, 22 June 1785, in *GWP, Conf. Series*, 3:70.

52. Catharine Macaulay to GW, 13 July 1785, in *GWP, Conf. Series*, 3:115.

53. *GWP, Diaries*, 15 June 1785, 4:153.

54. *GWP, Diaries*, 9 September 1785, 4:191.

55. *GWP, Diaries*, 8 July 1785, 4:161.

56. *JVHD*, 22 June 1784.

57. Benjamin Harrison to TJ, 20 July 1784, in *TJP, Main Series*, 7:378.

58. TJ to Benjamin Harrison, 12 January 1785, in *TJP, Main Series*, 7:599.

59. TJ to Benjamin Harrison, 12 January 1785, in *TJP, Main Series*, 7:599; John S. Hallam, "Houdon's Washington in Richmond: Some New Observations," *American Art Journal* 10, no 2 (1978): 79. The Virginia legislature also commissioned a bust of Gilbert du Motier, the marquis de Lafayette. They voted twice: the first vote in 1781 resolved that a bust of the marquis be made

and presented to him. The second vote, in 1784, stipulated that two busts would be made: one for the city of Paris (rather than for the marquis) and the other for the state of Virginia. In 1789, Houdon made a bust of Thomas Jefferson. Anne Poulet, *Jean-Antoine Houdon: Sculptor of the Enlightenment* (Washington, DC: National Gallery of Art, 2003). Houdon made several plaster copies of his various busts.

60. BF to GW, 20 September 1785, in *GWP, Conf. Series*, 3:266. Houdon also planned to bring with him several copies of his work for sale in Philadelphia. Unfortunately, the items did not arrive until after he returned to France. Robert Edge Pine took them into his gallery and offered them for sale. Wayne Craven, "The Origins of Sculpture in America: Philadelphia, 1785–1830," *American Art Journal* 9, no. 2 (November 1977): 8; Edward Biddle, *George Washington: Jean-Antoine Houdon, Sculptor* (Providence, RI: Gorham, 1932).

61. GW to Jean-Antoine Houdon, 26 September 1785, in *GWP, Conf. Series*, 3:279; GW to David Humphreys, 30 October 1785, in *GWP, Conf. Series*, 3:328.

62. *GWP, Diaries*, 2 October 1785, 4:200. Joseph Marie Perrin was a merchant in Alexandria. His name was usually spelled Perrin. Hugh Howard, *The Painter's Chair: George Washington and the Making of American Art* (New York: Bloomsbury, 2009), 96. Howard provides a description of Houdon's visit and technique.

63. Charles Henry Hart and Edward Biddle, *Memoirs of the Life and Works of Jean-Antoine Houdon: The Sculptor of Voltaire and of Washington* (Philadelphia: printed for the authors, 1911), 218.

64. *GWP, Diaries*, 9 October 1785, 4:203.

65. *GWP, Diaries*, 7 October 1785, 4:202.

66. Elkanah Watson, *Men and Times of the Revolution; or, Memoirs of Elkanah Watson, Including Journals of Travel in Europe and America from 1777 to 1842*, ed. Winslow Warren (New York: Dana, 1856), 119. Only three sculptors modeled Washington from life: Joseph Wright, Jean-Antoine Houdon, and Giuseppe Ceracchi. Nicholas B. Clark, "An Icon Preserved: Continuity in the Sculptural Images of Washington," in *George Washington: American Symbol*, ed. Barbara J. Minnick (Lexington, MA: Museum of Our National Heritage, 1999), 41; Giuseppe Ceracchi to GW, 31 October 1791, unnumbered note, in *GWP, Pres. Series*, 9:132.

67. *GWP, Diaries*, 10 October 1785, 4:203.

68. Nelly Custis Lewis to George Washington Parke Custis, 3 December 1849, George Washington Library, Mount Vernon.

69. *GWP, Diaries*, 19 October 1785, 4:208.

70. The bust remains at Mount Vernon. "Jean-Antoine Houdon," George Washington's Mount Vernon, https://www.mountvernon.org/library/digital history/digital-encyclopedia/article/jean-antoine-houdon/.

71. Charles Thomson to TJ, 2 November 1785, in *TJP, Main Series*, 9:9–10.

72. TJ to GW, 4 January 1786, in *GWP, Conf. Series*, 3:490; Poulet, *Jean-Antoine Houdon*, 267; Charles Thomson to TJ, 2 November 1785, in *TJP, Main Series*, 2:9.

73. To capitalize on his work, Houdon made and sold several terra-cotta copies of the Washington bust. Clark, "Icon Preserved," 42.

74. TJ to GW, 4 January 1786, in *GWP, Conf. Series*, 3:490.

75. GW to TJ, 1 August 1786, in *GWP, Conf. Series*, 4:183.

76. GW to TJ, 1 August 1786, in *GWP, Conf. Series*, 4:183.

77. TJ to GW, 14 August 1787, in *GWP, Conf. Series*, 5:290.

78. For a view of the history of the statue, see *Houdon's Washington: An Address by W. A. Day before the Eleventh Annual Convention of the General Agency Association of the Equitable Life Insurance Society of the United States* (Atlantic City, NJ: n.p., 1922); John S. Hallam, "Houdon's Washington in Richmond: Some New Observations," *American Art Journal* 10, no. 2 (1978): 72–80; Gilbert Chinard, ed., *Houdon in America* (Baltimore: Johns Hopkins University Press, 1930).

79. John Marshall interview with Jared Sparks, 9 May 1826, in *Papers of John Marshall*, 12 vols., ed. Herbert A. Johnson (Chapel Hill: University of North Carolina Press, 1974–2006), 10:289.

80. JM to Henry Sherburne, 28 April 1825, in *JMP, Ret. Series*, 3:522.

81. The longer inscription, written by James Madison, was added in 1813. Since its unveiling, more than thirty-seven bronze and plaster copies have been made for presentation in the United States and abroad. My thanks to Mark Greenough at the Virginia State Capitol for information on the statue.

CHAPTER 7. FARMER

1. Located on the Harvard College campus, Wadsworth House had been the residence of the college president. When the college decamped to Concord, the house became available for Washington. Wadsworth House, however, proved inadequate; Washington moved a few blocks to the west on Brattle Street and established his headquarters at Vassall House. Its owner, John Vassall, a Tory, had fled. It is now the Longfellow House–Washington's Headquarters National Historic Site. "The Early History of 105 Brattle Street,"

Longfellow House, Washington's Headquarters National Historic Site, U.S. National Park Service, https://www.nps.gov/long/learn/historyculture/early -history-of-105-brattle-street.htm.

2. Samuel Powel, October 1787, quoted in Susan P. Schoelwer, "Design, Construction, Decoration, and Furnishing the New Room," George Washington's Mount Vernon, https://www.mountvernon.org/the-estate-gardens /the-mansion/the-new-room/design-construction-decoration-and-furnishing -the-new-room.

3. GW to Alexander Spotswood, 13 February 1788, in *GWP, Conf. Series*, 6:110.

4. GW to Arthur Young, 4 December 1788, in *GWP, Pres. Series*, 1:159.

5. John Rawlins to GW, 15 November 1785, in *GWP, Conf. Series*, 3:359; Tench Tilghman to GW, 1 March 1786, in *GWP, Conf. Series*, 3:576; Robert F. Dalzell and Lee Baldwin Dalzell, *George Washington's Mount Vernon: At Home in Revolutionary America* (New York: Oxford University Press, 1998), 114–15, 119–21; Thomas Reinhart, director of Preservation Mount Vernon, to author, 28 July 2020. Lawrence named the plantation Mount Vernon in honor of Admiral Edward Vernon, under whom he had served in the 1741 expedition against Cartagena.

6. "Will of Lawrence Washington," in *Wills of George Washington and His Immediate Ancestors*, ed. Worthington C. Ford (Brooklyn, NY: Historical Printing Club, 1891), 73–79.

7. Frank E. Grizzard Jr., "Lawrence Washington," in *George! A Guide to All Things Washington* (Buena Vista, VA: Mariner, 2005), 332; "Lease of Mount Vernon," 17 December 1754, in *GWP, Col. Series*, 1:232.

8. Robert Dinwiddie to GW, January 1754, in *GWP, Col. Series*, 1:65.

9. GW to Robert Dinwiddie, 3 June 1754, in *GWP, Col. Series*, 1:122.

10. GW to JAW, 31 May 1754, in *GWP, Col. Series*, 1:118.

11. GW to Henry Bouquet, 2 August 1758, in *GWP, Col. Series*, 5:353; GW to Francis Halkett, 2 August 1758, in *GWP, Col. Series*, 5:360.

12. Robert Orme to GW, 10 November 1755, in *GWP, Col. Series*, 2:165.

13. For an assessment of the Custis estate, see "Complete Inventory, by County, of the Estate, January 1759," in *"Worthy Partner": The Papers of Martha Washington*, comp. Joseph E. Fields (Westport, CT: Greenwood, 1994), 61–75; "Settlement of the Daniel Parke Custis Estate, Schedule B: General Account of the Estate, c. 1759," editorial note, in *GWP, Col. Series*, 6:252–57.

14. *JVHD*, 2 April 1759.

15. GW to John Alton, 5 April 1759, in *GWP, Col. Series*, 6:200.

16. GW to Richard Washington, 15 April 1757, in *GWP, Col. Series*, 4:32; GW to Richard Washington, 7 May 1759, in *GWP, Col. Series*, 6:319. Richard Washington was a London merchant with whom Washington dealt. He was not a relative. William Fairfax to GW, 14 April 1756, in *GWP, Col. Series*, 2:351.

17. Cary had been the agent for Martha before her marriage to Washington. Martha Custis to Richard Cary and Company, 20 August 1757, in Fields, *"Worthy Partner,"* 5–6.

18. GW to Robert Cary and Company, 1 May 1759, in *GWP, Col. Series*, 6:315.

19. GW to Robert Stewart, 27 April 1763, in *GWP, Col. Series*, 7:205.

20. Alan Fusonie and Donna Jean Fusonie, *George Washington: Pioneer Farmer* (Mount Vernon, VA: Mount Vernon Ladies Association, 1998), 12.

21. A Country Gentleman, *A New System of Agriculture, or, A Plain, Easy and Demonstrative Method of Speedily Growing Rich* (London: Millar, 1755), 2, 70.

22. GW to Robert Cary, 1 May 1759, in *GWP, Col. Series*, 6:315; Alan and Donna Jean Fusonie, eds., *A Selected Bibliography on George Washington's Interest in Agriculture* (Davis: University of California Press, 1976).

23. *GWP, Diaries*, 14 April 1760, 1:266.

24. Washington never completely abandoned tobacco. GW to GAW, 31 March 1789, in *GWP, Pres. Series*, 1:472.

25. "Washington's Farewell Address to the Army," 2 November 1783, FOL.

26. Fusonie and Fusonie, *George Washington*, 12.

27. GW to Arthur Young, 6 August 1786, in *GWP, Conf. Series*, 4:196.

28. Names of the farms vary a bit. I am using the names provided by Mary V. Thompson, *"The Only Unavoidable Subject of Regret": George Washington, Slavery, and the Enslaved Community at Mount Vernon* (Charlottesville: University of Virginia Press, 2019); GW to Arthur Young, 12 December 1793, in *GWP, Pres. Series*, 14:504.

29. GW to William Fairfax, 30 June 1785, in *GWP, Conf. Series*, 3:87.

30. GW to William Fairfax, 30 June 1785, in *GWP, Conf. Series*, 3:87. One of the few books on the subject published in America was John Bordley, *A Summary View of the Course of Crops in the Husbandry of England and Maryland with a Comparison of Their Products and a System of Improved Courses Proposed for Farms in America* (Philadelphia: Cist, 1784); "George Washington's Library," in *DEGW*, https://www.mountvernon.org/library/digitalhistory/digital-ency clopedia/article/george-washington-s-library.

31. William Fairfax to GW, 23 January 1786, in *GWP, Conf. Series*, 3:523.

32. "Agreement," 31 May 1786, in *GWP, Conf. Series*, 4:86.

33. James Bloxham to William Peacey, 23 July 1786, enclosure, in GW to William Peacey, 5 August 1786, in *GWP, Conf. Series*, 4:192.

34. On 18 June 1792, Washington wrote Young a long letter, later published, describing farming conditions in America, including the use of enslaved Africans. In his letter he noted, "Blacks are capable of much labor, but having (I am speaking generally) no ambition to establish a good name, they are too regardless of a bad one." George Washington, *Letters on Agriculture from His Excellency George Washington to Arthur Young Esq, F.R.S. and Sir John Sinclair, Bart, M.P.*, ed. Franklin Knight (Washington, DC: published by the editor, 1847), 60–65. See also GW to Arthur Young, 12 December 1793, FOL. In several letters to Young, Washington repeats his misgivings about slave labor. See also Thompson, *"The Only Unavoidable Subject of Regret,"* 98–99.

35. William Peacey to GW, 2 February 1787, in *GWP, Conf. Series*, 5:14. For Washington's views on Bloxham, see GW to William Peacey, 5 August 1786, FOL.

36. William Peacey to GW, 2 February 1787, in *GWP, Conf. Series*, 5:6; GW to William Peacey, 7 January 1788, in *GWP, Conf. Series*, 6:13; Wilbur Cortez Abbott, "James Bloxham, Farmer," *Proceedings of the Massachusetts Historical Society*, 3rd ser., 59 (October 1925–June 1926): 199.

37. John Adams to James Warren, in *Warren Adams Letters: Being Chiefly a Correspondence among John Adams, Samuel Adams, and James Warren* (Boston: Massachusetts Historical Society, 1917), 2:277.

38. Elizabeth A. Mosimann, *Promoting Agriculture in a Changing World: 225 Years of the Philadelphia Society for Promoting Agriculture, 1785–2010* (Philadelphia: Philadelphia Society for Promoting Agriculture, 2012).

39. Samuel Powel to GW, 5 July 1785, in *GWP, Conf. Series*, 3:105.

40. GW to James Warren, 7 October 1785, in *GWP, Conf. Series*, 3:298.

41. GW to William Drayton, 25 March 1786, in *GWP, Conf. Series*, 3:605.

42. GW to ML, 18 June 1788, in *GWP, Conf. Series*, 6:335.

43. At the same time, Washington also built an icehouse. While adding to the distinctiveness of Mount Vernon, the building was not unusual. He copied the design from one he had seen at Robert Morris's house in Philadelphia. Robert Morris to GW, 15 June 1784, in *GWP, Conf. Series*, 1:450.

44. GW to Tench Tilghman, 11 August 1784, in *GWP, Conf. Series*, 2:30.

45. John Adams, *Diary and Autobiography*, ed. Lyman Butterfield (Cambridge, MA: Harvard University Press, 1961), 2:260.

46. Tench Tilghman to GW, 18 August 1784, in *GWP, Conf. Series*, 2:42.

47. Mount Vernon Ladies Association, "The Rebuilding of the Greenhouse—Quarters," in *Mount Vernon Ladies Association Annual Report* (Mount

Vernon, VA: Mount Vernon Ladies Association, 1952), 19–26. In 1791–1792, wings were added to provide slave quarters. The original was destroyed by a fire in 1835. The present reconstruction was completed in 1951. "The Four Gardens at Mount Vernon," George Washington's Mount Vernon, https://www.mountvernon.org/the-estate-gardens/gardens-landscapes/four-gardens-at-mount-vernon/.

48. Quoted in Mount Vernon Ladies Association, *George Washington's Mount Vernon Official Guidebook* (Mount Vernon, VA: Mount Vernon Ladies Association, n.d.), 114.

49. Rodney C. Loehr, "Arthur Young and American Agriculture," *Agricultural History* 43, no. 1 (1969): 45; GW to William Peacey, 5 August 1786, in *GWP, Conf. Series*, 4:192. For Washington's association with the Philadelphia Society, see Olive Moore Gambrill, "John Beale Bordley and the Early Years of the Philadelphia Agricultural Society," *PMH and B* 65, no. 4 (1942): 410–39.

50. William Fairfax to GW, 23 January 1786, in *GWP, Conf. Series*, 3:517.

51. Stanley Ellis Cushing, *The George Washington Library Collection* (Boston: Boston Athenaeum, 1997), 32; Arthur Young to GW, 7 January 1786, in *GWP, Conf. Series*, 3:498.

52. GW to Arthur Young, 6 August 1786, in *GWP, Conf. Series*, 4:196. In his letters to Young, Washington shared his thoughts on animal husbandry, the West, farming practices, price of commodities, and several other topics.

53. At the time of his death, Washington had thirty-one volumes of the *Annals* in his library as well as copies of Young's books. Arthur Young to GW, 7 January 1786, note 2, in *GWP, Conf. Series*, 3:498.

54. GW to Arthur Young, 4 December 1788, in *GWP, Pres. Series*, 1:159.

55. GW to Alexander Spotswood, 13 February 1788, in *GWP, Conf. Series*, 6:110–13; "Washington's Crops," George Washington's Mount Vernon, https://www.mountvernon.org/george-washington/farming/washingtons-crops/.

56. To bring up the mud, Washington employed a device called the "Hippopotamus." GW to Levi Hollingsworth, 20 September 1785, in *GWP, Conf. Series*, 3:267; GW to Arthur Donaldson, 16 October 1785, in *GWP, Conf. Series*, 3:307.

57. GW to William Fairfax, 30 June 1785, in *GWP, Conf. Series*, 3:87.

58. GW to Arthur Young, 4 December 1788, in *GWP, Pres. Series*, 1:159; *GWP, Diaries*, 16 November 1785, 4:228; *GWP, Diaries*, 18 November 1785, 4:232; *GWP, Diaries*, 24 November 1785, 4:236. The actual numbers varied from time to time.

59. Fusonie and Fusonie, *George Washington*, 25.

60. Arthur Young to GW, 19 May 1789, in *GWP, Pres. Series*, 2:341; GW to Sir John Sinclair, 20 July 1794, in *GWP, Pres. Series*, 16:394.

61. GW to Harry Dorsey Gough, 23 August 1797, in *GWP, Ret. Series*, 1:316.

62. Arthur Young to GW, 1 July 1788, in *GWP, Conf. Series*, 6:368.

63. GW to Arthur Young, 15 August 1789, in *GWP, Pres. Series*, 3:472.

64. Arthur Young to GW, 19 May 1789, in *GWP, Pres. Series*, 2:341.

65. GW to Harry Dorsey Gough, 23 August 1797, in *GWP, Ret. Series*, 1:316.

66. Mount Vernon Ladies Association, *George Washington's Mount Vernon Official Guidebook*, 89. Flax grown on the estate was also processed.

67. Figures can vary. These numbers are taken from Fusonie and Fusonie, *George Washington*, 30–31.

68. Lewis Cecil Gray, *History of Agriculture in the Southern United States to 1860*, 2 vols. (Washington, DC: Carnegie Institute, 1933), 1:204.

69. GW to Arthur Young, 1 November 1787, in *GWP, Conf. Series*, 5:402.

70. Arthur Young to GW, 19 May 1789, in *GWP, Pres. Series*, 2:341.

71. Washington owned a variety of breeds; most were working dogs, including "Madame Moose," a coach dog. GW to GAW, 12 August 1787, in *GWP, Conf. Series*, 5:286. Other names included were Mopsey, Tarter, Jupiter, Tipler, Truelove, Juno, Duchess, and Lady.

72. GW to Thomas Mifflin, 18 March 1777, in *GWP, Rev. Series*, 8:598.

73. Marquis de Chastellux, *Travels in North America for the Years 1780, 1781, and 1782 by the Marquis de Chastellux*, 2 vols., ed. Howard C. Rice Jr. (Chapel Hill: University of North Carolina Press, 1963), 1:111.

74. TJ to Walter Jones, 2 January 1814, in *TJP, Ret. Series*, 7:100.

75. Robert Hunter Jr., "An Account of a Visit Made to Washington at Mount Vernon, by an English Gentleman, in 1785," *PMH and B* 17 (1893): 80. Portraits include *Washington before Yorktown*, by Rembrandt Peale (1824); *Washington at Verplanck's Point*, by John Trumbull (1790); *General Washington at Trenton*, by John Trumbull (1792); *Washington Rallying the Americans at the Battle of Princeton*, by William Tylee Ranney (1848).

76. GW to Elizabeth French Dulany, 23 November 1785, in *GWP, Conf. Series*, 3:381.

77. George Washington Parke Custis, *Recollections and Private Memoirs of Washington* (Philadelphia: Benson Lossing, 1861), 249.

78. Arthur Young to GW, 19 May 1789, in *GWP, Pres. Series*, 2:341.

79. GW to Robert Townshend Hooe, 18 July 1784, in *GWP, Conf. Series*, 2:1.

80. GW to Robert Townshend Hooe, 18 July 1784, in *GWP, Conf. Series*, 2:1.

81. Conde Floridablanca to William Carmichael, 24 November 1784, enclosure, and William Carmichael to GW, 3 December 1784, in *GWP, Conf. Series*, 2:163.

82. GW to John Fairfax, 26 October 1785, in *GWP, Conf. Series*, 3:320. At the time, Washington was not certain how many jacks had been sent.

83. *GWP, Diaries*, 5 December 1785, 4:244; Samuel Holton to William Carmichael, 6 October 1785, in *LD*, 22:664.

84. ML to GW, 16 April 1785, note 4, in *GWP, Conf. Series*, 2:503; James McHenry to GW, 5 November 1786, in *GWP, Conf. Series*, 4:330; GW to ML, 19 November 1786, in *GWP, Conf. Series*, 4:385. Lafayette also sent pheasants and partridges.

85. GW to Arthur Young, 4 December 1788, in *GWP, Pres. Series*, 1:159; Arthur Young to GW, 19 May 1789, in *GWP, Pres. Series*, 2:341.

86. Arthur Young to GW, 19 May 1789, in *GWP, Pres. Series*, 2:341.

87. "Royal Gift and the Knight of Malta, Two Valuable Jack Asses," *Maryland Journal*, 23 March 1787.

88. "Fox Hunting," George Washington's Mount Vernon, https://www .mountvernon.org/george-washington/athleticism/foxhunting/.

89. ML to GW, 13 May 1785, in *GWP, Conf. Series*, 2:556.

90. *GWP, Diaries*, 24 August 1785, 4:185; William Grayson to GW, 5 September 1785, in *GWP, Conf. Series*, 3:229.

91. *GWP, Diaries*, 19 September 1785, 4:195.

92. GW to Arthur Young, 6 August 1786, in *GWP, Conf. Series*, 4:196.

CHAPTER 8. ANNAPOLIS

1. *GWP, Diaries*, 26 August 1785, 4:186.

2. *GWP, Diaries*, 28 and 29 August 1785, 4:187.

3. *GWP, Diaries*, 29 August 1785, 4:187.

4. *GWP, Diaries*, 30 August 1785, 4:188.

5. *GWP, Diaries*, 3 September 1785, 4:189.

6. Benjamin H. Hibbard, *A History of the Public Land Policies* (Madison: University of Wisconsin Press, 1965), 10–11.

7. Claims of Virginia, Massachusetts, Connecticut, and New York conflicted. South Carolina and Georgia claimed land south of Virginia. For a brief

history, see "Motion Regarding the Western Lands," 6 September 1780, editorial note, in *JMP, Cong. Series*, 2:72.

8. The conditions:

- Reimburse the state for the costs of the expedition led by George Rogers Clark to capture the British forts west of the Ohio River.
- Affirm the boundaries defined by the state (including the Kentucky district, which became the state of Kentucky in 1792) and all the Ohio River to the low-water mark on the northern shore.
- Affirm land claims of Virginians already in the contested area.
- Reject all claims by private companies/individuals in the cession area, if the claim was based on arrangements with Native Americans that had not been ratified by Virginia.

Source: "Virginia's Cession of the Northwest Territory," Virginia Places, http://www.virginiaplaces.org/boundaries/cessions.html.

9. *JVHD*, 2 January 1781. In 1783, one proviso remained, which Congress accepted: "that lands be reserved out of those hereby proposed to be ceded sufficient to make good the several military bounties agreed to be given to sundry officers by resolutions of both Houses of Assembly: the lands hitherto reserved being insufficient for that purpose." *JVHD*, 8 December 1783.

10. *JCC*, 26:117; William Grayson to JM, 1 May 1785, note 8, in *JMP, Cong. Series*, 8:274; Rufus King to Timothy Pickering, 8 May 1785, in *LD*, 22:386.

11. *JCC*, 26:119.

12. *JCC*, 26:119.

13. TJ to JM, 25 April 1784, in *JMP, Cong. Series*, 8:23. For concern over congressional voting practices, see *JCC*, 26:245–46; Peter Onuf, *Statehood and Union* (Bloomington: Indiana University Press, 1987); Andro Linklater, *Measuring America* (New York: Walker, 2002), 61–73.

14. *JCC*, 26:356.

15. Thomas Jefferson was in Paris by the time the Ordinance of 1785 was enacted.

16. Virginia did not receive compensation until after the establishment of the republic.

17. Shortly after arriving in Congress, James Madison authored instructions to John Jay, the American representative in Madrid, insisting "on the navigation of the Mississippi for citizens of the United States." *JCC*, 18:935–47.

18. East and West Florida are described in the Treaty of Aranjuez. "Treaty of Alliance between France and Spain, Concluded at Aranjuez," 12 April 1779,

in *European Treaties Bearing on the History of the United States and Its Dependencies,* ed. Frances Gardiner Davenport and Charles Oscar Paullin (Washington, DC: Carnegie Institution, 1937), 4:144, https://archive.org/details/europeantreat ies04daveuoft/page/144/mode/2up.

19. In a separate treaty, Spain did recover Minorca and the Floridas. Great Britain retained Gibraltar.

20. The Definitive Treaty of Peace, 1783. "British–American Diplomacy: The Paris Peace Treaty of September 30, 1783," Avalon Project, Yale Law School, https://avalon.law.yale.edu/18th_century/paris.asp.

21. RHL to Patrick Henry, 14 February 1785, in *LD,* 22:195.

22. *JVHD,* 3 November 1784.

23. Francisco Rendon to the President of Congress, 16 November 1784, in *JCC,* 27:689. The United States had claimed free navigation of the Mississippi as early as 5 August 1779; *JCC,* 14:926.

24. Charles Thomson to JJ, 2 July 1784, in *JJP,* 3:590; *JCC,* 27:661.

25. *JCC,* 27:655; "Interfering Claims to the Mississippi River," n.d., in *JJP,* 4:141.

26. "Report of Congress," 15 February 1785, in *JJP,* 4:55; William Carmichael to GW, 25 March 1785, in *GWP, Conf. Series,* 2:460.

27. RHL to GW, 14 February 1785, in *GWP, Conf. Series,* 2:361. Two years later, Lee reversed himself, writing to Washington that opening the Mississippi would "depopulate and ruin the Old States." RHL to GW, 15 July 1787, in *GWP, Conf. Series,* 5:258.

28. RHL to Patrick Henry, 14 February 1785, in *LD,* 22:195.

29. "Account of John Jay's Conferences with Diego de Gardoqui and Bernardo del Campo," 3–4 September 1780, in *JJP,* 2:232.

30. James Monroe to JM, 12 July 1785, in *JMP, Cong. Series,* 8:317.

31. Henry Lee to GW, 2 March 1786, in *GWP, Conf. Series,* 3:578; James Monroe to JM, 2 October 1786, note 8, in *JMP, Cong. Series,* 9:138. Lee had served as a cavalry commander in the Revolution, earning the sobriquet "Light Horse." He is perhaps best known for the eulogy he delivered for Washington describing him as "first in war, first in peace, and first in the hearts of his countrymen."

32. See, for example, RHL to JM, 27 December 1784, in *JMP, Cong. Series,* 8:202; RHL to JM, 30 May 1785, in *JMP, Cong. Series,* 8:288.

33. JM to ML, 20 March 1785, in *JMP, Cong. Series,* 8:250.

34. JM to James Monroe, 8 January 1785, in *JMP, Cong. Series,* 8:220.

35. James Monroe to Patrick Henry, 12 August 1786, in *LD,* 23:463.

36. *JCC,* 29:658.

37. JJ to President of Congress (RHL), 15 August 1785, in *JJP*, 4:156.

38. Charles Ellis Dickson, "James Monroe's Defense of Kentucky's Interests in the Confederation Congress: An Example of Early North/South Party Alignment," *The Register of the Kentucky Historical Society* 74, no. 4 (October 1976): 268.

39. Loan officers were appointed by Congress. They were usually local citizens with their own parochial interests.

40. GW to ML, 25 July 1785, in *GWP, Conf. Series*, 3:151. In a letter to Henry Knox, Washington hinted at his concerns that the new lands might compete with his own plans. GW to HK, 18 June 1785, in *GWP, Conf. Series*, 3:61. His cautious attitude may also be seen in GW to William Grayson, 25 April 1785, in *GWP, Conf. Series*, 2:519, and GW to William Grayson, 22 June 1785, in *GWP, Conf. Series*, 3:69.

41. GW to Anne-César de La Luzerne, 5 September 1785, in *GWP, Conf. Series*, 3:231.

42. GW to David Humphreys, 25 July 1785, in *GWP, Conf. Series*, 3:148.

43. GW to Comte de Rochambeau, 7 September 1785, in *GWP, Conf. Series*, 3:237.

44. GW to David Humphreys, 25 July 1785, in *GWP, Conf. Series*, 3:148.

45. John Adams to Benjamin Rush, 11 November 1806, FOL; GW to Bushrod Washington, 9 November 1787, in *GWP, Conf. Series*, 5:420.

46. Shortly after Madison left New York, a Grand Committee was appointed "to expedite the settlement of public accounts." Joseph Gardner to John Dickinson, 1 October 1785, note 3, in *LD*, 22:652.

47. "Report on Negotiations with Gardoqui," 3 August 1786, in *JJP*, 4:378.

48. JM to TJ, 3 October 1785, in *JMP, Cong. Series*, 8:373.

49. GW to Thomas Blackburne, 10 October 1785, in *GWP, Conf. Series*, 3:301; GW to Jonathan Trumbull Jr., 1 October 1785, in *GWP, Conf. Series*, 3:289.

50. *GWP, Diaries*, 13 October 1785, 4:205.

51. GW to Chastellux, 5 September 1785, in *GWP, Conf. Series*, 3:228.

52. On 1 July 1785, Richard Dobbs Spaight, representative from North Carolina, visited Mount Vernon. *GWP, Diaries*, 1 July 1785, 4:157; "Spaight, Richard Dobbs," in *Biographical Directory of the United States Congress, 1774–1961* (Washington, DC: Government Printing Office, 1961), https://bioguideretro.congress.gov/Home/MemberDetails?memIndex=S000693.

53. GW to James Warren, 7 October 1785, in *GWP, Conf. Series*, 3:298.

54. Elbridge Gerry to TJ, 12 September 1785, in *TJP, Main Series*, 8:515.

55. This idea is suggested by Irving Brant, *James Madison: The Nationalist, 1780–1787* (Indianapolis, IN: Bobbs-Merrill, 1948), 376.

56. William Grayson to GW, 27 May 1786, in *GWP, Conf. Series*, 4:81.

57. JJ's report, in *JCC*, 31:480.

58. JJ to RHL, 15 August 1785, in *JJP*, 4:156; "Negotiations with Gardoqui Reach an Impasse," editorial note, in *JJP*, 4:364.

59. Henry Lee to GW, 3 July 1786, in *GWP, Conf. Series*, 4:147.

60. Henry Lee to GW, 21 April 1786, in *GWP, Conf. Series*, 4:25.

61. GW to Benjamin Harrison, 10 October 1784, in *GWP, Conf. Series*, 2:86; GW to Henry Lee, 18 June 1786, *GWP, Conf. Series*, 4:116.

62. JM to TJ, 4 December 1786, in *JMP, Cong. Series*, 9:189.

63. Henry Lee to GW, 7 August 1786, in *GWP, Conf. Series*, 4:200.

64. JM to TJ, 4 December 1786, in *JMP, Cong. Series*, 9:189.

65. JJ to John Hancock, 29 May 1786, in *JJP*, 4:347. Although elected, President Hancock never served. Ill health caused him to resign. *JCC*, 30:328.

66. *JCC*, 31:457.

67. There is no evidence that Washington and Jay communicated directly on this issue; however, in his letter of 21 April 1786, Lee wrote, "I have taken the liberty to shew in some private circles your observations with respect to the present prospect of our fœderal affairs." Henry Lee to GW, 21 April 1786, in *GWP, Conf. Series*, 4:25. The quotation is from GW to Henry Lee, 18 June 1786, in *GWP, Conf. Series*, 4:116.

68. "The United States, Spain and the Navigation of the Mississippi," in *DHRC*, https://archive.csac.history.wisc.edu/mississippi_essay.pdf; Frederick A. Ogg, *The Opening of the Mississippi: A Struggle for Supremacy in the American Interior* (New York: Macmillan, 1904), 418.

69. The report is in *JCC*, 31:537–52. Debates took place on 10, 17, 18, 21, and 22 August 1786.

70. *JCC*, 29:658.

71. James Monroe to Patrick Henry, 12 August 1786, in *LD*, 23:463.

72. Timothy Bloodworth to Richard Caswell, 24 August 1786, in *LD*, 23:521.

73. [*Secret*] *JCC*, 3 August–29 August 1786, 4:44–127; "Report on the State of Negotiations with Gardoqui," 11 April 1787, in *JJP*, 4:496.

74. "Report on the State of Navigation," 11 April 1787, in *JJP*, 4:496; Ogg, *Opening of the Mississippi*, 400–459.

75. JM to TJ, 19 March 1787, in *TJP, Main. Series*, 11:219.

76. *JCC*, 34:535.

77. James Monroe to JM, 14 August 1786, in *JMP, Cong. Series*, 9:104.

78. James Monroe to Patrick Henry, 12 August 1786, in *LD*, 23:463; James Monroe to TJ, 16 June 1786, unnumbered note, in *TJP, Main Series*, 9:652; JM to TJ, 4 December 1786, in *JMP, Cong. Series*, 9:189.

79. GW to Henry Lee, 18 June 1786, in *GWP, Conf. Series*, 4:116.

80. Quoted in Ogg, *Opening of the Mississippi*, 437.

81. James Monroe to Patrick Henry, 12 August 1786, in *LD*, 23:463. Officially, the meeting was called the "Meeting of Commissioners to Remedy Defects of the Federal Government."

82. *JVHD*, 21 January 1786. While a vocal supporter of the resolution, Madison did not present it. JM to GW, 9 December 1785, note 5, in *GWP, Conf. Series*, 3:439; JM to Noah Webster, 12 October 1804, in *JMP, Sec. State Series*, 8:159.

83. Jones and Smith did not accept appointment, leaving Madison, St. George Tucker, and Randolph as commissioners.

84. Mervin B. Whealy, "'The Revolution Is Not Over': The Annapolis Convention of 1786," *Maryland Historical Magazine* 81 (Fall 1986): 230.

85. Stephen Higginson, quoted in the introduction to *DHRC*, 1:177.

86. "The Annapolis Convention," September 1786, editorial note, in *JMP, Cong. Series*, 9:115.

87. JM to TJ, 12 August 1786, in *JMP, Cong. Series*, 9:93; JM to James Monroe, 22 January 1786, in *JMP, Cong. Series*, 8:482; "Notes on Ancient and Modern Confederacies," in *JMP, Cong. Series*, 9:3.

88. JM to James Monroe, 19 March 1786, in *JMP, Cong. Series*, 8:504.

89. JJ to GW, 16 March 1786, in *GWP, Conf. Series*, 3:601.

90. GW to JJ, 18 May 1786, in *GWP, Conf. Series*, 4:55.

91. JM to TJ, 12 August 1786, in *JMP, Cong. Series*, 9:93. In this scenario, the northern states were in the majority.

92. For some time, Madison had been studying "the general constitution and the droit public of the several confederations which have existed." "Report on Books for Congress," in *JMP, Cong. Series*, 6:62–115; Brant, *James Madison*, 309.

93. JM to Ambrose Madison, 8 September 1786, in *JMP, Cong. Series*, 9:120.

94. Quoted in Louis Ottenberg, "A Fortunate Fiasco: The Annapolis Convention of 1786," *American Bar Association Journal* 45, no. 8 (1959): 876.

95. JM to Noah Webster, 12 October 1804, in *JMP, Sec. State Series*, 8:159.

96. Ottenberg, "A Fortunate Fiasco," 876; *JCC*, 31:677–80.

97. JM to Noah Webster, 12 October 1804, in *JMP, Sec. State Series*, 8:159.

98. Quoted in Whealy, "'The Revolution Is Not Over,'" 236.

99. *JCC*, 31:680.

100. GW to John Fitzgerald, 9 September 1786, in *GWP, Conf. Series*, 4:241.

CHAPTER 9. PHILADELPHIA

1. JM to Ambrose Madison, 8 September 1786, in *JMP, Cong. Series*, 9:120; JM to James Monroe, 11 September 1786, note 3, in *JMP, Cong. Series*, 9:121.

2. *GWP, Diaries*, 16 September 1786, 5:40.

3. Charles Lee was a merchant in Alexandria and the younger brother of Henry (Harry) "Light Horse" Lee. Cole was also a merchant in Alexandria and secretary to the Masonic Lodge no. 39 in Alexandria. In 1752, Washington was initiated as an entered apprentice freemason (first degree) in the Lodge at Fredericksburg, Virginia. He was made an honorary member of the Alexandria lodge in 1784.

4. *GWP, Diaries*, 23 September 1786, 5:43.

5. GW to JJ, 15 August 1786, in *GWP, Conf. Series*, 4:212; GW to JM, 18 November 1786, in *GWP, Conf. Series*, 4:382.

6. *JCC*, 31:678–80.

7. Rufus King to Elbridge Gerry, 17 September 1786, in *LD*, 23:563; Rufus King to John Adams, 2 October 1786, in *LD*, 23:579.

8. James Monroe to JM, 3 September 1786, in *JMP, Cong. Series*, 9:112.

9. *JCC*, 31:770; Henry Lee to St. George Tucker, 20 October 1786, in *LD*, 23:609.

10. James Monroe to JM, 11 August 1786, note 5, in *JMP, Cong. Series*, 9:91; James Monroe to JM, 7 October 1786, in *JMP, Cong. Series*, 9:142.

11. *GWP, Diaries*, 23 October 1786, 5:56.

12. *GWP, Diaries*, 24 October 1786, 5:56.

13. *JCC*, 32:72.

14. *JVHD*, 30 October 1786.

15. *JVHD*, 1 November 1786; JM to GW, 1 November 1786, in *GWP, Conf. Series*, 4:326.

16. JM to GW, 8 November 1786, in *GWP, Conf. Series*, 4:344.

17. GW to JM, 18 November 1786, in *GWP, Conf. Series*, 4:382.

18. Circular Letter to Society of the Cincinnati, 31 October 1786, in *GWP, Conf. Series*, 4:316.

19. GW to Society of the Cincinnati, 31 October 1786, in *GWP, Conf. Series*, 4:316; GW to JM, 18 November 1786, in *GWP, Conf. Series*, 4:382.

20. While attending the Constitutional Convention, Washington never complained about his health.

21. *JVHD*, 4 December 1786. The quote may be apocryphal, but it does represent Henry's views.

22. *JVHD*, 4 December 1786; Edmund Randolph to JM, 22 March 1787, note 4, in *JMP, Cong. Series*, 9:328; William Pierce, "Anecdote," in "Character Sketches of Delegates to the Federal Convention," in Farrand, 3:95; *GWP, Diaries*, 17 May 1787, 5:158.

23. JM to GW, 7 December 1786, in *GWP, Conf. Series*, 4:448.

24. GW to JM, 16 December 1786, in *GWP, Conf. Series*, 4:457.

25. JM to GW, 24 December 1786, in *GWP, Conf. Series*, 4:474.

26. HK to GW, 14 January 1787, in *GWP, Conf. Series*, 4:518.

27. GW to David Humphreys, 26 December 1786, in *GWP, Conf. Series*, 4:447.

28. Henry Lee to GW, 1 October 1786, in *GWP, Conf. Series*, 4:281; David Humphreys to GW, 24 September 1786, in *GWP, Conf. Series*, 4:264.

29. GW to David Humphreys, 22 October 1786, in *GWP, Conf. Series*, 4:296; Michael Lienesch, "Remembering Rebellion: The Influence of Shays's Rebellion on American Political Thought," in *In Debt to Shays: The Bicentennial of an Agrarian Rebellion*, ed. Robert A. Gross, Colonial Society of Massachusetts Collections 65 (Charlottesville: University of Virginia Press, 1986), 170–74. For a more complete analysis of the rebellion, see David Szatmary, *Shays' Rebellion: The Making of an Agrarian Insurrection* (Amherst: University of Massachusetts Press, 1980).

30. Szatmary, *Shays' Rebellion*, 83–84.

31. GW to HK, 26 December 1786, in *GWP, Conf. Series*, 4:481.

32. HK to GW, 17 December 1786; 14, 21, 25, 29, 30, 31 January 1787; and 1, 8, 12, 15, 22 February 1787, in *GWP, Conf. Series*, vol. 4.

33. HK to GW, 23 October 1786, in *GWP, Conf. Series*, 4:300.

34. HK to GW, 17 December 1786, in *GWP, Conf. Series*, 4:460.

35. GW to HK, 3 February 1787, in *GWP, Conf. Series*, 5:7.

36. Lincoln sent Washington a full account of the rebellion, 4 December 1786–4 March 1787, in *GWP, Conf. Series*, 4:418–35.

37. GW to HK, 26 December 1786, in *GWP, Conf. Series*, 4:481.

38. HK to GW, 14 January 1787, in *GWP, Conf. Series*, 4:518.

39. GW to HK, 3 February 1787, in *GWP, Conf. Series*, 5:7.

40. "Introduction," in *DHRC*, 1:195–223.

41. *JCC*, 32:39.

42. *JCC*, 32:71–72.

43. JM to James Monroe, 19 March 1786, in *JMP, Cong. Series*, 8:504.

44. Stuart Leibiger, *Founding Friendship: George Washington, James Madison and the Creation of the American Republic* (Charlottesville: University of Virginia Press, 1999), 67.

45. Edmund Randolph to GW, 11 March 1787, in *GWP, Conf. Series*, 5:112–14.

46. GW to HK, 8 March 1787, in *GWP, Conf. Series*, 5:74.

47. HK to GW, 19 March 1787, in *GWP, Conf. Series*, 5:95.

48. GW to Edmund Randolph, 28 March 1787, in *GWP, Conf. Series*, 5:112. For Washington's ongoing association with the society, see GW to HK, 2 April 1787, note 2, in *GWP, Conf. Series*, 5:119. In addition to Washington, other members of the delegation included John Blair, James Madison, Edmund Randolph, George Mason, George Wythe, and James McClurg. Wythe and McClurg left the convention before its conclusion. Three days after writing Randolph, Washington wrote a detailed letter describing his views on national problems. Nowhere in that letter did he mention that he had agreed to go to Philadelphia. GW to JM, 31 March 1787, in *GWP, Conf. Series*, 5:114. In a letter to Randolph, Washington tacitly admitted that he was likely to continue as president general of the Society of the Cincinnati. GW to Edmund Randolph, 9 April 1787, in *GWP, Conf. Series*, 5:135.

49. *GWP, Diaries*, various entries, April 1787 (see https://founders.archives .gov/about/Washington).

50. Edmund Randolph to JM, 4 April 1787, in *JMP, Cong. Series*, 9:364.

51. JM to TJ, 6 June 1787, in *JMP, Cong. Series*, 10:28.

52. In Thomas Jefferson's first presidential administration, Beckley was appointed librarian of Congress.

53. *GWP, Diaries*, 26 April 1787, 5:143. On the same day he left for Fredericksburg, Washington wrote a lengthy letter to Henry Knox explaining that he would attend both the convention and the meeting of the Society of the Cincinnati. GW to HK, 27 April 1787, in *GWP, Conf. Series*, 5:157.

54. *GWP, Diaries*, 27 April 1787, 5:144. Although she survived this crisis, Mary Ball Washington continued to suffer from cancer. She died on 25 August 1789. Martha Sexton, *The Widow Washington: The Life of Mary Washington* (New York: Farrar, Straus & Giroux, 2019), 282, 284.

55. *GWP, Diaries*, 2 May 1787, 5:148.

56. Edmund Randolph to JM, 4 April 1787, in *JMP, Cong. Series*, 9:364; *GWP, Diaries*, 15 May 1787, 5:156.

57. *GWP, Diaries*, 3 May 1787, 5:149.

58. JM to GW, 16 April 1787, in *GWP, Conf. Series*, 5:144.

59. JM to GW, 16 April 1787, in *GWP, Conf. Series*, 5:144.

60. JJ to GW, 7 January 1787, in *GWP, Conf. Series*, 4:502; HK to GW, 14 January 1787, in *GWP, Conf. Series*, 4:518; "Notes on the Sentiments of Gov-

ernment: John Jay, Henry Knox and James Madison," April 1787, in *GWP, Conf. Series,* 5:163.

61. *GWP, Diaries,* 9 May 1787, 5:193; Ron Chernow, *Washington: A Life* (New York: Penguin, 2010), 526; GW to Robert Morris, 5 May 1787, in *GWP, Conf. Series,* 5:171. Giles and Paris remained with Washington after his election as president, as did Billy Lee. Mary V. Thompson, *"The Only Unavoidable Subject of Regret": George Washington, Slavery, and the Enslaved Community at Mount Vernon* (Charlottesville: University of Virginia Press, 2019), 58.

62. *GWP, Diaries,* 13 May 1787, 5:155.

63. *Pennsylvania Packet,* 14 May 1787.

64. Robert Morris to GW, 23 April 1787, note 2, in *GWP, Conf. Series,* 5:153–54; GW to Robert Morris, 5 May 1787, *GWP, Conf. Series,* 5:171.

65. *GWP, Diaries,* 13 May 1787, 5:155; Leibiger, *Founding Friendship,* 70. This was the same house that would later serve as the President's House. At the time, Benjamin Franklin was president of the Supreme Executive Council of Pennsylvania.

66. *GWP, Diaries,* 14 May 1787, 5:156. Since the Pennsylvania General Assembly was not in session and Congress was meeting in New York, the chamber was available.

67. *GWP, Diaries,* 14 May 1787, 5:156.

68. *GWP, Diaries,* 15 May 1787, 5:156.

69. *GWP, Diaries,* 15 May 1787, 5:156; Arthur Lee to GW, 13 May 1787, note 1, in *GWP, Conf. Series,* 5:185; George Turner to GW, 22 May 1787, note 1, in *GWP, Conf. Series,* 5:194; *Proceedings of the Society of the Cincinnati,* vol. 1, *1784–1884,* ed. John C. Davies (Philadelphia: Review Printing House, 1887), 20.

70. BF to Thomas Jordan, 18 May 1787, in Farrand, 3:A21.

71. *GWP, Diaries,* 23 May 1787, 5:160.

72. The editors of the Washington Papers note, "None of George Augustine Washington's letters to GW in Philadelphia has been found, but GW's letters to his nephew confirm that George Augustine followed the instructions to make weekly reports." George Washington's surviving letters to George Augustine during the summer of 1787 are dated 17 and 27 May; 3, 10, and 15 June; 1, 8, 15, 24, and 29 July; 12 and 26 August; and 2 and 9 September. Information about what George Augustine wrote not only comes from George Washington's letters but also can be found in the weekly farm reports that he prepared for George Washington. It might also be possible that he wrote earlier to Martha. If so, it is likely that those letters and others

were among those destroyed by her. GW to GAW, 17 May 1787, note 2, in *GWP, Conf. Series*, 5:189.

73. *GWP, Diaries*, 17 May 1787, 5:158.

74. GW to Arthur Lee, 20 May 1787, in *GWP, Conf. Series*, 5:191.

75. George Mason to George Mason Jr., 20 May 1787, in Farrand, 3:22–23.

76. The states present were Massachusetts, New York, New Jersey, Pennsylvania, Delaware, Virginia, and North Carolina. Eventually all states would be represented except Rhode Island.

77. JM, "Notes," 25 May 1787, in Farrand, 1:4.

78. Pierce, "Anecdote," in Farrand, 3:94.

79. *Pennsylvania Gazette*, 30 May 1787.

80. *GWP, Diaries*, 25 May 1787, 5:162.

81. William Shippen to Thomas Shippen, 14 May 1787, in *Supplement to Max Farrand's* The Records of the Federal Convention of 1787, ed. James H. Hutson (New Haven, CT: Yale University Press, 1987), 1.

82. William Jackson's "Official Journal of the Convention" provides only a bare and incomplete outline of the convention's proceedings. The most important source are the notes taken by James Madison. For a review of sources, see *DHRC*, 1:25–38.

83. *GWP, Diaries*, 25 May 1787, 5:162.

84. *GWP, Diaries*, 27 May 1787, 5:163; "Diary of John Adams," 29 August 1774, FOL; Walter Staib, *The City Tavern Cookbook: Recipes from the Birthplace of American Cuisine* (Philadelphia: Running Press, 2009), 8, 20, 24.

85. Prior to the adoption of the "one state, one vote" rule, the Pennsylvania delegation, led by Robert Morris and Gouverneur Morris (not related), tried to persuade other large states that votes ought to be apportioned by size. Although Virginia would have benefited from such an arrangement, the delegates argued that such discrimination would drive open a wide breach between the large and the small states and likely cause the latter to walk out. JM, "Notes," 28 May 1787, in Farrand, 1:10–11, note 4.

86. "Journal," 29 May 1787, in Farrand, 1:16. Although more detailed, rules adopted by the convention were similar to those employed by the Continental Congress. *JCC*, 1:25–26.

87. "Frame of the Government of Pennsylvania, May 5, 1682," Avalon Project, Yale Law School, https://avalon.law.yale.edu/17th_century/pa04.asp.

88. GW to TJ, 30 May 1787, in *GWP, Conf. Series*, 5:203.

89. JM, "Notes," 28 May 1787, in Farrand, 1:12.

90. For George Washington's views, see GW to HK, 8 March 1787, in *GWP, Conf. Series,* 5:74; GW to David Humphreys, 8 March 1787, in *GWP, Conf. Series,* 5:72; GW to David Stuart, 1 July 1787, in *GWP, Conf. Series,* 5:239.

91. Pierce, "Anecdote," in Farrand, 3:85–86n.

92. Pierce, "Anecdote," in Farrand, 3:85.

93. John Dickinson to Polly Dickinson, 29 May 1787, Historical Society of Pennsylvania, https://www.consource.org/document/john-dickinson-to -polly-dickinson-1787-5-29/.

94. JM, "Notes," 29 May 1787, in Farrand, 1:18.

95. "James McHenry before the Maryland House of Delegates," 29 November 1787, in Farrand, 3:146.

96. "Resolutions," 29 May 1787, in Farrand, 1:20–22; original copy not found. "The Virginia Plan," 29 May 1787, editorial note, in *GWP, Cong. Series,* 5:202. As governor, Randolph was the de facto senior member of the delegation. Since George Washington was certain to be elected president, it was inappropriate that he should take the floor. JM to John Tyler [no date], in Farrand, 3:525.

97. W. R. Davie to James Iredell, 30 May 1787, in Farrand, 3:31.

98. JM to John Tyler, n.d., in Farrand, 3:524–25.

99. No evidence exists as to who wrote the resolutions that Randolph read to the convention, and the original manuscript has never been located. Since the delegates were not presented with printed copies of documents until they received the draft constitution of 6 August, they made copies for their own use during the debates. Several copies exist, but Max Farrand, the editor of *The Records of the Federal Convention,* concluded that the copy in Madison's "Notes of Debates" "is an accurate copy of the original." "The Virginia Resolutions," 29 May 1787, in Farrand, 3:593–94. Madison himself was not certain of events. Madison to Edmund Randolph, 21 August 1789, in *JMP, Cong. Series,* 12:348.

100. JM, "Notes," 29 May 1787, in Farrand, 1:23.

CHAPTER 10. PRESIDENT

1. Farrand, 1:29.

2. "Notes," James McHenry, 29 May 1787, in Farrand, 1:26.

3. Robert Yates, "Secret Proceedings," 16 June 1787, in Farrand, 1:257.

4. JM, "Notes," 15 June 1787, in Farrand, 1:242.

5. For an analysis of the factions within the convention, see David Brian Robertson, "Madison's Opponents and Constitutional Design," *American Political Science Review* 99, no. 2 (May 2005): 225–43.

6. JM, "Notes," 15 June 1787, in Farrand, 1:242.

7. *GWP, Diaries*, 27 May 1787, 5:163. On 4 July, he attended the Calvinist church to hear "an Oration on the Anniversary of Independence" (*GWP, Diaries*, 4 July 1787, 5:174). White was the second Anglican bishop serving in America after the Revolution; Samuel Seabury was first. "The House of Deputies," Archives of the Episcopal Church, https://www.episcopalarchives.org /house-of-deputies/leadership/william-white.

8. JM, "Notes," 19 June 1787, in Farrand, 1:322.

9. JM, "Notes," 19 June 1787, in Farrand, 1:322.

10. GW to David Stuart, 1 July 1787, in *GWP, Conf. Series*, 5:239.

11. William Pierce, "Anecdote," in Farrand, 3:96.

12. Robert Yates, 2 July 1787, in Farrand, 1:510–16. Members of the committee were Elbridge Gerry (Massachusetts), Roger Sherman (Connecticut), Robert Yates (New York), William Paterson (New Jersey), Benjamin Franklin (Pennsylvania), Gunning Bedford (Delaware), Luther Martin (Maryland), George Mason (Virginia), William Davie (North Carolina), John Rutledge (South Carolina), and Abraham Baldwin (Georgia). Yates, 2 July 1787, in Farrand, 1:520.

13. *GWP, Diaries*, 2, 3, 4 July 1787, 5:173–74.

14. *GWP, Diaries*, 2 and 3 July 1787, 5:173.

15. *GWP, Diaries*, 3 July 1787, unnumbered note, 5:173.

16. *Journal*, 5 July 1787, in Farrand, 1:524. Deliberations in the committee may be followed in Elbridge Gerry to Vice President of the Convention of Massachusetts, 21 January 1788, in Farrand, 3:263–67; Luther Martin, "Genuine Information," n.d., in Farrand, 3:172–232.

17. Hugh Williamson to James Iredell, 8 July 1787, in Farrand, 3:55.

18. GW to Alexander Hamilton, 10 July 1787, in *GWP, Conf. Series*, 5:257.

19. JM, "Notes," 14 July 1787, in Farrand, 2:4.

20. *Journal*, 16 July 1787, in Farrand, 2:13. While the convention was debating, in New York the Confederation Congress adopted the Northwest Ordinance providing "for the Government of the Territory of the United States, Northwest of the river Ohio"; *JCC*, 32:334–43.

21. Hugh Williamson to James Iredell, 22 July 1787, in Farrand, 3:61.

22. JM, "Notes," 26 July 1787, in Farrand, 2:128. The committee consisted of John Rutledge (South Carolina, chair), Edmund Randolph (Virginia), Na-

thaniel Gorham (Massachusetts), Oliver Ellsworth (Connecticut), and Hugh Williamson (North Carolina).

23. *GWP, Diaries*, 30 July 1787, 5:178.

24. GW to Elizabeth Powel, 30 July 1787, note 5, in *GWP, Conf. Series*, 5:279.

25. *GWP, Diaries*, 31 July 1787, 5:179.

26. *GWP, Diaries*, 3 August 1787, 5:179.

27. *Journal*, 6 August 1787, in Farrand, 2:176–89.

28. JM, "Notes," 6 August 1788, in Farrand, 2:177–89; Elbridge Gerry to Ann Gerry, 26 August 1787, in *Supplement to Max Ferrand's* The Records of the Federal Convention, ed. James Hutson (New Haven, CT: Yale University Press, 1987), 241.

29. *Journal*, 6 August 1787, in Farrand, 2:196.

30. On 24 August, they agreed to adjourn at three o'clock. *Journal*, 24 August 1787, in Farrand, 2:399.

31. Arthur N. Holcombe, "The Role of Washington in the Framing of the Constitution," *Huntington Library Quarterly* 19, no. 4 (1956): 332.

32. GW to GAW, 17 May 1787, in *GWP, Conf. Series*, 5:189. Although mentioned in the *GWP*, none of the letters from George Augustine during this period have survived, nor do any letters to or from Martha during Washington's stay in Philadelphia exist. Martha Washington, *"Worthy Partner": The Papers of Martha Washington*, comp. Joseph E. Fields (Westport, CT: Greenwood, 1994), xxviii–xxxv.

33. GW to ML, 15 August 1787, in *GWP, Conf. Series*, 5:294.

34. JM, "Notes," 13 August 1787, in Farrand, 2:278.

35. GW to HK, 19 August 1787, in *GWP, Conf. Series*, 5:297.

36. Committee of Detail, 19 June–23 July 1787, in Farrand, 2:129–89.

37. ? to TJ, 11 October 1787, in Farrand, 3:104; Elbridge Gerry to Ann Gerry, 26 August 1787, in Hutson, *Supplement*, 241.

38. JM, "Notes," 30 August 1787, in Farrand, 2:468–69.

39. JM, "Notes," 30 August 1787, in Farrand, 2:470.

40. JM, "Notes," 31 August 1787, in Farrand, 2:482.

41. JM, "Notes," 31 August 1787, in Farrand, 2:478.

42. JM, "Notes," 8 September 1787, in Farrand, 2:547.

43. GW to GAW, 9 September 1787, in *GWP, Conf. Series*, 5:321.

44. *Journal*, 12 September 1787, in Farrand, 2:582.

45. *GWP, Diaries*, 15 September 1787, 5:185.

46. Rob Reep, "Jacob Shallus: Penman of the United States Constitution," Fossil HD, 29 September 2011, https://fossilhd.wordpress.com/2011/09/29/jacob-shallus-penman-of-the-united-states-constitution/.

47. JM, "Notes," 17 September 1787, in Farrand, 2:644. On only one other occasion did Washington speak. It occurred when a careless member dropped a copy of the proceedings in the State House. Washington chastised the members "to be more careful, lest our transactions get in the newspapers." William Pierce, "Anecdote," n.d., in Farrand, 3:86.

48. JM, "Notes," 17 September 1787, in Farrand, 2:644.

49. JM, "Notes," 17 September 1787, in Farrand, 2:648.

50. JM, "Notes," 17 September 1787, in Farrand, 2:649.

51. James McHenry, 17 September 1787, in Farrand, 2:650.

52. James McHenry, 17 September 1787, in Farrand, 2:650.

53. Nicholas Gilman to Joseph Gilman, 18 September 1787, in Farrand, 3:82.

54. GW to President of Congress, 17 September 1787, note 7, in *GWP, Conf. Series*, 5:330.

55. Farrand, "Introduction," in Farrand, 1:xi; William Jackson to GW, 17 September 1787, in *GWP, Conf. Series*, 5:329; *GWP, Diaries*, 17 September 1787, unnumbered note, 5:185. Joined with Washington's own papers, this addition created the most important private archive in America. In 1796, Washington deposited the convention papers with the Department of State.

56. *GWP, Diaries*, 17 September 1787, 5:185.

57. GW to TJ and ML, 18 September 1787, in *GWP, Conf. Series*, 5:333, 5:334.

58. GW to ML, 1 February 1784, in *GWP, Conf. Series*, 1:87. He also used this phrase in letters to René-Marie, vicomte de Darrot, 25 September 1785, in *GWP, Conf. Series*, 3:272; Charles Vaughan, 18 November 1785, in *GWP, Conf. Series*, 3:372; Comte de Rochambeau, 7 September 1785, in *GWP, Conf. Series*, 3:237; Charles Thomson, 22 January 1784, in *GWP, Conf. Series*, 1:71; Marquis de Chastellux, 1 February 1784, in *GWP, Conf. Series*, 1:85.

59. ML to GW, 1 January 1788, in *GWP, Conf. Series*, 6:5.

60. *GWP, Diaries*, 19 September 1787, 5:186.

61. *GWP, Diaries*, 22 September 1787, 5:186–87.

62. *GWP, Diaries*, 23 September 1787, 5:187.

63. William Bingham to Thomas Fitzsimons, 21 September 1787, in *LD*, 24:435; *JCC*, 33:488–503.

64. *JCC*, 33:549.

65. *JCC*, 33:549.

66. *Pennsylvania Packet*, 19 September 1787.

67. For Washington's sentiments on the need for a strong central government, see GW to JJ, 15 August 1786, in *GWP, Conf. Series*, 4:212; GW to Thomas Johnson, 12 November 1786, in *GWP, Conf. Series*, 4:359.

68. GW to David Humphreys, 10 October 1787, in *GWP, Conf. Series*, 5:365. Humphreys's opinion on the convention vacillated. David Humphreys to GW, 11 February 1787, in *GWP, Conf. Series*, 5:21; 9 April 1787, in *GWP, Conf. Series*, 5:131; 13 August 1787, in *GWP, Conf. Series*, 5:289.

69. GW to Catharine Macaulay, 16 November 1787, in *GWP, Conf. Series*, 5:440.

70. James Monroe to TJ, 12 July 1787, FOL.

71. Douglas Southall Freeman, *George Washington: A Biography*, 7 vols. (New York: Scribner, 1948–1957), 6:112.

72. For Washington's views on state sovereignty, see GW to JJ, 10 March 1787, in *GWP, Conf. Series*, 5:79; GW to JM, 31 March 1787, in *GWP, Conf. Series*, 5:114; "Notes on the Sentiments of John Jay, Henry Knox, and James Madison," [?] April 1787, in *GWP, Conf. Series*, 5:163; GW to HK, 2 April 1787, in *GWP, Conf. Series*, 5:119; GW to Edmund Randolph, 9 April 1787, in *GWP, Conf. Series*, 5:135; GW to Robert Morris, 5 May 1787, in *GWP, Conf. Series*, 5:171.

73. GW to JJ, 10 March 1787, in *GWP, Conf. Series*, 5:79.

74. JM, "Notes," 5 July 1787, in Farrand, 1:533.

75. *GWP, Diaries*, 24 September 1787, 5:188.

76. *GWP, Diaries*, 27 September 1787, 5:188; GW to Benjamin Harrison, 24 September 1787, in *GWP, Conf. Series*, 5:339.

77. *GWP, Diaries*, 9 October 1787, 5:192; GW to George William Fairfax, 27 February 1785, in *GWP, Conf. Series*, 2:386.

78. Alexander Donald to TJ, 12 November 1787, in *TJP, Main Series*, 12:345.

79. Pennsylvania, Connecticut, Massachusetts, Georgia, Virginia, New Jersey, Delaware, Maryland, North Carolina, and New Hampshire. South Carolina called conventions in January and New York in February.

80. HK to GW, 3 October 1787, in *GWP, Conf. Series*, 5:351.

81. GW to David Stuart, 30 November 1787, in *GWP, Conf. Series*, 5:466.

82. GW to HK, 15 October 1787, in *GWP, Conf. Series*, 5:375.

83. JM to GW, 14 October 1787, in *GWP, Conf. Series*, 5:373.

84. Patrick Henry to GW, 19 October 1787, in *GWP, Conf. Series*, 5:384.

85. George Mason to GW, 7 October 1787, in *GWP, Conf. Series*, 5:355.

86. JM to GW, various dates, 30 September–31 December 1787, in *GWP, Conf. Series*, 5:345–499.

87. "Resolution Calling the State Convention," 31 October 1787, in *DHRC*, 8:118.

88. Of the six letters Stuart wrote to Washington (17 October 1787–23 June 1788), only one survives: 17 February 1788. *GWP, Conf. Series*, 6:115. The remainder are described as "not found." Nine letters from Washington to Stuart are in the *GWP*. The letter of 17 February as well as Washington's responses indicate clearly that Stuart was keeping Washington well informed. During this same period, Madison wrote twenty letters to Washington, who replied five times.

89. David Stuart to GW, 17 February 1788, in *GWP, Conf. Series*, 6:115; Pauline Maier, *Ratification: The People Debate the Constitution, 1787–1788* (New York: Simon & Schuster, 2010), 214–319.

90. JM to GW, 18 November 1787, in *GWP, Conf. Series*, 5:444–45. Between October 1787 and May 1788, eighty-five essays were published, authored by Madison, Hamilton, and Jay. Of the seven Madison sent to Washington, four were by Jay and three by Hamilton. "Full Text of the Federalist Papers," LC, https://guides.loc.gov/federalist-papers/full-text.

91. JM to GW, 18 November 1787, in *GWP, Conf. Series*, 5:444. The essays were written under the pen name of "Publius."

92. GW to David Humphreys, 10 October 1787, in *GWP, Conf. Series*, 5:365–66.

93. GW to David Stuart, 30 November 1787, in *GWP, Conf. Series*, 5:466, 468. For a discussion of ratification in Virginia, see Maier, *Ratification*, 254–319.

94. GW to Charles Carter, 14 December 1787, in *GWP, Conf. Series*, 5:489.

95. GW to Charles Carter, 12 January 1788, note 2, in *GWP, Conf. Series*, 6:37.

96. John Armstrong to GW, 20 February 1788, in *GWP, Conf. Series*, 6:118.

97. David Humphreys to GW, 28 September 1787, in *GWP, Conf. Series*, 5:365.

98. Gouverneur Morris to GW, 30 October 1787, in *GWP, Conf. Series*, 5:398; *GWP, Diaries*, 19 November 1787, 5:217.

99. John Armstrong to GW, 2 March 1787, in *GWP, Conf. Series*, 5:59; ML to GW, 3 August 1787, in *GWP, Conf. Series*, 5:280; Comte de Rochambeau to GW, 18 January 1787, in *GWP, Conf. Series*, 6:46.

100. "George Washington's Birthday," in *The American Book of Days*, 3rd ed., ed. Jane M. Hatch (New York: Wilson, 1978), 197–204. In the Julian calendar, Washington's birthday was reckoned to be 11 February. Conversion to the Gregorian calendar (1752) moved the date ahead to 22 February.

101. Freeman, *George Washington*, 6:146–47; Benjamin Lincoln to GW, 24 September 1787, in *GWP, Pres. Series*, 1:5.

102. GW to Henry Lee, 22 September 1788, in *GWP, Conf. Series*, 6:528; GW to Benjamin Lincoln, 26 October 1788, in *GWP, Conf. Series*, 1:70. Freeman, *George Washington*, 6:149, summarized Washington's thought.

103. GW to ML, 28 May 1788, in *GWP, Conf. Series*, 6:297.

104. JM to GW, 25 June 1788, in *GWP, Conf. Series*, 6:356.

105. GW to Tobias Lear, 29 June 1788, in *GWP, Conf. Series*, 6:364.

106. Henley had been Washington's spymaster during the Revolution.

107. GW to Tobias Lear, 29 June 1788, in *GWP, Conf. Series*, 6:364.

108. *JCC*, 34:281.

109. *JCC*, 34:523.

110. Article 2, United States Constitution.

111. Order of Ratification:

Delaware: 7 December 1787

Pennsylvania: 12 December 1787

New Jersey: 18 December 1787

Georgia: 2 January 1788

Connecticut: 9 January 1788

Massachusetts: 6 February 1788

Maryland: 28 April 1788

South Carolina: 23 May 1788

New Hampshire: 21 June 1788 (with this state's ratification, the Constitution was ratified)

Virginia: 25 June 1788

New York: 26 July 1788

North Carolina: 21 November 1789

Rhode Island: 29 May 1790

112. Benjamin Lincoln to GW, 24 September 1788, in *GWP, Pres. Series*, 1:5.

113. *The Works of John Adams*, 10 vols., ed. Charles F. Adams (Boston: Little, Brown, 1850–1856), 2:416–17.

114. Quoted in David McCullough, *John Adams* (New York: Simon & Schuster, 2001), 383.

115. Abigail Adams to John Quincy Adams, 10 February 1788, in McCullough, *John Adams*, 384–85.

116. United States Constitution, Article 2, section 1. Each elector had two votes. The Twelfth Amendment altered this procedure.

117. *Journal of the First Session of the Senate of the United States of America, Begun and Held at the City of New York, March 4, 1789* (Washington, DC: Gales and Seaton, 1820), 1:9.

118. GW to HK, 1 April 1789, in *GWP, Pres. Series*, 2:2.

119. *GWP, Diaries*, 16 April 1789, 5:445.

120. *GWP, Diaries*, 16 April 1789, 5:445.

BIBLIOGRAPHY

NEWSPAPERS

American Herald (Boston)
Maryland Gazette
Maryland Journal
Pennsylvania Gazette
Pennsylvania Packet
Virginia Journal and Alexandria Advertiser

MOUNT VERNON, ONLINE SOURCES

"Alexandria Academy." In *Digital Encyclopedia of George Washington*. https:// www.mountvernon.org/library/digitalhistory/digital-encyclopedia/article /alexandria-academy.

Blaakman, Michael A. "Dismal Swamp Company." In *Digital Encyclopedia of George Washington*. https://www.mountvernon.org/library/digitalhistory /digital-encyclopedia/article/dismal-swamp-company.

Digital Encyclopedia of George Washington. George Washington's Mount Vernon. https://www.mountvernon.org/library/digitalhistory/digital-encyclopedia.

"Dogs." In *Digital Encyclopedia of George Washington*. https://www.mountver non.org/library/digitalhistory/digital-encyclopedia/article/dogs.

Fields, Mason Faulkner. "Fairfax Family." In *Digital Encyclopedia of George Washington*. https://www.mountvernon.org/library/digitalhistory/digital -encyclopedia/article/fairfax-family.

"The Four Gardens at Mount Vernon." George Washington's Mount Vernon. https://www.mountvernon.org/the-estate-gardens/gardens-landscapes/four-gardens-at-mount-vernon/.

"Fox Hunting." George Washington's Mount Vernon. https://www.mountvernon.org/george-washington/athleticism/foxhunting/.

"George Washington's Library." In *Digital Encyclopedia of George Washington.* https://www.mountvernon.org/library/digitalhistory/digital-encyclopedia/article/george-washington-s-library.

"George Washington's Study." In *Digital Encyclopedia of George Washington.* https://www.mountvernon.org/library/digitalhistory/digital-encyclopedia/article/george-washingtons-study.

Hillman, Joseph. "Resignation of Military Commission." In *Digital Encyclopedia of George Washington.* https://www.mountvernon.org/library/digitalhistory/digital-encyclopedia/article/resignation-of-military-commission.

"HMS *Savage.*" In *Digital Encyclopedia of George Washington.* https://www.mountvernon.org/library/digitalhistory/digital-encyclopedia/article/h-m-s-savage.

"Jean-Antoine Houdon." George Washington's Mount Vernon. https://www.mountvernon.org/library/digitalhistory/digital-encyclopedia/article/jean-antoine-houdon/.

"Library on the Potomac." George Washington's Mount Vernon. https://www.mountvernon.org/george-washington/take-note/library-on-the-potomac/.

Pokorski, Robin. "George Washington's Library." In *Digital Encyclopedia of George Washington.* https://www.mountvernon.org/library/digitalhistory/digital-encyclopedia/article/george-washington-s-library.

Schoelwer, Susan P. "Design, Construction, Decoration, and Furnishing the New Room." George Washington's Mount Vernon. https://www.mountvernon.org/the-estate-gardens/the-mansion/the-new-room/design-construction-decoration-and-furnishing-the-new-room.

Smucker, Philip, "Fox Hunting in the 18th Century." George Washington's Mount Vernon. https://www.mountvernon.org/george-washington/athleticism/foxhunting.

Thompson, Mary V. "Christmas at Mount Vernon." In *Digital Encyclopedia of George Washington.* https://www.mountvernon.org/library/digitalhistory/digital-encyclopedia/article/christmas-at-mount-vernon.

———. "Eleanor 'Nelly' Parke Custis." In *Digital Encyclopedia of George Washington.* https://www.mountvernon.org/library/digitalhistory/digital-encyclopedia/article/eleanor-nelly-parke-custis.

"Washington's Crops." George Washington's Mount Vernon. https://www
.mountvernon.org/george-washington/farming/washingtons-crops/.

White, Gwendolyn. "Ferry Farm." In *Digital Encyclopedia of George Washington.*
https://www.mountvernon.org/library/digitalhistory/digital-encyclopedia
/article/ferry-farm.

OTHER SOURCES

Abbott, Wilbur Cortez. "James Bloxham, Farmer." *Proceedings of the Massa-chusetts Historical Society*, 3rd ser., 59 (October 1925–June 1926): 177–203.

Achebach, Joel. *The Grand Idea: George Washington's Potomac and the Race to the West.* New York: Simon & Schuster, 2014.

Adams, John. *Diary and Autobiography.* Edited by Lyman Butterfield. 4 vols. Cambridge, MA: Harvard University Press, 1961.

———. *The Works of John Adams.* Edited by Charles Francis Adams. 10 vols. Boston: Little, Brown, 1850–1856.

Adams, John, and Benjamin Rush. *The Spur of Fame: Dialogues of John Adams and Benjamin Rush, 1805–1813.* Edited by John A. Schutz and Douglass Adair. San Marino, CA: Huntington Library, 1966.

Alberts, Robert C. *A Charming Field for an Encounter.* Washington, DC: National Park Service, 1975.

Allen, Gardner W. *A Naval History of the American Revolution.* 2 vols. Williamstown, MA: Corner House, 1970.

APS Members Bibliography. "Motier Theodore Lafayette (402)." https://membib.amphilsoc.org/member/pub/402.

Asbury, Francis. *The Journal and Letters of the Rev. Francis Asbury, Bishop.* Edited by Elmer T. Clark. 3 vols. London: Epworth, 1958.

Bacon-Foster, Corra. *Early Chapters in the Development of the Potomac Route to the West.* Washington, DC: Columbia Historical Society, 1912.

Biddle, Edward. *George Washington: Jean-Antoine Houdon, Sculptor.* Providence, RI: Gorham, 1932.

Blanton, Wyndham. *Medicine in Virginia in the Eighteenth Century.* 2 vols. Richmond, VA: Byrd, 1930.

Bordley, John. *A Summary View of the Course of Crops in the Husbandry of England and Maryland with a Comparison of Their Products and a System of Improved Courses Proposed for Farms in America.* Philadelphia: Cist, 1784.

Brackenridge, Hugh Henry. *Law Miscellanies.* Philadelphia: Byrne, 1814.

Brant, Irving. *James Madison: The Nationalist, 1780–1787.* Indianapolis, IN: Bobbs-Merrill, 1948.

Bridenbaugh, Carl. "Baths and Watering Places of Colonial America." *William and Mary Quarterly* 3, no. 2 (1946): 161.

"A Brief History." Georgetown Presbyterian Church. https://www.gtown pres.org/history.

"British-American Diplomacy: The Paris Peace Treaty of September 30, 1783." Avalon Project, Yale Law School. https://avalon.law.yale.edu/18th _century/paris.asp.

Bryan, Helen. *Martha Washington: First Lady of Liberty.* New York: Wiley, 2002.

Buck, Solon, and Elizabeth Buck. *The Planting of Civilization in Western Pennsylvania.* Pittsburgh: University of Pittsburgh Press, 1939.

Burke, Aenanus. *Consideration on the Society or Order of Cincinnati; Lately Instituted by the Major-Generals, Brigadier-Generals and Officers of the American Army Proving That It Creates a Race of Hereditary Patricians, or Nobility.* Philadelphia: Bell, 1783.

Calloway, Colin. *The Indian World of George Washington.* New York: Oxford University Press, 2018.

"Catharine Macaulay (née Sawbridge)." National Portrait Gallery. https:// www.npg.org.uk/collections/search/portrait/mw07627/Catharine-Macau lay-ne-Sawbridge.

Chapman, Craig S. *Disaster on the Spanish Main.* Lincoln, NB: Potomac Books, 2021.

Chastellux, Marquis de. *Travels in North America in the Years 1780, 1781, and 1782 by the Marquis de Chastellux.* Edited by Howard C. Rice Jr. 2 vols. Chapel Hill: University of North Carolina Press, 1963.

Chernow, Ron. *Washington: A Life.* New York: Penguin, 2010.

Chinard, Gilbert, ed. *Houdon in America.* Baltimore: Johns Hopkins University Press, 1930.

Clark, C. "Rev. Stephen Bloomer Balch: A Pioneer Preacher of Georgetown." *Records of the Columbia Historical Society* 15 (1912): 73–95.

Clark, Nicholas B. "An Icon Preserved: Continuity in the Sculptural Images of Washington." In *George Washington: American Symbol,* edited by Barbara J. Minnick, 39–53. Lexington, MA: Museum of Our National Heritage, 1999.

Colbourn, Trevor. *The Lamp of Experience: Whig History and the Origins of the American Revolution.* Chapel Hill: University of North Carolina Press, 1965.

Conway, Moncure Daniel. *Barons of the Potomack and the Rappahannock.* New York: Grolier Club, 1892.

A Country Gentleman. *A New System of Agriculture; or, A Plain, Easy and De-monstrative Method of Speedily Growing Rich.* London: Millar, 1755.

Craven, Wayne. "The Origins of Sculpture in America: Philadelphia, 1785–1830." *American Art Journal* 9, no. 2 (November 1977): 4–33.

Crumine, Boyd. *History of Washington County.* Philadelphia: Everts, 1882.

Crump, Nancy Carter. "Yorkshire Christmas Pie." In *Dining with the Washingtons,* edited by Stephen A. McLeod, 152–53. Mount Vernon, VA: Mount Vernon Ladies Association, 2011.

Cushing, Stanley Ellis. *The George Washington Library Collection.* Boston: Boston Athenaeum, 1997.

Custis, Eleanor Parke. *George Washington's Beautiful Nelly: The Letters of Eleanor Parke Custis to Elizabeth Bordley Gibson, 1794–1851.* Edited by Patricia Brady. Columbia: University of South Carolina Press, 1991.

Custis, George Washington Parke. *Recollections and Private Memoirs of Washington.* Philadelphia: Benson Lossing, 1861.

Dalzell, Robert, and Lee Baldwin Dalzell. *George Washington's Mount Vernon: At Home in Revolutionary America.* New York: Oxford University Press, 1998.

Darnton, Robert. *Mesmerism and the End of the Enlightenment in France.* Cambridge, MA: Harvard University Press, 1968.

Davenport, Frances Gardiner, and Charles Oscar Paullin, eds. *European Treaties Bearing on the History of the United States and Its Dependencies.* 4 vols. Washington, DC: Carnegie Institution, 1937. https://archive.org/details/europe antreaties04daveuoft/page/144/mode/2up.

Davies, Kate. *Catharine Macaulay and Mercy Otis Warren: The Revolutionary Atlantic and the Politics of Gender.* Oxford: Oxford University Press, 2005.

Day, W. A. *Houdon's Washington: An Address by W. A. Day before the Eleventh Annual Convention of the General Agency Association of the Equitable Life Insurance Society of the United States.* Atlantic City, NJ: n.p., 1922.

Dickinson, John. "John Dickinson to Polly Dickinson May 29, 1787." ConSource. https://www.consource.org/document/john-dickinson-to-polly -dickinson-1787-5-29/20130122080330/.

Dickson, Charles Ellis. "James Monroe's Defense of Kentucky's Interests in the Confederation Congress: An Example of Early North/South Party Alignment." *The Register of the Kentucky Historical Society* 74, no. 4 (October 1976): 261–80.

The Documentary History of the Ratification of the Constitution. Edited by Merrill Jensen and John P. Kaminski. 37 vols. Madison: University of Wisconsin Press, 1976–2017.

Donnelly, Lucy Martin. "The Celebrated Mrs. Macaulay." *William and Mary Quarterly* 6 (1949): 173–207.

Dunlap, William. *A History of the Rise and Progress of the Arts of Design in the United States.* Edited by Frank William Bayley and Charles Eliot Goodspeed. New ed. New York: Bloom, 1965.

"The Early History of 105 Brattle Street." Longfellow House, Washington's Headquarters National Historic Site. U.S. National Park Service. https://www.nps.gov/long/learn/historyculture/early-history-of-105-brattle-street.htm.

Evans, Griffith. "Journal of Griffith Evans, 1784–1785." Notes and Documents, *Pennsylvania Magazine of History and Biography* 65 (1941): 202–33.

Farrand, Max, ed. *The Records of the Federal Convention of 1787.* 3 vols. New Haven, CT: Yale University Press, 1937.

Flexner, Thomas. *Steamboats Come True: American Inventors in Action.* New York: Viking, 1944.

Founders Online. "Correspondence and Other Writings of Seven Major Shapers of the United States: George Washington, Benjamin Franklin, John Adams (and Family), Thomas Jefferson, Alexander Hamilton, John Jay, and James Madison." National Archives. https://founders.archives.gov/.

———. "Editorial Note: George Washington's Resignation as Commander-in-Chief." National Archives. https://founders.archives.gov/documents/Jefferson/01-06-02-0319-0001.

Fowler, William M., Jr. *American Crisis: George Washington and the Dangerous Two Years after Yorktown, 1781–1783.* New York: Walker, 2011.

"Frame of the Government of Pennsylvania, May 5, 1682." Avalon Project, Yale Law School. https://avalon.law.yale.edu/17th_century/pa04.asp.

Franklin, Benjamin. *Writings of Benjamin Franklin.* Edited by Albert H. Smyth. 10 vols. New York: Macmillan, 1905–1907.

Freeman, Douglas Southall. *George Washington: A Biography.* 7 vols. New York: Scribner, 1948–1957.

"Full Text of the Federalist Papers." Library of Congress. https://guides.loc.gov/federalist-papers/full-text.

Fusonie, Alan, and Donna Jean Fusonie. *George Washington: Pioneer Farmer.* Mount Vernon, VA: Mount Vernon Ladies Association, 1998.

———, eds. *A Selected Bibliography on George Washington's Interest in Agriculture.* Davis: University of California Press, 1976.

Gaines, James. *Liberty and Glory: Washington, Lafayette and Their Revolutions.* New York: Norton, 2007.

Gambrill, Olive Moore. "John Beale Bordley and the Early Years of the Philadelphia Agricultural Society." *Pennsylvania Magazine of History and Biography* 65, no. 4 (1942): 410–39.

Gillispie, Charles. *The Montgolfier Brothers and the Invention of Aviation.* Princeton, NJ: Princeton University Press, 1983.

Glenn, Justin. *The Washingtons: A Family History.* Vol. 1, *Seven Generations of a Presidential Branch.* Hagerstown, MD: Savas, 2014.

Goodman, Dana. *The Republic of Letters.* Ithaca, NY: Cornell University Press, 1994.

Gottschalk, Louis. *Lafayette between the American and the French Revolution (1783–1789).* Chicago: University of Chicago Press, 1950.

Gray, Lewis Cecil. *History of Agriculture in the Southern United States to 1860.* 2 vols. Washington, DC: Carnegie Institute, 1933.

Grieve, George. "Notes on Conversation with Lund Washington." In *Travels in North America in the Years 1780, 1781, and 1782 by the Marquis de Chastellux*, vol. 2, edited by Howard C. Rice Jr. Chapel Hill: University of North Carolina Press, 1963.

Grizzard, Frank, Jr. "Lawrence Washington." In *George! A Guide to All Things Washington*, 332. Buena Vista, VA: Mariner, 2005.

———. "Mary Ball Washington." In *George! A Guide to All Things Washington*, 335–37. Buena Vista, VA: Mariner, 2005.

Hallam, John S. "Houdon's Washington in Richmond: Some New Observations." *American Art Journal* 10, no. 2 (1978): 72–80.

Hart, Charles Henry, and Edward Biddle. *Memoirs of the Life and Works of Jean-Antoine Houdon: The Sculptor of Voltaire and of Washington.* Philadelphia: Printed for the authors, 1911.

Hatch, Jane M., ed. *The American Book of Days.* 3rd ed. New York: Wilson, 1978.

Hay, Carla. "Catharine Macaulay and the American Revolution." *Historian* 56, no. 2 (Winter 1994): 301–16.

Hayes, Kevin J. *George Washington: A Life in Books.* New York: Oxford University Press, 2017.

Hening, William Waller. *Statutes at Large, 1619–1792.* Richmond, VA: Printed for the editor by George Cochran, 1819–1823.

Hibbard, Benjamin H. *A History of the Public Land Policies.* Madison: University of Wisconsin Press, 1965.

Higginbotham, Don. *Daniel Morgan: Revolutionary Rifleman.* Chapel Hill: University of North Carolina Press, 1961.

Hill, Bridget. *The Republican Virago: The Life and Times of Catharine Macaulay, Historian*. Oxford: Clarendon, 1992.

Holcombe, Arthur N. "The Role of Washington in the Framing of the Constitution." *Huntington Library Quarterly* 19, no. 4 (1956): 317–34.

Holmes, Oliver W. "Suter's Tavern: Birthplace of the Federal City." *Records of the Columbia Historical Society* 49 (1973–1974).

"The House of Deputies." Archives of the Episcopal Church. https://www .episcopalarchives.org/house-of-deputies/leadership/william-white.

Howard, Hugh. *The Painter's Chair: George Washington and the Making of American Art*. New York: Bloomsbury, 2009.

Humphreys, David. "An Address to the Armies of the United States of America." New Haven, CT: T. and S. Green, 1780.

———. *Life of General Washington*. Edited and with an introduction by Rosemary Zagarri. Athens: University of Georgia Press, 1991.

Humphreys, Frank Landon. *Life and Times of David Humphreys*. New York: Putnam, 1917.

Hunter, Robert, Jr. "An Account of a Visit Made to Washington at Mount Vernon by an English Gentleman in 1785." *Pennsylvania Magazine of History and Biography* 17 (1893): 76–82.

Hutson, James H., ed. *Supplement to Max Farrand's* The Records of the Federal Convention of 1787. New Haven, CT: Yale University Press, 1987.

Idzerda, Stanley J., ed. *Lafayette in the Age of the American Revolution: Selected Letters and Papers, 1776–1790*. 5 vols. Ithaca, NY: Cornell University Press, 1977–.

Jaffe, Irma. *John Trumbull: Patriot Artist of the American Revolution*. New York: Graphic Society, 1975.

"James Nourse of Virginia." *Virginia Magazine of History and Biography* 8, no. 2 (1900): 199–202.

James Nourse of Virginia (website). http://www.noursefamily.net/.

Jay, John. *Selected Papers of John Jay*. Edited by Elizabeth M. Nuxoll. 7 vols. New York: Columbia University Press, 2010–2021.

Jefferson, Thomas. *Notes on the State of Virginia*. Richmond, VA: Randolph, 1853.

———. *The Papers of Thomas Jefferson, Main Series*. Various editors. 44 vols. Princeton, NJ: Princeton University Press, 1950–2019.

———. *Papers of Thomas Jefferson, Retirement Series*. Various editors. 20 vols. to date. Princeton, NJ: Princeton University Press, 2005.

John Dickinson to Polly Dickinson, 29 May 1787. Historical Society of Pennsylvania. https://www.consource.org/document/john-dickinson-to-polly -dickinson-1787-5-29/.

Journal of the First Session of the Senate of the United States of America, Begun and Held at the City of New York, March 4, 1789. Washington, DC: Gales and Seaton, 1820.

Journals of the Continental Congress, 1774–1789. Edited by Worthington C. Ford. 34 vols. Washington, DC: Government Printing Office, 1904–1937.

Kahler, Gerald Edward. "Gentlemen of the Family: General George Washington's Aides-de-Camp and Military Secretaries." MA thesis, University of Richmond, 1997. https://scholarship.richmond.edu/cgi/viewcontent.cgi?article=1623&context=masters-theses.

Knollenberg, Bernard. *George Washington: The Virginia Period*. Durham: Duke University Press, 1964.

Le Mayeur, Jean Pierre. "From the City of New York, Dentist, Notes and Queries." *Virginia Magazine of History and Biography* 10 (1902–1903): 325.

Leibiger, Stuart. *Founding Friendship: George Washington, James Madison and the Creation of the American Republic*. Charlottesville: University of Virginia Press, 1999.

Letters of Delegates to Congress, 1774–1789. Edited by Paul M. Smith. 25 vols. Washington, DC: Library of Congress, 1976–2000.

Lienesch, Michael. "Remembering Rebellion: The Influence of Shays's Rebellion on American Political Thought." In *In Debt to Shays: The Bicentennial of an Agrarian Rebellion*, edited by Robert A. Gross, 161–82. Colonial Society of Massachusetts Collections 65. Charlottesville: University of Virginia Press, 1986.

Linklater, Andro. *Measuring America*. New York: Walker, 2002.

Littlefield, Douglas R. "Eighteenth-Century Plans to Clear the Potomac River: Technology, Expertise, and Labor in a Developing Nation." *Virginia Magazine of History and Biography* 93, no. 3 (1986): 291–322.

Loehr, Rodney C. "Arthur Young and American Agriculture." *Agricultural History* 43, no. 1 (1969): 43–56.

Longmore, Paul K. *The Invention of George Washington*. Berkeley: University of California Press, 1989.

Lossing, Benson John. *Life and Times of Philip Schuyler*. New York: Sheldon, 1873.

Ludlum, David. *Early American Winters, 1604–1820*. Boston: American Meteorological Society, 1966.

Macaulay, Catharine. *Address to the People of England, Ireland, and Scotland*. New York: Holt, 1775.

———. *Loose Remarks on Certain Propositions to Be Found in Mr. Hobbes's Philosophical Rudiments of Government and Society with a Short Sketch of a*

Democratical Form of Government in a Letter to Signor Paoli. London: Printed for T. Davies, 1767.

"Macaulay [nee Sawbridge; Other Married Name Graham], Catharine." In *Oxford Dictionary of National Biography*. https://www.oxforddnb.com/dis play/10.1093/ref:odnb/9780198614128.001.0001/odnb-9780198614128 -e-17344?rskey=m6osvx&result=2.

Madison, James. *The Papers of James Madison, Congressional Series*. Edited by William T. Hutchinson et al. 17 vols. Charlottesville: University of Virginia Press, 1962–1991.

———. *The Papers of James Madison, Retirement Series*. Edited by David B. Mattern et al. 4 vols. to date. Charlottesville: University of Virginia Press, 2009–.

———. *The Papers of James Madison, Secretary of State Series*. Edited by Robert J. Brugger et al. 12 vols. to date. Charlottesville: University of Virginia Press, 1986–.

Maier, Pauline. *Ratification: The People Debate the Constitution, 1787–1788*. New York: Simon & Schuster, 2010.

Mariners Museum. "HMS *Savage*, Waters of Despair, Waters of Hope." https://www.marinersmuseum.org/sites/micro/waters/war/war04.htm.

Marshall, John. *Papers of John Marshall*. Edited by Herbert A. Johnson. 12 vols. Chapel Hill: University of North Carolina Press, 1974–2006.

Martin, Lawrence. *The George Washington Atlas*. Washington, DC: George Washington Bicentennial Commission, 1932.

Maryland House of Delegates. *Votes and Proceedings*. 22 and 27 December 1784.

Mason, George. *The Papers of George Mason*. Edited by Robert A. Rutland. 3 vols. Chapel Hill: University of North Carolina Press, 2011.

Mathews, Catherine Van Cortlandt. *Andrew Ellicott: His Life and Letters*. New York: Grafton, 1908.

McCullough, David. *John Adams*. New York: Simon & Schuster, 2001.

McLeod, Stephen, ed. *Dining with the Washingtons*. Mount Vernon, VA: Mount Vernon Ladies Association, 2011.

Meschutt, David. "Life Portraits of George Washington." In *George Washington: American Symbol*, edited by Barbara J. Mitnick, 25–37. New York: Hudson Hills, 1990.

Miller, John C. *Origins of the American Revolution*. Boston: Little, Brown, 1943.

Morgan, John. "Air Balloons" (June 19, 1784). *Early Proceedings of the American Philosophical Society for the Promotion of Useful Knowledge Compiled by One of the Secretaries Manuscript Minutes of Its Meetings from 1744 to 1838* (Philadelphia, 1884): 126.

Mosimann, Elizabeth A. *Promoting Agriculture in a Changing World: 225 Years of the Philadelphia Society for Promoting Agriculture, 1785–2010*. Philadelphia: Society for Promoting Agriculture, 2012.

Mount Vernon Ladies Association. *George Washington's Mount Vernon Official Guidebook*. Mount Vernon, VA: Mount Vernon Ladies Association, n.d.

———. "The Rebuilding of the Greenhouse—Quarters." In *Mount Vernon Ladies Association Annual Report*, 19–26. Mount Vernon, VA: Mount Vernon Ladies Association, 1952.

Myers, Minor. *Liberty without Anarchy: A History of the Society of the Cincinnati*. Charlottesville: University of Virginia Press, 1983.

Newlin, Claude Milton. *The Life and Writings of Hugh Henry Brackenridge*. Princeton, NJ: Princeton University Press, 1932.

Nolan, J. Bennett. "Lafayette and the American Philosophical Society." *Proceedings of the American Philosophical Society* 73, no. 2 (1934): 117–26.

Ogg, Frederick A. *The Opening of the Mississippi: A Struggle for Supremacy in the American Interior*. New York: Macmillan, 1904.

Onuf, Peter. *Statehood and Union*. Bloomington: Indiana University Press, 1987.

Ottenberg, Louis. "A Fortunate Fiasco: The Annapolis Convention of 1786." *American Bar Association Journal* 45, no. 8 (1959): 834–37, 877–82.

Paine, Thomas. *Common Sense*. Philadelphia: Bell, 1776.

Pape, T. "Appleby Grammar School and Its Washington Pupils." *William and Mary Quarterly* 40, no. 4 (1940): 498–501.

Pine, Robert Edge. "America: To Those Who Wish to Sheathe the Desolating Sword of War." Library of Congress, Prints and Photographs Online Catalog. https://www.loc.gov/pictures/item/2003690788.

"Pine, Robert Edge." In *Oxford Dictionary of National Biography*. https://www.oxforddnb.com/view/10.1093/ref:odnb/9780198614128.001.0001/odnb-9780198614128-e-22294.

Pogue, Dennis. "Drink and Be Merry: Liquor and Wine at Mount Vernon." In *Dining with the Washingtons*, edited by Stephen A. McLeod, 96–112. Mount Vernon, VA: Mount Vernon Ladies Association, 2011.

Polwhelve, Richard. *Traditions and Recollections*. 2 vols. London: Nichols, 1826.

Poulet, Anne. *Jean-Antoine Houdon: Sculptor of the Enlightenment*. Washington, DC: National Gallery of Art, 2003.

Proceedings of the Society of the Cincinnati. Vol. 1, *1784–1884*. Edited by John C. Davies. Philadelphia: Review Printing House, 1887.

Reep, Rob. "Jacob Shallus: Penman of the United States Constitution." Fossil HD, 29 September 2011. https://fossilhd.wordpress.com/2011/09/29/jacob-shallus-penman-of-the-united-states-constitution/.

Reinhart, Thomas, Director of Preservation Mount Vernon, to author, 28 July 2020.

"Robert Edge Pine." National Gallery of Art. https://www.nga.gov/collec tion/artist-info.1788.html.

Robertson, David Brian. "Madison's Opponents and Constitutional Design." *American Political Science Review* 99, no. 2 (May 2005): 225–43.

"Rosegill." National Register of Historic Places. www.rosegill.com/Library /HistoricPlaces/HistoricPlaces.html.

Rossie, Jonathan Gregory. *The Politics of Command in the American Revolution.* Syracuse, NY: Syracuse University Press, 1975.

Rowland, Kate Mason. "The Mount Vernon Convention." *Pennsylvania Maga-zine of History and Biography* 11, no. 4 (January 1888): 410–25.

"Samuel Washington." Family Search. https://ancestors.familysearch.org/en /L4BC-1J8/samuel-washington-1734-1781.

"Samuel Washington—Marriages and Children." Liquisearch. www.liqui search.com/samuel_washington/marriages_and_children.

Schoepf, Johann David. *Travels in the Confederation, 1783–1784.* Edited and translated by Alfred Morrison. Philadelphia: Campbell, 1911.

Seelye, John. *Beautiful Machine: Rivers and the Republican Plan, 1755–1825.* New York: Oxford University Press, 1991.

Sexton, Martha. *The Widow Washington: The Life of Mary Washington.* New York: Farrar, Straus & Giroux, 2019.

Shirley, Craig. *Mary Ball Washington: The Untold Story of George Washington's Mother.* New York: HarperCollins, 2019.

Smith, Paul M., comp. *English Defenders of American Freedoms, 1774–1778.* Washington, DC: Library of Congress, 1972.

Smith, Philip C. F. *The Empress of China.* Philadelphia: Philadelphia Maritime Museum, 1984.

Smith, W. P. *A History and Description of the Baltimore and Ohio Railroad.* Balti-more: Murphy, 1853.

Society of the Cincinnati Archives. Washington, DC.

"Spraight, Richard Dobbs." In *Biographical Directory of the United States Congress, 1774–1961.* Washington, DC: Government Printing Office, 1961. https:// bioguideretro.congress.gov/Home/MemberDetails?memIndex=S000693.

Staib, Walter. *The City Tavern Cookbook: Recipes from the Birthplace of American Cuisine.* Philadelphia: Running Press, 2009.

Stiles, Ezra. *Literary Diary of Ezra Stiles.* Edited by Franklin Bowditch. 3 vols. New York: Scribner, 1901.

"Stephen Bloomer Balch." Georgetown Presbyterian Church. https://www
.gtownpres.org/stephen-bloomer-balch.

Stewart, Robert G. *Robert Edge Pine: A British Portrait Painter in America, 1784–1788.* Washington, DC: Smithsonian Institution Press, 1979.

Szatmary, David. *Shays's Rebellion: The Making of an Agrarian Insurrection.* Amherst: University of Massachusetts Press, 1980.

Thacher, James. *American Medical Biography; or, Memoirs of Eminent Physicians Who Have Flourished in America.* 2 vols. Boston: Richardson and Lord, 1828.

Thompson, Mary V. *"The Only Unavoidable Subject of Regret": George Washington, Slavery, and the Enslaved Community at Mount Vernon.* Charlottesville: University of Virginia Press, 2019.

———. "Visitors to Mount Vernon, 1784–1789: A Study Undertaken for the Bill of Rights Institute and the Mount Vernon Education Department." Unpublished paper, Mount Vernon Ladies Association, July 2003.

United States National Archives, Pieces of History. "Constitution 225: To Errata Is Human." https://prologue.blogs.archives.gov/2012/09/14/consti tution-225-to-errata-is-human/.

University of Pennsylvania. *Biographical Catalogue of the Matriculates of the College, 1749–1893.* Philadelphia: Society of the Alumni, 1894.

"Virginia's Cession of the Northwest Territory." Virginia Places. http://www
.virginiaplaces.org/boundaries/cessions.html.

Virginia House of Delegates. *Journal of the House of Delegates of the Commonwealth of Virginia.* Richmond: Commonwealth of Virginia, 1828–. https:// onlinebooks.library.upenn.edu/webbin/serial?id=vahousej.

Virginians' Petition to Prevent the Emancipation of Slaves, Citizens of Mecklenburg, Amelia, and Pittsylvania Counties (Virginia). *To the Honourable the General Assembly of Virginia, the Remonstrance and Petition of the Free Inhabitants of Amelia County, 8–10 November 1785.* Richmond, VA: Legislative Petitions, 1784–1785, Virginia State Library.

Voight, Heather. "Presidential Pets: George Washington's Dogs." Heather on History. https://heathervoight.com/2018/01/26/presidential-pets-george -washingtons-dogs/.

Warren, Mercy Otis. *Mercy Otis Warren: Selected Letters.* Edited by Jeffrey H. Richards and Sharon M. Harris. Athens: University of Georgia Press, 2009.

Warren Adams Letters: Being Chiefly a Correspondence among John Adams, Samuel Adams, and James Warren. 2 vols. Boston: Massachusetts Historical Society, 1917–1925.

Washington, George. "Circular Letter to States on the Distress of the Army, Headquarters." Newburgh, NY, 18 June 1783.

————. *The Diaries of George Washington.* Edited by Donald Jackson and Dorothy Twohig. 6 vols. Charlottesville: University of Virginia Press, 1976–1979.

————. "From George Washington to United States Congress, 23 December 1783." Founders Online. https://founders.archives.gov/documents/Washington/99-01-02-12223.

————. *General Orders of George Washington Issued at Newburgh on the Hudson, 1782–1783.* Compiled by Major Edward C. Boynton. Harrison, NY: Harbor Hill Books, 1973.

————. *Letters on Agriculture from His Excellency George Washington to Arthur Young Esq, F.R.S. and Sir John Sinclair, Bart. M.P.* Edited by Franklin Knight. Washington, DC: Published by the editor, 1847.

————. *Newburgh Address.* Boston: Massachusetts Historical Society, 1966.

————. *The Papers of George Washington, Colonial Series.* Edited by W. W. Abbot and Dorothy Twohig. 10 vols. Charlottesville: University of Virginia Press, 1983–1995.

————. *The Papers of George Washington, Confederation Series.* Edited by W. W. Abbot and Dorothy Twohig. 6 vols. Charlottesville: University of Virginia Press, 1992–1997.

————. *The Papers of George Washington, Presidential Series.* Edited by W. W. Abbot, Philander D. Chase, and Dorothy Twohig. 19 vols. to date. Charlottesville: University of Virginia Press, 1987–.

————. *The Papers of George Washington, Retirement Series.* Edited by W. W. Abbot. 4 vols. Charlottesville: University of Virginia Press, 1998–1999.

————. *The Papers of George Washington, Revolutionary War Series.* Edited by W. W. Abbot, Dorothy Twohig, Philander D. Chase, and Theodore Crackel. 26 vols. Charlottesville: University of Virginia Press, 1985–.

————. *Wills of George Washington and His Immediate Ancestors.* Edited by Worthington C. Ford. Brooklyn, NY: Historical Printing Club, 1891.

Washington, Martha. *"Worthy Partner": The Papers of Martha Washington.* Compiled by Joseph E. Fields. Westport, CT: Greenwood, 1994.

Watson, Elkanah. *Men and Times of the Revolution; or, Memoirs of Elkanah Watson, Including Journals of Travel in Europe and America from 1777 to 1842.* Edited by Winslow Warren. New York: Dana, 1856.

Whealy, Mervin B. "'The Revolution Is Not Over': The Annapolis Convention of 1786." *Maryland Historical Magazine* 81 (Fall 1986): 228–40.

Whiteley, Emily Stone. *Washington and His Aides-de-Camp.* New York: Macmillan, 1936.

INDEX

148; and presidency, 198–99; and
stock gift, 75; and western lands,
24–25, 139–41, 250n20
Constitutional Convention, 159–78,
179–89; Annapolis meeting
and, 78; arrivals for, 170–73;
defining ratification, 186–87;
delegates to, characteristics of,
176; and ratification, 189, 193–97,
255n111; rules committee, 174–
75; secretary of, 168–69, 174; and
signing, 188
convention proposals: for Annapolis,
147–48, 153–57; for Philadelphia,
156–57
Conway, Thomas, 71
Conway Cabal, 6, 71
corporal punishment, 95–97
Coxe, Tench, 155, 156
Craik, James, 38, 42–43, 48, 52, 97,
225n63
Craik, Marianne Ewell, 43
Cresap, Michael, 53
Cresap, Thomas, 52–53
Croghan, George, 55
Crosby, Brass, 106
Custis, Daniel, 8, 125
Custis, Daniel Parke, II, 8
Custis, Eleanor Calvert, 9
Custis, Eleanor Parke "Nelly," 8, 9,
34, 89, 109, 117
Custis, Elizabeth Parke "Eliza," 9,
109
Custis, Frances Parke, 8
Custis, George Washington Parke
"Wash," "Tub," 8, 9, 34, 85, 89,
105, 109, 113; on horses, 134–35
Custis, John Parke "Jacky," 8–9, 124

Custis, Martha Parke "Patsy," 8–9,
49, 109, 124

Dade, Parthenia, 93
dancing, 91
Dandridge, Anna Maria, 85–86
Davie, W. R., 177
Deane, Silas, 29
Delaware, 155, 166
dentistry, 103–5
Dickinson, John, 155, 156, 157, 160;
Constitutional Convention and,
177, 185, 186
Dinwiddie, Robert, 123
discretion: Constitutional
Convention and, 175, 189;
Washington and, 36, 146, 185
dogs, 34, 137, 237n71
Donald, Alexander, 193
Drayton, William, 161
Dulany, Benjamin Tasker, 134
Dunlap, John, 191
Dunmore, Lord (governor), 16
duty, Washington and, 164, 167,
199

education: Washington and, 90–97;
of women, 92, 110
Ellicott, Andrew, 53
Ellsworth, Oliver, 183, 198
enslaved Africans: Billy Lee, 6,
170, 247n61; Bloxham and,
128; British and, 16; at Mount
Vernon, 12, 101, 127, 235n34;
and Philadelphia, 170, 247n61;
and Potomac Company, 83; in
western lands, 207n71
Epple, Henry, 182